MORE PRAISE FOR *UNDER AFRICAN SKIES*

An invigorating cacophony of involved and compassionate voices . . . This rich collection offers a fascinating composite image of a society perhaps eternally in transition. —BRUCE ALLEN, *The Boston Sunday Globe*

These 27 stories, spanning 50 years across the continent, show an astonishing range, from forms rooted in the oral tradition to postcolonial and post-apartheid fiction. —*Booklist*

A marvelous collection that brings together the best stories by writers young and old from every corner of the African continent.

—BERNTH LINDFORS

Professor of English and African

Literatures, University of Texas at Austin

These stories bring to life the conflicting family ties, the calls of the ancestors, the grinding poverty, corruption and personal resiliency that make up life in much of modern Africa. —NEELY TUCKER, *Detroit Free Press*

A sampling of the variety and power of writing from Africa which I would hope will inspire eager readers to ask for more.

—NADINE GORDIMER

An invaluable handbook for readers of African fiction in the twenty-first century, indeed a twentieth-century literary collector's treasure.

—ERNEST N. EMENYONU

Professor of African and African-American

Literatures, Kalamazoo College

Under African

EDITED AND WITH AN INTRODUCTION BY CHARLES R. LARSON

Skies · MODERN AFRICAN STORIES

The Noonday Press • Farrar, Straus and Giroux • New York

The Noonday Press
A division of Farrar, Straus and Giroux
19 Union Square West, New York 10003

Introduction copyright © 1997 by Charles R. Larson
All rights reserved
Distributed in Canada by Douglas & McIntyre Ltd.
Printed in the United States of America
Designed by Jonathan D. Lippincott
First published in 1997 by Farrar, Straus and Giroux
First Noonday paperback edition, 1998

The Library of Congress has catalogued the hardcover edition as follows:

Under African skies : modern African stories / edited and with an
introduction by Charles R. Larson. — 1st ed.
    p.   cm.
  ISBN 0-374-17659-0 (alk. paper)
  1. Short stories, African.   2. African fiction—20th century.
3. Short stories, African—Translations into English.   I. Larson,
Charles R.
PQ8011.U7   1997
808.83'10896—dc21
                                                    96-48601

See page 313 for permissions

For Roberta, Vanessa, and Joshua

Telephone Conversation

The price seemed reasonable, location
Indifferent. The landlady swore she lived
Off premises. Nothing remained
But self-confession. "Madam," I warned,
"I hate a wasted journey—I am African."
Silence. Silenced transmission of
Pressurized good-breeding. Voice, when it came,
Lipstick-coated, long gold-rolled
Cigarette-holder pipped. Caught I was, foully.
"HOW DARK? " . . . I had not misheard . . . "ARE YOU LIGHT
OR VERY DARK? " Button B. Button A. Stench
Of rancid breath of public hide-and-speak.
Red booth. Red pillar-box. Red double-tiered
Omnibus squelching tar. It *was* real! Shamed
By ill-mannered silence, surrender
Pushed dumbfoundment to beg simplification.
Considerate she was, varying the emphasis—
"ARE YOU DARK? OR VERY LIGHT? " Revelation came.
"You mean—like plain or milk chocolate? "
Her assent was clinical, crushing in its light
Impersonality. Rapidly, wave-length adjusted,
I chose. "West African sepia"—and as afterthought,
"Down in my passport." Silence for spectroscopic
Flight of fancy, till truthfulness clanged her accent
Hard on the mouthpiece. "WHAT'S THAT? " conceding
"DON'T KNOW WHAT THAT IS." "Like brunette."
"THAT'S DARK, ISN'T IT? " "Not altogether.
Facially, I am brunette, but madam, you should see
The rest of me. Palm of my hand, soles of my feet
Are a peroxide blond. Friction, caused—
Foolishly, madam—by sitting down, has turned
My bottom raven black—One moment, madam! "—sensing
Her receiver rearing on the thunderclap
About my ears—"Madam," I pleaded, "wouldn't you rather
See for yourself? "

—Wole Soyinka

CONTENTS

INTRODUCTION

Undoubtedly, the most extraordinary aspect of African literature—and particularly the fiction—of the past half century has been its resiliency. The ability of the African writer to overcome enormous obstacles and continue creating has been nothing less than astonishing—to borrow an important word from the title of one of Ben Okri's visionary novels. From near-total invisibility on the world literary scene four decades ago, African writers have moved to center stage in a remarkably short time. A Nobel Prize (Wole Soyinka), a Booker Award (Ben Okri), an internationally praised novel that has sold in the millions (Chinua Achebe)—and, most encouraging, the majority of them on the African continent—these are some of the impressive accomplishments garnered by black Africa's highly visible writers during the past two generations.

And yet all is not well on the African literary scene, nor has it ever been. The twentieth century has been a difficult time for writers in many areas of the world—not just in Africa, but in Asia and Latin America, as well as in some of the countries of the former Communist world. Too many international writers have been faced with obstacles their counterparts in the West have never had to worry about or at least confront as a ubiquitous presence. But African writers, including many represented in this volume, have suffered the indignities of censorship, of exile, of such high illiteracy in some places that many were unread in their own countries for years; of publishers who had privileged Western views of the continent—let alone the logistics of publishing "overseas" or in the so-called mother country before adequate means of book production existed on the continent itself. More recently, Ken Saro-Wiwa's death by hanging in Nigeria in 1995 sent shock waves throughout the intellectual community which will take years to subside.

Many of these issues were heatedly discussed at the Zimbabwe International Book Fair in Harare during the summer of 1996, as they tend to be on most occasions when African writers (and editors and publishers) are drawn together. The subject at the *indaba* which preceded the actual fair, "National Book Policy," may in general relate to questions of governmental support for textbooks for students in schools across the continent—who approves them, who produces them, who profits from their marketing—but as much as anything, the question centers on the most basic one of all: money. Books, and particularly literary works, are expensive in Africa, so expensive that Africans cannot afford them (even if they have the ability to read them), though literacy as we approach the end of the century is a lesser problem than cost. At the Book Fair a year earlier, in 1995, the Honorable Dumiso Dabengwa, Minister of Home Affairs for Zimbabwe, stated the dilemma much more starkly: "Concerns over freedom of expression are quite different to the middle-class urban professional in the highly developed consumer societies of Europe or the United States, with home library, newspapers, magazines, television, video, radio and personal computer, in comparison to the subsistence farmer in the rural areas of Africa, where the radio is something which sometimes operates when batteries can be found and paid for, where the two-week-old newspaper is read over and over by ten or twenty people and where a library is something not many, especially of the older generation, have actually seen. The same comparison needs to be made between our own relatively privileged urban elites and our peasant farmers."

Some of the pioneers (now the privileged elite) of African writing can clearly remember the difficulties they encountered when they first sent their manuscripts to European editors for possible publication, since there were virtually no publishers in tropical Africa with the capacity to print books. Chinua Achebe has recounted the story behind the publication of *Things Fall Apart* (1958) a number of times. Not only did he pay £30 to have the manuscript typed before it was sent off to England—an amount in that decade equal to what the average Nigerian subsisted on for an entire year—but the manuscript was almost lost in the mail. Fortunately, it was not. One cannot help asking, however, what would have happened to the continent's most distinguished novelist if he had not had the funds to pay for the typing, or if the mails had failed him. Imagine the topography of world literature without Achebe's presence. Imagine the topography of subsequent African literature without Achebe's enormous influence.

Several years earlier, the Nigerian writer Amos Tutuola had fewer resources available to him. As Bernth Lindfors has noted, Tutuola's novel was *lost* for thirty-some years because the writer miscalculated his choice of publisher. How, in fact, would an unpublished African writer in the 1950s know which European publisher would be most sympathetic to his work? How many African writers in that era gave up their dreams of seeing their works in print after the lengthy delays in submission via colonial mails, after the loss of the only copy (most likely handwritten) of a manuscript, or after rejection by a publisher or two? There is the apocryphal story of the writer from the continent who received a letter of rejection from a European publisher with the stark comment: "Not African enough."

Those fortunate enough at the time to have their work accepted tell stories of elation followed by acute frustration, typically a year or so later when the first printed copy of their book (or short story or poem) arrived. Writers may not always want to celebrate their earliest publication with family or friends, but such celebration is impossible if parents and, possibly, friends are illiterate. In such a context, who will read the writer's work? Fortunately, today that problem is not the most urgent one on the continent, as it was during the time when the first generation of African writers were writing their books. However, I can still recall Stanlake Samkange describing his horror on reading the first royalty statement he received from his publisher when he realized that his novel (*On Trial for My Country*, 1966) had sold few copies outside of Britain and his further chagrin that copies sold "abroad" (i.e., Africa) earned only half royalties because of the increased expenses of distribution.

These are anecdotes from the past, to be sure, but they are directly related to the issues of book policy in black Africa today, especially those of an economic nature. Books simply cost too much in Africa (and in many other parts of the world) and therefore fall within the domain of luxury items. In an article in *The Washington Post* of February 3, 1996, Eniwoke Ibagere identifies several grim examples of book sales in Nigeria (traditionally, an affluent country). "The economics of the collapsed Nigerian economy have turned what once was a thriving market for literature, reference works and other printed products into a disaster area. Soyinka's latest book, *Ibadan—the Pen-kelemes Years*, costs about 4,000 naira—more than the monthly salary of most civil servants.'' Ibagere further explains: ''The economy is so battered that people think more of how to survive. . . . The best that many authors can hope for is a lavish launch ceremony, where the publisher runs off a limited edition that is snapped up by Nigeria's rich and powerful for inflated prices of up to 20,000 naira ($250) a copy.'' For a family struggling to pay a child's school fees, the money to purchase a novel or even a textbook may result in deprivation of basic needs. The other side of the coin is no better. European publishers have been burned so many times by unpaid bills from their African distributors that some who were once eager to publish African writers have considerably retrenched, cutting back their plans for expansion in a market that by all logic should be exploding.

The African reading audience for creative writing has not exploded, though one hopes—if examples from India and certain Latin American markets can be replicated—in time it may, but many African writers and critics are not encouraging about this growth in spite of the literally hundreds of publishing outlets that exist on the continent today. Books remain luxury items. Presses have to be imported, and—worse—in most African countries, paper has to be imported. Sadly, even paper of the cheapest kind is expensive and, too often, highly taxed—one of the hidden burdens of book production in Africa today.

The reading audience has not mushroomed because in too many instances creative works are the last to be considered even by an affluent reader. Self-help books, textbooks, and technical works are, typically, of first importance (as they are throughout most of the world); a novel or a collection of poems or stories is purchased much later, if at all. The climate for the reading of creative works has to be nurtured, slowly and carefully. Some African writers and critics will state quite candidly that their fellow countrymen do not read books. Although the example is once again from Chinua Achebe, it cannot be laughed off as satirically as he implied. Chief Nanga, a character in *A Man of the People* (1966) who is identified as his country's Minister of Culture, ''announced in public that he had never heard of his country's most famous novel and received applause—as indeed he received again later when he prophesied that before long our great country would produce great writers like Shakespeare, Dickens, Jane Austen, Bernard Shaw and—raising his eyes off the script—Michael West and Dudley Stamp.''

The climate for reading is easily developed in a household or a classroom full of books or other printed material. But schools which are barren of the printed page rarely produce adults who are readers, even in the face of the most intense craving for the printed text. What a pity, given the way the eyes of children around the world shine when they are read aloud to, or the laughter and excitement of schoolchildren when they are presented with printed literature (magazines, even brochures or colorful advertisements) to take home.

Encountering the excitement of a group of African writers, especially those at the beginning of their careers, one would conclude that the scene for African writing is much more favorable than I have described here. At the 1996 Zimbabwe International Book Fair, the country's most distinguished novelist, Chenjerai Hove, signed copies of his latest book, a collection of essays called *Shebeen Tales,* with a cover price of sixty local dollars (U.S.$6). Copies of the paperback book were selling briskly, but one wonders how many of Hove's fellow writers find such a market for their works? Can Hove support himself, and presumably his family, solely by his writing? How many creative writers in Zimbabwe, which appears to have a thriving publishing market, are able to do so? How many writers in all of black Africa are able to support themselves solely by their work? My guess is that there may be two—or possibly three or four—in sub-Saharan Africa who belong to this exclusive club, and all of them are Nigerian. Revealingly, those few—the only ones I can be certain of—do not currently reside in Africa.

The mere idea of full-time creativity collapses in the face of censorship and the related indignities that many African writers have experienced once their careers were launched. In most instances, creative works pose little threat to African governments simply because so few copies of a newly released work are sold within a given country. The problems are much more likely to be encountered later. This was especially true for writers who began publishing before the independence of their countries, establishing themselves in part by criticizing the colonial power. What could be more logical than the writer/critic subsequently exposing the excesses of the new leaders, especially those Ayi Kwei Armah described in *The Beautyful Ones Are Not Yet Born* (1968): "How long will Africa be cursed with its leaders? There were men dying from the loss of hope, and others were finding gaudy new ways to enjoy power they did not have. We were ready here for big and beautiful things, but what we had was our own black men hugging new paunches scrambling to ask the white man to welcome them onto our backs. . . . There is something so terrible in watching a black man trying at all points to be the dark ghost of a European, and that is what we were seeing in those days.''

Stated more bluntly, politics and literature have been firmly intertwined within the panorama of African writing since the earliest days—and not just within the obvious context of apartheid in South Africa. Nadine Gordimer spoke disturbingly about the consequences of this bonding at the 1995 Zimbabwe Book Fair: ''There were raids on these [South African] writers' homes, their manuscripts were taken away to be buried in police files, sometimes even their typewriters were confiscated, so that the type-face might be compared with that appearing on revolutionary pamphlets. No manuscript was ever returned even though the type-face didn't match; the message was: Stop writing. Shut up.''

That same year at the Book Fair, Nigerian Wole Soyinka—currently an exiled writer—described an even more alarming situation with reference to the publication of one of his books: ''Two hundred armed police were there stopping the launching of a book.'' Of the brief introductory notes to each selection in this volume, too many include references to periods of censorship or exile for the writers themselves. One especially mourns almost an entire generation of exiled South African writers who drank themselves into oblivion as a result of the terror generated by apartheid's invisible reach. There was little optimism at all during those years; it looked as if apartheid would last forever.

The stories in this collection span a period of nearly fifty years. During that time, apartheid wreaked its havoc on an entire country (and perhaps indirectly on an entire continent) but finally came to an unexpectedly sudden and liberating halt. During that time, short stories by African writers moved from Amos Tutuola's spontaneous surrealism (perhaps more accurately identified as magic realism before the term was used to describe Latin American fiction) to Véronique Tadjo's ''The Magician and the Girl,'' which the author admits was influenced by writers of the Boom. Similarly, the movement has been from colonial to post-colonial, as well as from a literary topography dominated by men to one where women writers finally have a voice. Nevertheless, the short story has typically been regarded as the stepsister of African writing in large part because of the difficult logistics of placement, of first publication. Finding a serious magazine where literary fiction is admired is almost always a challenge for the African writer.

Forty years ago, Abioseh Nicol sent several of his short stories to the now-defunct *Encounter*, where they were praised for their misperceived quaintness and their humor. In Paris, *Présence Africaine* already existed as a potential outlet for Francophone writers. But other examples of African writers establishing their careers and their audience by publishing short stories in the little magazines or quarterlies and then collecting them in a volume (as many have done in the West) are not found with enough frequency to establish a meaningful pattern. To be sure, Ayi Kwei Armah, Bessie Head, Es'kia Mphahlele and, somewhat later, Ben Okri had occasional stories in highly visible publications at the onset of their writing careers. More typically, the short story in Africa has made only sporadic appearances, largely ignored by critics and academics, as F. Odun Balogun has indicated in *Tradition and Modernity in the African Short Story*.

As always—and as in so many cultures—short stories have appeared profusely in newspapers across the African continent, but they tend to be more journalistic than literary, more sensational than subtle. I met a young writer in Zimbabwe who had published more than a hundred such stories in his country's newspapers, but of the dozen or so that he offered me when I asked for his most important work, none was of more than passing significance; nearly all were closer to the news stories found in American tabloid newspapers than to literary fiction. I do not mean to denigrate this kind of writing but simply observe that few writers, historically, have made the transition from sensationalism (exaggerated sex and violence) to aesthetic realism of lasting value. The gap between the two (and the study of popular writing) has been a subject of critical debate in Western literature for years. Perhaps it is no surprise that similar patterns exist within the emergent African literature of the second half of the twentieth century. Again, to quote Nadine Gordimer: "Writers in Africa don't have enough readers; comic-book literacy does not mean an ability to read a story, poem or novel that has more than a vocabulary that consists largely of grunts and exclamatory syllables."

At the beginning of this introduction, I referred to the resiliency—the indomitable survival—of African fiction in the past half century. Its enormous variety, its versatility, should also be praised. One immediately thinks of the oral tradition out of which Amos Tutuola and the earliest writers began their careers, assuming incorrectly that that fine tradition of storytelling has somehow slipped away during the post-colonial era. But that is not true, as recent works by Ben Okri, Véronique Tadjo, and some of their peers demonstrate. The oral tradition is never lost, as cultures move from

being analphabetic and literature becomes written, as *griots* are comple-
mented by highly educated writers with international and cosmopolitan back-
grounds.

As much as possible, the stories in this collection have been arranged to
reflect the sequence of their writing, though the date at the end of each
story is the date of first publication. Any errors are mine alone. I must say,
however, that finding original publication dates for some of the stories included here was very difficult. This arrangement is intended to demonstrate
the changes that have taken place in African short fiction in the past several
decades, during the transition from colonial to post-colonial, as well as with
respect to the other issues mentioned earlier.

If the most recent South African short stories in this volume are any
indication, apartheid's long reach would finally appear to be broken. Es'kia
Mphahlele's "Mrs. Plum," the longest story in the collection, was published
when Mphahlele was in exile. Bessie Head's "The Prisoner Who Wore
Glasses" appeared in 1973, when Head was in exile in Botswana. Though
widely different, both stories give pessimistic accounts of black life in South
Africa; both also project the possibility that things will change. Don Mattera's
more recent story, "Afrika Road," would appear to be the apex of apartheid
horror, though Mattera's stark realism clearly extends beyond the confines
of his own country of birth.

With Sindiwe Magona's "I'm Not Talking About That, Now" and Mandla
Langa's "A Gathering of Bald Men" (1996), a change is in the works, as
South Africa itself moves from apartheid to post-apartheid. Magona's story,
the more traditional of the two, depicts the rapid disintegration of family
structures and values within her country. But Langa's story—certainly one
of the most invigorating in this volume—achieves a total turnaround, not
only reversing the situation of blacks and whites in post-apartheid South
Africa but, in its fast-paced narration, presenting us with a rare example of
African comedy. I mention this because for years readers have asked me to
direct them to African comedies (stories, poems, novels), and I have been
hard-pressed to find examples.

One other enormous change that I mentioned earlier is the literary lime-
light shared today by women writers. This change has not been sudden but
gradual, and at times has not occurred at all. Of the first generation of
African writers—those who emerged during the fifties and sixties—very few
were women, since education had largely been denied them. They were, by
my estimate, one out of twenty: five percent; and too many were published

solely because of their gender. In choosing the selections for this anthology, I reread stories by many of them and, I am sorry to say, was appalled at how poorly written some were. Consequently, few of the early selections in this anthology are by women writers.

Happily, this situation has changed in the last eight or ten years. The literary silence of African women has come to an abrupt end, as novelists such as Mariama Bâ and Calixthe Beyala have daringly shown us. Beyala's four extraordinary novels to date place her in the first rank of contemporary African writers. Unfortunately, the short-story form has yet to interest her. Not so with Sindiwe Magona, Yvonne Vera, and Véronique Tadjo—all of whom are represented in this volume. Nor is this proliferation likely to subside, as African women writers' networks across the continent demonstrate.

Finally, I must mention the increased presence of female characters in recent works by any number of younger African writers who happen to be men. Mzamane Nhlapo has staked out his identification with women's issues. Is it possible to forget Azaro's incredible mother (as well as her loving portrait) in Ben Okri's *The Famished Road* or *Songs of Enchantment*? Or Camara Laye's much earlier homage to his own mother in *L'enfant noir* (*The Dark Child*), for that matter? The most frequent theme of Western literature, romantic love, still remains offstage in the works of most African writers. But who knows but that women's increasing presence may soon alter the literary scene in a way that they—or we—have yet to imagine.

The art of African storytelling is no doubt as old as our common paleolithic ancestor Lucy's presence on the continent itself. What this collection hopes to demonstrate is the richness and wisdom of some of the most recent expressions of African writing.

—Charles R. Larson
Harare, Naxos, Washington
August 1996

Under African Skies

Amos Tutuola

(BORN 1920) NIGERIA

Amos Tutuola's writing career began in 1948, when he mailed *The Wild Hunter in the Bush of Ghosts* to the Focal Press in London. In an earlier letter, Tutuola had described the ghost narrative, claiming that the text would be accompanied by photographs of Nigerian spirits. According to Bernth Lindfors, when the Focal Press received the work, "the 77-page handwritten manuscript had been wrapped in brown paper, rolled up like a magazine, bound with twine, and sent via surface mail. When the sixteen negatives accompanying it were developed, all but one turned out to be snapshots of hand-drawn sketches of spirits and other phenomena featured in the story. Tutuola had hired a schoolboy to draw these illustrations and had photographed them. He had also included a photograph of a human being sitting by the lagoon in Lagos because he felt that she adequately represented 'the old woman who sat near the river' in the story."

In Tutuola's enchanting narrative, there are illegitimate and cannibalistic ghosts, a sixteen-headed ghost, and a Salvation Army ghost, plus an educated ghost who teaches the narrator to read and write. More disturbing, the Yoruba afterworld (the domain of the spirits described in the story) has become fully bureaucratic, so complicated in its red tape that it's surprising that anyone ever passes on.

The Focal Press—publishers of photography books—quickly lost interest in Tutuola's novel, which languished until Lindfors edited the work for publication in 1982. Well before that time, Tutuola had become a world-famous writer, primarily because of the publication of *The Palm-Wine Drin-kard*, in 1952. Reviewing the book, the Welsh poet Dylan Thomas noted: "This is the brief, thronged, grisly and bewitching story, written in young English by a West African, about a journey of an expert and devoted palm-wine drinkard through a nightmare of indescribable adventures, all simply and carefully described, in the spirit-bristling bush." The term "young English" confused the literary world, which quickly assumed that all subsequent Anglophone African writers would write in a similar style.

Clearly, Amos Tutuola's creative world is bewitching, extraordinarily vivid, and unforgettable. The Yoruba cosmology, which is central in each of the author's seven published books, often springs spontaneously alive when a character opens a door (perhaps in a tree) and enters into an entirely new world. As I wrote years ago, Tutuola's eschatology provides "a bridge between the internal and the external world (the ontological gap), between the real and the surreal, between the realistic and the supernatural."

Amos Tutuola was born in Abeokuta, Western Nigeria, in 1920. He completed six years of primary-school education, followed by training as a blacksmith, while serving in the R.A.F. in Lagos throughout World War II. *The Palm-Wine Drinkard* was written while Tutuola was working as a messenger for the Department of Labor. "The Complete Gentleman" has been excerpted from *The Palm-Wine Drinkard* as an example of oral storytelling incorporated into a written narrative. Other versions of this story exist in many West African languages. (See, for example, "The Chosen Suitor," from *Dahomean Narrative*, edited by Melville and Frances Herskovits, 1958.)

- Endurance and strength.
- The idea of Magical Realism: magical elements on illogical scenarios appears in an otherwise realistic narrative.
- Depicts appearence and beauty on a superficial basis.
- The complete Gentleman was perhaps there to teach a lesson. Not to go on someone's looks but on nature.
- A fairytale type of story.

*Beware of temptations. ↓ Don't give in. Relate to Tokyo.

- The journey of a hero and how he found his wife.
- There was something terrifying about the complete gentleman.

THE COMPLETE GENTLEMAN

THE DESCRIPTION OF THE CURIOUS CREATURE—

He was a beautiful "complete" gentleman, he dressed with the finest and most costly clothes, all the parts of his body were completed, he was a tall man but stout. As this gentleman came to the market on that day, if he had been an article or animal for sale, he would be sold at least for £2,000 (two thousand pounds). As this complete gentleman came to the market on that day, and at the same time that this lady saw him in the market, she did nothing more than to ask him where he was living, but this fine gentleman did not answer her or approach her at all. But when she noticed that the fine or complete gentleman did not listen to her, she left her articles and began to watch the movements of the complete gentleman about in the market and left her articles unsold.

By and by, the market closed for that day then the whole people in the market were returning to their destinations etc., and the complete gentleman was returning to his own too, but as this lady was following him about in the market all the while, she saw him when he was returning to his destination as others did, then she was following him (complete gentleman) to an unknown place. But as she was following the complete gentleman along the road, he was telling her to go back or not to follow him, but the lady did not listen to what he was telling her, and when the complete gentleman had tired of telling her not to follow him or to go back to her town, he left her to follow him.

DO NOT FOLLOW UNKNOWN MAN'S BEAUTY

But when they had traveled about twelve miles away from that market, they left the road on which they were traveling and started to travel inside an endless forest in which only the terrible creatures were living.

RETURN THE PARTS OF BODY TO THE OWNERS; OR HIRED PARTS OF THE COMPLETE GENTLEMAN'S BODY TO BE RETURNED

As they were traveling along in this endless forest then the complete gentleman in the market that the lady was following began to return the hired parts of his body to the owners and he was paying them the rentage money. When he reached where he hired the left foot, he pulled it out, he gave it to the owner and paid him, and they kept going; when they reached the place where he hired the right foot, he pulled it out and gave it to the owner and paid for the rentage. Now both feet had returned to the owners, so he began to crawl along on the ground, by that time that lady wanted to go back to her town or her father, but the terrible and curious creature or the complete gentleman did not allow her to return or go back to her town or her father again and the complete gentleman said thus: "I had told you not to follow me before we branched into this endless forest which belongs to only terrible and curious creatures, but when I become a half-bodied incomplete gentleman you wanted to go back, now that cannot be done, you have failed. Even you have never seen anything yet, just follow me."

When they went furthermore, then they reached where he hired the belly, ribs, chest, etc., then he pulled them out and gave them to the owner and paid for the rentage.

Now to this gentleman or terrible creature remained only the head and both arms with neck, by that time he could not crawl as before but only went jumping on as a bullfrog and now this lady was soon faint for this fearful creature whom she was following. But when the lady saw every part of this complete gentleman in the market was shared or hired and he was returning them to the owners, then she began to try all her efforts to return to her father's town, but she was not allowed by this fearful creature at all.

When they reached where he hired both arms, he pulled them out and gave them to the owner, he paid for them; and they were still going on in this endless forest, they reached the place where he hired the neck, he pulled it out and gave it to the owner and paid for it as well.

A FULL-BODIED GENTLEMAN REDUCED TO HEAD

Now this complete gentleman was reduced to head and when they reached where he hired the skin and flesh which covered the head, he returned them, and paid to the owner, now the complete gentleman in the market reduced to a SKULL and this lady remained with only Skull. When the lady saw that she remained with only Skull, she began to say that her father had been telling her to marry a man, but she did not listen to or believe him.

When the lady saw that the gentleman became a Skull, she began to faint, but the Skull told her if she would die she would die and she would follow him to his house. But by the time that he was saying so, he was humming with a terrible voice and also grew very wild and even if there was a person two miles away he would not have to listen before hearing him, so this lady began to run away in that forest for her life, but the Skull chased her and within a few yards, he caught her, because he was very clever and smart as he was only Skull and he could jump a mile to the second before coming down. He caught the lady in this way: so when the lady was running away for her life, he hastily ran to her front and stopped her as a log of wood.

By and by, this lady followed the Skull to his house, and the house was a hole which was under the ground. When they reached there both of them entered the hole. But there were only Skulls living in that hole. At the same time that they entered the hole, he tied a single cowrie on the neck of this lady with a kind of rope, after that, he gave her a large frog on which she sat as a stool, then he gave a whistle to a Skull of his kind to keep watch on this lady whenever she wanted to run away. Because the Skull knew already that the lady would attempt to run away from the hole. Then he went to the back yard to where his family were staying in the daytime till night.

But one day, the lady attempted to escape from the hole, and at the same time that the Skull who was watching her whistled to the rest of the Skulls that were in the back yard, the whole of them rushed out to the place where the lady sat on the bullfrog, so they caught her, but as all of them were rushing out, they were rolling on the ground as if a thousand petrol drums were pushing along a hard road. After she was caught, then they brought her back to sit on the same frog as usual. If the Skull who was watching her fell asleep, and if the lady wanted to escape, the cowrie that was tied on her neck would raise up the alarm with a terrible noise, so that the Skull who was watching her would wake up at once and then the rest of the

Skull's family would rush out from the back in thousands to the lady and ask her what she wanted to do with a curious and terrible voice.

But the lady could not talk at all, because as the cowrie had been tied on her neck, she became dumb at the same moment.

THE FATHER OF GODS SHOULD FIND OUT WHEREABOUTS THE DAUGHTER OF THE HEAD OF THE TOWN WAS

Now as the father of the lady first asked for my name and I told him that my name was "Father of gods who could do anything in this world," then he told me that if I could find out where his daughter was and bring her to him, then he would tell me where my palm-wine tapster was. But when he said so, I was jumping up with gladness that he should promise me that he would tell me where my tapster was. I agreed to what he said; the father and parent of this lady never knew whereabouts their daughter was, but they had information that the lady followed a complete gentleman in the market. As I was the "Father of gods who could do anything in this world," when it was at night I sacrificed to my juju with a goat.

And when it was early in the morning, I sent for forty kegs of palm wine. After I had drunk it all, I started to investigate whereabouts was the lady. As it was the market day, I started the investigation from the market. But as I was a juju-man, I knew all the kinds of people in that market. When it was exactly 9 o'clock a.m., the very complete gentleman whom the lady followed came to the market again, and at the same time that I saw him, I knew that he was a curious and terrible creature.

THE LADY WAS NOT TO BE BLAMED FOR FOLLOWING THE SKULL AS A COMPLETE GENTLEMAN

I could not blame the lady for following the Skull as a complete gentleman to his house at all. Because if I were a lady, no doubt I would follow him to wherever he would go, and still as I was a man I would jealous him more than that, because if this gentleman went to the battlefield, surely, enemy would not kill him or capture him and if bombers saw him in a town which was to be bombed, they would not throw bombs on his presence, and if they did throw it, the bomb itself would not explode until this gentleman would leave that town, because of his beauty. At the same time that I saw this gentleman in the market on that day, what I was doing was only to follow him about in the market. After I looked at him for so many hours, then I ran to a corner of the market and I cried for a few minutes because

Emphasizes the power and envy of beauty.

I thought within myself why was I not created that he was only a Skull, then I thanked God that He had created me without beauty, so I went back to him in the market, but I was still attracted by his beauty.) So when the market closed for that day, and when everybody was returning to his or her destination, this gentleman was returning to his own too and I followed him to know where he was living.

INVESTIGATION TO THE SKULL'S FAMILY'S HOUSE

When I traveled with him a distance of about twelve miles away to that market, the gentleman left the really road on which we were traveling and branched into an endless forest and I was following him, but as I did not want him to see that I was following him, then I used one of my juju which changed me into a lizard and followed him. But after I had traveled with him a distance of about twenty-five miles away in this endless forest, he began to pull out all the parts of his body and return them to the owners, and paid them.

After I had traveled with him for another fifty miles in this forest, then he reached his house and entered it, but I entered it also with him, as I was a lizard. The first thing that he did when he entered the hole (house) he went straight to the place where the lady was, and I saw the lady sat on a bullfrog with a single cowrie tied on her neck and a Skull who was watching her stood behind her. After he (gentleman) had seen that the lady was there, he went to the back yard where all his family were working.

THE INVESTIGATOR'S WONDERFUL WORK IN THE SKULL'S FAMILY'S HOUSE

When I saw this lady and when the Skull who brought her to that hole or whom I followed from the market to that hole went to the back yard, then I changed myself to a man as before, then I talked to the lady but she could not answer me at all, she only showed that she was in a serious condition. The Skull who was guarding her with a whistle fell asleep at that time.

To my surprise, when I helped the lady to stand up from the frog on which she sat, the cowrie that was tied on her neck made a curious noise at once, and when the Skull who was watching her heard the noise, he woke up and blew the whistle to the rest, then the whole of them rushed to the place and surrounded the lady and me, but at the same time that they saw me there, one of them ran to a pit which was not so far from that spot, the pit was filled with cowries. He picked one cowrie out of the pit, after that he was running toward me, and the whole crowd wanted to tie the cowrie on my neck too. But before they could do that, I had changed myself into air, they could not trace me out again, but I was looking at them. I believed that the cowries in that pit were their power and to reduce the power of any human being whenever tied on his or her neck and also to make a person dumb.

Over one hour after I had dissolved into air, these Skulls went back to the back yard, but there remained the Skull who was watching her.

After they had returned to the back yard, I changed to a man as usual, then I took the lady from the frog, but at the same time that I touched her, the cowrie which was tied on her neck began to shout; even if a person was four miles away he would not have to listen before hearing, but immediately the Skull who was watching her heard the noise and saw me when I took her from that frog, he blew the whistle to the rest of them who were in the back yard.

Immediately the whole Skull family heard the whistle when it blew to them, they were rushing out to the place and before they could reach there, I had left their hole for the forest, but before I could travel about one hundred yards in the forest, they had rushed out from their hole to inside the forest and I was still running away with the lady. As these Skulls were chasing me about in the forest, they were rolling on the ground like large stones and also humming with terrible noise, but when I saw that they had nearly caught me or if I continued to run away like that, no doubt, they would catch me sooner, then I changed the lady to a kitten and put her inside my pocket and changed myself to a very small bird which I could describe as a sparrow in English language.

After that I flew away, but as I was flying in the sky, the cowrie which was tied on that lady's neck was still making a noise and I tried all my best to stop the noise, but all were in vain. When I reached home with the lady, I changed her to a lady as she was before and also myself changed to man as well. When her father saw that I brought his daughter back home, he was exceedingly glad and said thus: "You are the 'Father of gods' as you had told me before."

But as the lady was now at home, the cowrie on her neck did not stop making a terrible noise once, and she could not talk to anybody; she showed only that she was very glad she was at home. Now I had brought the lady but she could not talk, eat, or loose away the cowrie on her neck, because the terrible noise of the cowrie did not allow anybody to rest or sleep at all.

THERE REMAIN GREATER TASKS AHEAD

Now I began to cut the rope of the cowrie from her neck and to make her talk and eat, but all my efforts were in vain. At last I tried my best to cut off the rope of the cowrie; it only stopped the noise, but I was unable to loose it away from her neck.

When her father saw all my trouble, he thanked me greatly and repeated again that as I called myself "Father of gods who could do anything in this world" I ought to do the rest of the work. But when he said so, I was very ashamed and thought within myself that if I return to the Skulls' hole or house, they might kill me and the forest was very dangerous travel always, again I could not go directly to the Skulls in their hole and ask them how to loose away the cowrie which was tied on the lady's neck and to make her talk and eat.

BACK TO THE SKULL'S FAMILY'S HOUSE

On the third day after I had brought the lady to her father's house, I returned to the endless forest for further investigation. When there remained about one mile to reach the hole of these Skulls, there I saw the very Skull who the lady had followed from the market as a complete gentleman to the hole of Skull's family's house, and at the same time that I saw him like that, I changed into a lizard and climbed a tree which was near him.

He stood before two plants, then he cut a single opposite leaf from the opposite plant; he held the leaf with his right hand and he was saying thus: "As this lady was taken from me, if this opposite leaf is not given her to eat, she will not talk forever." After that he threw the leaf down on the ground. Then he cut another single compound leaf with his left hand and said that if this single compound is not given to this lady, to eat, the cowrie on her neck could not be loosened away forever and it would be making a terrible noise forever.

After he said so, he threw the leaf down at the same spot, then he jumped away. So after he had jumped very far away (luckily, I was there when he was doing all these things, and I saw the place that he threw both leaves separately), then I changed myself to a man as before, I went to the place that he threw both leaves, then I picked them up and I went home at once.

But at the same time that I reached home, I cooked both leaves separately and gave her to eat; to my surprise the lady began to talk at once. After that, I gave her the compound leaf to eat for the second time and imme-

diately she ate that too, the cowrie which was tied on her neck by the Skull
loosened away by itself, but it disappeared at the same time. So when the
father and mother saw the wonderful work which I had done for them, they
brought fifty kegs of palm wine for me, they gave me the lady as wife and
two rooms in that house in which to live with them. So I saved the lady
from the complete gentleman in the market who was afterwards reduced to
a Skull and the lady became my wife since that day. This was how I got a
wife.

—1952

Camara Laye

(1928–80) GUINEA

On Tuesday, February 5, 1980, Léopold Sédar Senghor, the president of
Senegal and one of the earliest proponents of *négritude*, announced over Radio
Senegal that Camara Laye, the Guinean novelist, had died the day before.
The fifty-two-year-old writer had been ill for many years—much of the time
during his exile in Senegal, where he had resided for thirteen years as Senghor's guest. Laye was regarded as his continent's preeminent Francophone
novelist.

Most of Laye's career as a writer was a continuous struggle against hard-
ship, poverty, and government censorship. Laye had become a writer somewhat by accident. Born in Kouroussa, Guinea, in 1928, he distinguished
himself as a student and in time received a government scholarship to a
technical school in France. At the end of the year overseas, when Laye
decided that he wanted to continue his studies and pursue a baccalaureate,
his government abruptly cut off his funds.

Impoverished, Laye took whatever work he could to support himself. Out
of loneliness, frustration, and a fear that he would forget his African heritage,
he began writing down memories of his childhood in Guinea. Although he
never intended his writing to be published, he was persuaded by a Parisian
woman who had befriended him to show the material to a publisher. The
work appeared in 1954, as *L'enfant noir* (*The Dark Child*, or *The African Child*,
as it is translated in the two English-language versions), still perhaps the most

beautiful account of traditional African life ever published—in large part because of the haunting portrait of Laye's mother.

Laye's first novel, *Le regard du roi* (*The Radiance of the King*), was published two years later, in 1956, by which time he had decided that he wanted to be a full-time writer. This novel—a lengthy narrative about a white man who undergoes a spiritual transformation and becomes an African—has repeatedly been cited, along with Chinua Achebe's *Things Fall Apart*, as one of the masterpieces of African fiction. Laye—a firm believer in the positive aspects of cultural syncretism, in ethnic reciprocity—was an optimist, in spite of the unsettling difficulties that were about to unfold in his own life.

Back home in Guinea, Laye was given an innocuous position in the civil service, which permitted him time to write. But when Sékou Touré, the president of Guinea, read the author's work-in-progress, Laye was given two options: not publish the book or go into exile. Laye chose the latter, and *Dramouss* (a sequel to *L'enfant noir*) was published in Paris in 1966, after being postponed for several years.

In exile in Senegal, Laye was a haunted man. Sékou Touré ordered Laye's wife imprisoned, apparently in retaliation for the books her husband had published. Laye agonized about his wife and children in Guinea while suffering recurrent physical and psychological illnesses. Like other African writers of his generation, he discovered that his fame as a writer did not bring commensurate economic rewards or intellectual freedom.

Laye's writing suffered, though more in quantity than in quality. His final work, *Le Maître de la Parole* (1979), was published in Paris the year before his death. Though the volume chronicles the life and death of Sundiata, the first Emperor of the ancient Malian empire, *The Guardian of the Word* (the English-language title) is equally a celebration of the traditional African storyteller, the *griot*. In the narrative itself, Laye warns the reader not to confuse the true *griot* with contemporary storytellers, "those music merchants, those choristers or guitarists who wander through the big cities looking for recording studios."

Rather, Laye tells us, the true *griot*, "one of the important members of that ancient, clearly defined hierarchical society, is . . . preceding his status as a historian . . . above all an artist, and, it follows, his chants, his epics, and his legends are works of art."

Camara Laye was such a custodian of the word.

THE EYES OF THE STATUE

Translated from the French by Una Maclean

She stopped walking for a moment—ever since she set out she had been feeling as though she had earned a moment's rest—and she took stock of her surroundings. From the top of the hill on which she stood she saw spread out before her a great expanse of country.

Far away in the distance was a town, or, rather, the remains of a town, for there was no trace of movement to be seen near it, none of the signs of activity which would suggest the presence of a town. Perhaps it was merely distance which hid from her sight all the comings and goings, and possibly once within the town she would be borne along on the urgent flood of activity. Perhaps.

"From this distance anything is possible," she was surprised to hear herself say aloud.

She mused on how, from such a vast distance, it seemed still as though anything could happen, and she fervently believed that if any changes were to take place they would occur in the intervals when the town was hidden by the trees and undergrowth.

There had been many of these intervals and they were nearly always such very long intervals, so long that it was now by no means certain that she was approaching the town by the most direct route, for there was absolutely nothing to guide her and she had to struggle continually against the intertwining branches and tangled thorns and pick her way around a maze of swamps. She had tried very hard to cross the swamps but all she had succeeded in doing was getting her shoes and the hem of her skirt soaking wet and she had been obliged to retrace her steps hurriedly, so treacherous was the surface of the ground.

She couldn't really see the town and she wasn't going straight toward it except for the rare moments when she topped a rise. There the ground was sparsely planted with broom and heath and she was far above the thickly wooded depths of the valleys. But no sooner had she finished scrambling up the hills than she had to plunge once more into the bushes and try to force her way through the impenetrable undergrowth where everything was in her way, cutting off her view and making her walk painful and dangerous again.

"Perhaps I really ought to go back," she said to herself; and certainly that would have been the most sensible thing to do. But in fact she didn't slacken her pace in the least, as though something away over there was calling to her, as though the distant town were calling. But how could an empty town summon her. A silent deserted town!

For the closer she came to it the more she felt that it must really be a deserted city, a ruined city in fact. The height of the bushes and the dense tangled undergrowth about her feet convinced her. If the town had still been inhabited, even by a few people, its surroundings would never have fallen into the confusion through which she had been wandering around for hours; surely she would have found, instead of this tangled jungle, the orderly outskirts of which other towns could boast. But here there were neither roads nor paths; everything betokened disorder and decay.

Yet once more she wondered whatever forced her to continue her walk, but she could find no reply. She was following an irresistible urge. She would have been hard put to it to say how this impulse had arisen or indeed to decide just how long she had been obeying it. And perhaps it was the case that if only she followed the impulse for long enough she would no longer be capable of defying it, although there was no denying that it was grossly irrational. At any rate the urge must have been there for a very long time, as she could tell from the tiredness of her limbs, and moreover it was still very close. Couldn't she feel it brimming up within her, pressing on her breast with each eager breath she drew. Then all of a sudden she realized that she was face-to-face with it.

"The urge is me," she cried.

She proclaimed it defiantly but without knowing what she was defying, and triumphantly although unaware of her opponent. Whom had she defied, and what could she be triumphing over? It was not simply that she was identifying herself with the strange compulsion in order to get to know more of it and of herself. She was obliged to admit that the urge was indefinable, as her own being forever escaped definition.

After one final struggle with the branches and obstacles, and after skirting one more morass, she suddenly emerged in front of the city, or what remained of it. It was really only the traces of a town, no more than the traces, and in fact just what she had feared to find ever since she set out, but so sad, so desolate, she could never have imagined such desolation. Scarcely anything but rough heaps of walls remained. The porticoes were crumbling and most of the roofs had collapsed; only a column here or a fragment of a wall there proclaimed the former splendor of the peristyles. As for the remaining buildings, they seemed to waver uncertainly, as though on the very point of tumbling. Trees had thrust their branches through broken windows, great tufts of weeds pushed upwards the blocks and the marble slabs, the statues had fallen from their niches, all was ruined and burst asunder.

"I wonder why these remains seem so different from the forests and bush I have come through already?" she said to herself. There was no difference except for the desolation and loss, rendered all the more poignant by the contrast with what had once been. "What am I searching for here?" she asked herself once more. "I ought never to have come."

"Many people used to come here once," said an old man who appeared out of the ruins.

"Many people?" she said. "I have not seen a single soul."

"Nobody has been here for a very long time," said the old man. "But there was a time when crowds of people visited the ruins. Is that what you have come for?"

"I was coming toward the city."

"It certainly was a great city once. But you have arrived too late. Surely you must have been delayed on the road."

"I should not have been so late but for my battles with the trees and undergrowth and all my detours around the swamps. If only they hadn't held me back . . ."

"You should have come by the direct route."

"The direct route?" she exclaimed. "You cannot have any idea of the wilderness round this place."

"All right, all right," he said. "I do have some idea of it. As a matter of fact, when I saw that people had stopped coming, I guessed how it was. Perhaps there isn't any road left?"

"There isn't even a bush path!"

"What a pity," he said. "It was such a fine town, the most beautiful city in all the continent."

"And now, what is it?" she said.

"What is it?" he replied dismally.

With his stick he began to mow down the nettles which rose thick and menacing about them.

"Look at this," he said.

She saw in the midst of the nettles a fallen statue, green with moss, a humiliated statue. It cast upon her a dead, gray glance. Presently she became aware that the look was not really dead, only blind, as the eyes were without pupils, and it was in fact a living gaze, as alive as a look could be. A cry came from it, an appealing cry. Was the statue bewailing its loneliness and neglect? The lips drooped pitiably.

"Who is it?" she asked.

"He was the ruler who lived in this place. His rooms can still be seen."

"Why don't you set up the statue over there?" she said. "It would be better there than among all these nettles."

"That is what I wanted to do. As soon as the statue fell from its alcove I wanted to put it back, but I simply hadn't the strength. These stone sculptures are terribly heavy."

"I know," she replied, "and after all it is merely a stone sculpture."

But was it merely carved stone? Could sculptured stone have cast upon her such a piercing glance? Perhaps, then, it wasn't mere stone. And even if it were nothing more than mere stone, the fact remained that for all the nettles and moss and the vagaries of fortune which it had endured, this stone would still outlast man's life. No, it could not be mere stone. And with this sort of distress in its look, this cry of distress . . .

"Would you care to visit his rooms?" asked the old man.

"Yes, take me there," she answered.

"Pay particular attention to the columns," he told her. "No doubt there is only one hall left here now, but when you consider the number of broken and fallen columns it does look as though there used to be at least ten halls."

With the end of his stick he pointed out the marble stumps and debris of broken slabs buried in the grass.

"This gateway must have been exceedingly high," he said, gazing upwards.

"It can't have been higher than the palace, surely," she said.

"How can we tell? I have never seen it any more than you have. By the time I arrived here, it had already fallen into the grass; but those who were here before my time declared that it was an astonishing entrance. If you could put all this debris together again I dare say you would get a surprise. But who could tackle such a task?"

He shrugged his shoulders and continued: "You would need to be a giant, to have the hands and the strength of a giant."

"Do you really believe that a giant . . ."

"No," he replied. "Only the ruler himself, who had it erected, could do it. He could certainly manage it."

She gazed at the niches where great tufts of grass had been bold enough to replace the statues. There was one space, larger than all the rest, where the weeds grew particularly ostentatiously, like a flaming torch.

"That is the niche, over there, where he used to stand before his fall among the nettles," he remarked.

"I see," she said. "But now there is nothing left but wild grass and the memory of his agony."

"He used to find this city and his palace trying enough. He personally supervised the building of the entire place. He intended this town to be the biggest and this palace the highest. He wanted them built to his own scale. Now he is dead, his heart utterly broken."

"But could he have died any other way?"

"No, I suppose he carried his own death within him, like us all. But he had to carry the fate of a felled Goliath."

By this time they had reached the foot of a staircase and he pointed out a little door at the end of the corridor on the left.

"That is where I live," he told her. "It is the old porter's lodge. I suppose I could have found somewhere a little more spacious and less damp, but after all, I am not much more than a cartetaker. In fact, a guide is only a caretaker."

So saying, he began to make his way painfully up the steps. He was a decrepit old man.

"You are looking at me? I know I'm not much better than the palace! All this will crumble down one day. Soon all this will crumble down on my head and it won't be a great loss! But perhaps I shall crumble before the palace."

"The palace is older," she said.

"Yes, but it is more robust. They don't build like that nowadays."

"What have you been saying?" she demanded. "You are not stone! Why compare your body to a palace?"

"Did I compare myself to a palace? I don't think so. My body is certainly no palace, not even a ruined one. Perhaps it is like the porter's lodge where I live, and perhaps I was wrong to call it damp and dark, perhaps I should have said nothing about it. But I must pause for breath. These stairs. At my age no one likes climbing stairs."

And he wheezed noisily, pressing his hand over his heart as though to subdue its frantic beating.

"Let us go," he said at last, "up the few remaining steps."

They climbed a little higher and reached a landing with a great door opening off it, a door half wrenched from its hinges.

"Here are the rooms," he said.

She saw an immense apartment, frightfully dilapidated. The roof had partly collapsed, leaving the rafters open to the sky. Daylight streamed in upon the debris of tiles and rubbish strewn upon the floor. But nothing could take from the chamber its harmonious proportions, with its marble panels, its tapestry and paintings, the bold surge of its columns, and the deep alcoves between them. It was all still beautiful, in spite of being three-quarters ruined. The torn and rotten tapestries and the peeling paintings were still beautiful: so were the cracked stained-glass windows. And although the paneling was practically torn away, the grandeur of the original conception remained.

"Why have you let everything deteriorate so far?" she asked.

"Why indeed? But now it is too late to do anything about it."

"Is it really too late?"

"Now that the master is no longer here . . ." He tapped the panels with his stick.

"I don't know how the walls are still standing," he said. "They may last a fair time yet. But the rain deluges through the roof and windows and loosens the stones. And then when the winter storms come! It is those violent storms that destroy everything."

He dislodged a scrap of mortar. "Just look, it's no more than a bit of gray dust. I can't think why the blocks don't fall apart. The damp has destroyed everything."

"Was this the only room the master had?" she asked.

"He had hundreds of them and all of them richly furnished. I've pushed the movable stuff into one of the smaller rooms which were less damaged."

He opened a door concealed in the paneling. "Here is some of it," he said.

She beheld a jumble of carved furniture, ornaments, carpets, and crockery.

"Gold dishes, please note. The master would eat off nothing but gold. And look at this. Here he is in his robes of state." He pointed to a canvas where the face of the statue was portrayed.

The eyes were marvelously expressive. They were so even in the statue, although the sculptor had given them no pupils, but here they were infinitely more expressive and the look which they gave was one of anguish. "Is no one left near me?" they seemed to ask. And the droop of the mouth replied, "No one." The man had known they would all forsake him, he had long foreseen it. Nevertheless, she, she had come! She had fought through the bush and she had wandered round the swamps, she had felt fatigue and despair overwhelming her, but she had triumphed over all these obstacles and she had come, she had come at last. Had he not guessed she would come? Yet possibly this very foresight had but accentuated the bitter line of his set lips. "Yes," said those lips, "someone will come, when all the world has ceased to call. But someone who will be unable to soothe my distress."

She swung round. This reproach was becoming unbearable, and not only this reproach, which made all her goodwill seem useless, but the cry of abandonment, the wild lonely appeal in his look.

"We can do nothing, nothing at all for him," the old man declared. And she replied: "Is there ever anything we can do?" She sighed. In her innermost being she felt the anguish of this look; one might have thought it was she who cried, that the cry of loneliness welled from her own lonely heart.

"Perhaps you can do something," he said. "You are still young. Although you may not be able to do anything for yourself, you might perhaps help others."

"You know very well that I cannot even do that," she said.

She seemed overwhelmed, as though she bore the ruins on her own shoulders.

"Are there still more rooms?" she asked him.

"Lots of them. But it is getting late, the sun is sinking."

Daylight was fading fast. The light had become a soft, rosy glow, a light which was kinder to details, and in it the great room took on a new aspect. The paintings and panels regained a freshness which was far from theirs by right. This sudden glow was the gentlest of lights. But not even this light could calm a tormented heart.

"Come along," called the old man.

"Yes," she said.

She imagined that once she went out of this hall and its adjoining storeroom her heart would perhaps calm down. She thought that perhaps she might forget the great cry coming from the storeroom. Yes, if only she could get away from this palace, leave these ruins, surely she could forget it. But was not the cry inside herself?

"The cry is within me," she exclaimed.

"Stop thinking about it," advised the old man. "If you hear anything it's just because the silence has got on your nerves. Tomorrow you will hear nothing."

"But it is a terrible cry."

"The swans have an awful cry, too," he remarked.

"Swans?"

"Yes, the swans. To look at them gliding over the water you might never believe it. Have you ever happened to hear them cry? But of course not, you are scarcely more than a child and with less sense than one, and you probably imagine that they sing. Listen, formerly there were lots of swans here, they were at the very gate of the palace. Sometimes the lake was covered with them like white blossoms. Visitors used to throw scraps to them. Once the tourists stopped coming, the swans died. No doubt they had lost the habit of searching for food themselves and so they died. Very well, never, do you hear me, never did I hear a single song coming from the pond."

"Why do you have to tell me all this? Have I ever told you I believe in the swan's song? You didn't need to speak to me like that."

"No, maybe I shouldn't have said it, or I should have said it less suddenly at least. I'm sorry. I even believed in the swan's song myself once. You know how it is, I am old and lonely and I have got into the habit of talking to myself, then. I once believed that the lord of this palace, before he died, sang a swan's song. But no, he cried out. He cried so loudly that . . ."

"Please tell me no more," she begged.

"All right, I suppose we shouldn't think about all that. But let's go."

He carefully closed the storeroom door and they made their way toward the exit.

"Did you mean to leave the door of the big room open?" she asked, once they had reached the landing.

"It hasn't been shut for a long time," he replied. "Besides, there is nothing to fear. No one comes here now."

"But I came."

He glanced at her. "I keep wondering why you came," he said. "Why did you?"

"How can I tell?" she said.

Her visit was futile. She had crossed a desert of trees, and bush and swamps. And why? Had she come at the summoning of that anguished cry from the depth of the statue's and the picture's eyes? What way was there of finding out? And moreover it was an appeal to which she could not respond, an appeal beyond her power to satisfy. No, this impulse which had moved her to hasten toward the town had been mad from the start.

"I don't know why I came," she repeated.

"You shouldn't take things to heart like that. These painters and carvers are so crafty, you know, they can make you realize things you would never have considered. Take that statue and the portrait, for instance. Have you noticed the look in the eyes? We begin by wondering where they found such a look and eventually we realize they have taken it from ourselves; and these are the paradoxes they would be the first to laugh at. You should laugh, too."

"But these paradoxes, as you call them, which come from the depth of our being, what if we cannot find them there?"

"What do you find within yourself?" he answered her.

"I have already told you: unbearable loneliness."

"Yes," he said, "there is something of that in each one of us."

"But in me . . ."

"No, not more than in anyone else," he insisted. "Don't imagine that others are any less alone. But who wants to admit that? All the same, it is not an unendurable state of affairs. It is quite bearable in fact. Solitude! Listen, solitude isn't what you imagine. I don't want to run away from my solitude. It is the last desirable thing left me, it is my only wealth, a great treasure, an ultimate good."

"Is he just saying that to comfort me?" she wondered. "But it is no

consolation, a shared solitude can be no consolation. The sharing only makes
the solitude doubly lonely.''

Aloud she said: "That doesn't console me in the least.''

"I didn't think it would,'' he replied. They had by now reached the foot
of the staircase and the old man showed her the little corridor leading to
his room.

"My lodge is here.''

"Yes, I know,'' she said. "You've told me already.''

"But I haven't told you everything. I didn't say that my room is right
beneath the staircase. When visitors used to climb up there in throngs they
were walking over my lodge. Do you understand?''

"Yes.''

"No, you don't understand at all, you don't realize that they were marching on my head, wiping their feet on my hair. I had plenty of hair in those
days.''

"But they weren't really wiping their feet,'' she said, "they . . .''

"Don't you think it was humiliating enough anyway?''

She did not know how to reply. The old man seemed slightly crazed:
some of what he said was very sensible but a lot of it was sheer nonsense.
"The solitude has gone to his head,'' she told herself, and she looked at
him afresh. He was certainly very old. There must be times when age and
loneliness together . . . Aloud she remarked: "I don't know.'' And then,
all of a sudden: "What made you say that solitude is an ultimate good?''

"How very young you are'' was his only reply. "You should never have
come here.'' He made off toward his lodge, saying: "I'm going to prepare
a meal.''

"I shall rest here awhile,'' she said as she climbed the steps.

"Yes, do have a rest, you've certainly earned one. I shall call you when
the food is ready.''

She sat down and gazed at the evil weeds. The nettles were by far the
most numerous and reminded her of the ocean. They were like a great green
sea which surged around the palace trying to drown it, and ultimately they
would completely engulf it. What could mere stones do against such a powerful wave? A wave with the deceptive smoothness of velvety leaves, a wave
which hid its poisons and its sorcery beneath a velvet touch. It seemed to
her fevered imagination that the wave was already rising. Or was it simply
the darkness? Was it night which was burying the lowest steps? No, it was
really the wave of nettles, imperceptibly advancing in its assault upon the

palace. A transient attack, no doubt. Probably this sea of nettles had tides like the ocean. And perhaps it wasn't merely a simple tide. Perhaps . . .

She leapt to her feet. The tide was about her ankles. She climbed several steps and the tide rose as quickly.

"Caretaker!" she screamed.

But she could no longer see the porter's lodge. Perhaps the sea had already entered the room while she was sitting down. She couldn't be certain now whether it had a door which shut. Even suppose it did have, how could a door stop such a wave?

"What is to become of me?" she asked herself. She climbed a few more steps, but the tide continued to pursue her, it really was following her. She paused; perhaps if she stopped, the tide in its turn might stop rising. But instead it flowed right up to her, covering her shoes. Feverishly she resumed her upward flight and gained the landing opposite the doorway of the main hall. But to her horror she realized that the wave was there almost as soon. It was inches away. Must she drown in those horrible weeds?

She rushed to open the storeroom door, only to find that the sea had beaten her and had borne everything away, literally washed off the face of the earth. There was no longer any storeroom left! It had been engulfed beneath the flood of nettles, with its furniture and tapestries and dishes, and the portrait as well. Only the cry, the great cry of anguish remained, and it had become vaster and louder, more piercing and heartrending than ever. It swelled to fill the whole earth! It seemed to her as though nothing could silence it anymore and that whatever she did she could never escape. Her heart could never escape again. Yet at the same time she tried to bolt the door upon it as though in spite of all she knew she might evade it yet. But what could she escape to? There was no way of escape left open, it was either the cry or the flood. She was a prey to this cry and in no time she would be the victim of the flood. She was trapped between two floods, the one which swallowed up the storeroom and was lying in wait menacingly on its threshold, and the other one which had pursued her step by step up the stairs and across the great hall. She had no choice but to cast herself into one of these two floods which were soon to merge. Placed as she was, she could neither advance nor retreat.

"Caretaker!" she cried.

But did she actually shriek? No sound came from her lips. Terror was throttling her; it had her by the throat. She only imagined she had shouted.

At the second attempt she could not even pretend to herself that she had shouted. She no longer even had the will to cry out. She realized that her terror was so extreme that she could never shout again. Nevertheless, she continued to struggle hopelessly, she fought and struggled silently and in vain.

And meanwhile the flood was steadily rising beyond her ankles and up her legs. Confident of its power, it rose more rapidly than ever.

Then, while she was struggling and trying desperately to regain her voice, she suddenly caught sight of the statue. The sea of weeds had lifted it and was tossing it on its waves.

She stopped struggling to watch it and at once she could see that its eyes were looking at her just as they had done when the old man had first thrust aside the nettles. It was the same look, the same cry of distress and bitter loneliness.

She longed to awake from her nightmare and she tried once more to call for help, but in vain. Must she really die alone beneath the flood of weeds, all alone? She hid her face in her arms.

A little later she felt a blow on her forehead and she felt as if her skull was bursting.

—1959

Birago Diop

(BORN 1906) SENEGAL

Birago Diop's early schooling was at the Lycée Faidherbe in St. Louis. He continued his education in France, at the University of Toulouse, where he studied veterinary science. Removed from his homeland during his advanced studies, he began writing down the stories he had heard as a child. Many of these were published in 1947 as *Les contes d'Amadou Koumba (Tales of Amadou Koumba)*. His first positions in Africa as a veterinarian were in the Ivory Coast and Upper Volta. A second collection of tales appeared in 1958: *Les nouveaux contes d'Amadou Koumba (The New Tales of Amadou Koumba)*. Diop has also published poetry and served in his country's diplomatic corps.

In his most typical stories, Diop has tapped the oral tradition of his Wolof people, especially their animal tales. Dorothy S. Blair (one of Diop's translators) has commented on the author's cosmology: "In the traditional animistic beliefs and mythology of Africa there is no dividing line between life and death, between animate and inanimate objects, between animals and humans. Everything lives and possesses a soul: tree, arrow, antelope, pebble, man. All these partake of the same essence and contribute to each other's total experience of existence. An animal, a child, or a wooden statuette can contain the spirit of a dead ancestor." Because of the mystical, animistic world of Diop's stories, his work has been compared to the writings of the *négritude* poets of the 1930s and 1940s. Diop had, in fact, associated with some of these writers during his years as a student in France.

Joyce A. Hutchinson has written specifically of the story included here:

"His [veterinary] travels in connection with his work enabled him to keep in touch with the traditional customs and stories of his people and also to observe the effects of increasing French penetration on their way of life. . . . The obligation to respect traditions, to respect the ancestors and customary beliefs, and to pay attention to the teachings of one's parents and elders . . . figures as a leitmotif in many of Diop's stories. The harshest social sanctions are those imposed on characters who fail to show respect in these matters. . . ."

SARZAN

Translated from the French by Ellen Conroy Kennedy

It was hard to distinguish the piles of ruins from the termite mounds, and only an ostrich shell, cracked and yellowed by the weather, still indicated at the tip of a tall column what once had been the mirab of the mosque El Hadj Omar's warriors had built. The Toucouleur conqueror had shorn the hair and shaved the heads of the forebears of those who are now the village elders. He had decapitated those who would not submit to Koranic law. Once again, the village elders wear their hair in braids. The sacred woods long ago burned by the fanatic Talibés have long since grown tall again, and still harbor the cult objects, pots whitened from the boiling of millet or browned by the clotted blood of sacrificed chickens and dogs.

Like grain felled at random beneath the flail, or ripe fruits that drop from branches filled with sap, whole families left Dougouba to form new villages, Dougoubanis. Some of the young people would go off to work in Ségou, in Bamako, in Kayes, or Dakar; others went to work the Senegalese groundnut fields, returning when the harvest was in and the product had been shipped. All knew the root of their lives was still in Dougouba, which had long ago erased all traces of the Islamic hordes and returned to the teachings of the ancestors.

One son of Dougouba had ventured farther and for a longer time than any of the others: Thiemokho Keita. From Dougouba he went to the local capital, from there to Kati, from Kati to Dakar, from Dakar to Casablanca, from Casablanca to Fréjus, and then to Damascus. Leaving the Sudan to be a soldier, Thiemokho Keita had been trained in Senegal, fought in Morocco, stood guard in France, and patrolled in Lebanon. He returned to Dougouba a sergeant, catching a lift in my medical caravan.

I had been making my veterinarian's rounds in the heart of the Sudan when I met Sergeant Keita in a local administrator's office. He had just been discharged from the service and wanted to enlist in the local police, or to be taken on as an interpreter.

"No," the local commandant told him. "You can do more for the administration by returning to your village. You who have traveled so much and seen so much, you can teach the others something about how white men live. You'll 'civilize' them a bit. Say there, Doctor," he continued, turning to me. "Since you're going in that direction, won't you take Keita with you? It will spare him the wear and tear of the road and save him some time. It's fifteen years he's been gone."

So we set out. The driver, the sergeant, and I occupied the front seat of the little truck, while behind, the cooks, medical aides, driver's helper, and the civil guard were crowded together among the field kitchen, the camp bed, and the cases of serum and vaccine. The sergeant told me about his life as a soldier, then as a noncommissioned officer. I heard about the Riff Wars from the viewpoint of a Sudanese rifleman; he talked about Marseilles, Toulon, Fréjus, Beirut. He seemed no longer to see the road in front of us. Rough as a corrugated tin room, it was paved with logs covered with a layer of clay, disintegrating into dust now because of the torrid heat and the extreme dryness. It was an unctuous oily dust that stuck to our faces like a yellow mask, making our teeth gritty and screening from our view the chattering baboons and frightened does that leaped about in our wake. Through the choking haze, Keita seemed to see once more the minarets of Fez, the teeming crowds of Marseilles, the great tall buildings of France, the blue sea.

By noon we reached the town of Madougou, where the road ended. To reach Dougouba by nightfall, we took horses and bearers.

"When you come back this way again," Keita said, "you'll go all the way to Dougouba by car. Tomorrow I'm going to get started on a road."

The muffled rolling of a tom-tom announced that we were nearing the village. A gray mass of huts appeared, topped by the darker gray of three palm trees against a paler gray sky. The rumbling was accompanied now by the sharp sound of three notes on a flute. We were in Dougouba. I got down first and asked for the village chief.

"Dougou-tigui, here is your son, the Sergeant Keita."

Thiemokho Keita jumped down from his horse. As if the sound of his shoes on the ground had been a signal, the drumming stopped and the flute was silent. The aged chief took Keita's two hands while other old men examined his arms, his shoulders, his decorations. Some old women ran up and began fingering the puttees at his knees. Tears shone on the dark faces, settling in the wrinkles that crossed their ritual scars.

Everyone was saying: "Keita, Keita, Keita!"

"Those," the old man quavered at last, "those who brought your steps back to our village on this day are generous and good."

It was in fact a day unlike other days in Dougouba. It was the day of the Kotéba, the day of the Testing.

The drum resumed its rumbling, pierced by the sharp whistles of the flute. Inside the circle of women, children, and grown men, bare-chested youngsters, each carrying a long branch of balazan wood stripped clean and supple as a whip, were turning about to the rhythm of the tom-tom. In the center of this moving circle, crouching with his knees and elbows on the ground, the flute player gave forth three notes, always the same. Above him a young man would come to stand, legs apart, arms spread in the shape of a cross, while the others, passing close to him, let their whips whistle. The blows fell on his chest, leaving a stripe wide as a thumb, sometimes breaking the skin. The sharp voice of the flute would go a note higher, the tom-tom would grow softer, as the whips whistled and the blood ran. Firelight gleamed on the black-brown body and light from the embers leaped to the tops of the palm trees, softly creaking in the evening wind. Kotéba! the test of endurance, the testing for insensibility to pain. The child who cries when he hurts himself is only a child; the child who cries when he is hurt will not make a man.

Kotéba! to offer one's back, receive the blow, turn around, and give it back to someone else. Kotéba!

"This, these are still the ways of savages!"

I turned round. It was Sergeant Keita who had come to join me by the drum.

The ways of savages? This testing, which among other things produced men who were hard and tough! What was it that had enabled the forebears of these youngsters to march with enormous burdens on their heads for whole days without stopping? What had made Thiemokho Keita himself, and others like him, able to fight valiantly beneath skies where the sun itself is very often sickly, to labor with heavy packs on their backs, enduring cold, thirst, and hunger?

The ways of savages? Perhaps. But I was thinking that elsewhere, where I came from, we had left these initiations behind. For our adolescents there was no longer a "house of men" where the body, the mind, and the character were tempered, where the ancient *passines*, the riddles and conundrums, were learned by dint of beatings on the bent back and the held-out fingers, and where the *kassaks*, the age-old memory-training songs whose words and wisdom descend to us from the dark nights, were assured their place in our heads by the heat of live coals that burned the palms of our hands. I was thinking that as far as I could see we had still gained nothing, that perhaps we had left these old ways behind without having caught up with the new ones.

The tom-tom murmured on, sustaining the piercing voice of the flute. The fires died and were born again. I went to the hut that had been prepared for me. Inside, mixed with the thick smell of *banco*—the dried clay kneaded with broken rotten straw that made the hut rainproof—a subtler odor hung, the fragrance of the dead, whose number, three, was indicated by animal horns fixed to the wall at the level of a man's height. For, in Dougouba, the cemetery too had disappeared, and the dead continued to live with the living. They were buried in the huts.

The sun was already warm when I took my leave, but Dougouba was still asleep: drunk, both from fatigue and from the millet beer that had circulated in calabashes from hand to mouth and mouth to hand the whole night long.

"Goodbye," said Keita. "The next time you come there will be a road, I promise you."

The work in other sectors and localities kept me from returning to Dougouba until the following year.

It was late in the afternoon after a hard journey. The air seemed a thick mass, hot and sticky, that we pushed our way through with great effort.

Sergeant Keita had kept his word; the road went all the way to Dougouba. As in all the villages, at the sound of the car a swarm of naked children appeared at the end of the road, their little bodies gray-white with dust, and on their heels came the reddish-brown dogs with cropped ears and bony flanks. In the midst of the children a man was gesticulating, waving a cow's tail attached to his right wrist. When the car stopped, I saw it was the sergeant, Thiemokho Keita. He wore a faded fatigue jacket, without buttons or stripes. Underneath were a *boubou* and pants made of strips of khaki-colored cotton, like the ones worn by the village elders. His pants stopped above the knee and were held together with pieces of string. His puttees were in rags. He was barefoot but wore a képi on his head.

"Keita!"

The children scattered like a volley of sparrows, chirping: "Ayi! Ayi!" (No! No!)

Thiemokho Keita did not take my hand. He looked at me, but seemed not to see me. His gaze was so distant that I couldn't help turning around to see what his eyes were fixed upon through mine. Suddenly, agitating his cowtail, he began to cry out in a hoarse voice:

> *Listen to things*
> *More often than beings*
> *Hear the voice of fire*
> *Hear the voice of water*
> *Listen in the wind to the sighs of the bush*
> *This is the ancestors breathing.*

"He's mad," said my driver, whom I silenced with a gesture. The sergeant was still chanting, in a strange, singsong voice:

> *Those who are dead are not ever gone*
> *They are in the darkness that grows lighter*
> *And in the darkness that grows darker*
> *The dead are not down in the earth*
> *They are in the trembling of the trees*
> *In the moaning of the woods*
> *In the water that runs*
> *In the water that sleeps*
> *They are in the hut, they are in the crowd.*

> *The dead are not dead.*
> *Listen to things*

More often than beings
Hear the voice of fire
Hear the voice of water
Listen in the wind
To the bush that is sighing
This is the breathing of ancestors
Who have not gone away
Who are not under earth
Who are not really dead.

Those who are dead are not ever gone
They are in a woman's breast
In a child's wailing
and the log burning
in the moaning rock and
in the weeping grasses
in the forest in the home
The dead are not dead.

Hear the fire speak
Hear the water speak
Listen in the wind to
the bush that is sobbing
This is the ancestors breathing.

Each day they renew ancient bonds
Ancient bonds that hold fast
Binding our lot to their law
To the will of the spirits stronger than we are
Whose covenant binds us to life
Whose authority binds to their will
The will of the spirits that move
In the bed of the river, on the banks of the river
The breathing of ancestors
Wailing in the rocks and weeping in the grasses.

Spirits inhabit
the darkness that lightens, the darkness that darkens

the quivering tree, the murmuring wood
the running and the sleeping waters
Spirits much stronger than we are
The breathing of the dead who are not really dead
Of the dead who are not really gone
Of the dead now no more in the earth.
Listen to things
More often than beings . . .

The children returned, circling round the old chief and the village elders. After the greetings, I asked what had happened to Sergeant Keita.

"Ayi! Ayi!" said the old men. "Ayi! Ayi!" echoed the children.

"No, not Keita!" said the old father, "Sarzan,* just Sarzan. We must not rouse the anger of the departed. Sarzan is no longer a Keita. The Dead and the Spirits have punished him for his offenses."

It had begun the day after his arrival, the very day of my departure from Dougouba.

Sergeant Keita had wanted to keep his father from sacrificing a white chicken to thank the ancestors for having brought him home safe and sound. Keita declared that if he had come home it was quite simply that he had had to, and that the ancestors had had nothing to do with it.

"Leave the dead be," he had said. "They can no longer do anything for the living."

The old chief had paid no attention and the chicken had been sacrificed.

When it was time to work the fields, Thiemokho had called it useless and even stupid to kill black chickens and pour their blood into a corner of the fields. The work, he said, was enough. Rain would fall if it was going to. The millet, corn, groundnuts, yams, and beans would grow all by themselves, and would grow better if the villagers would use the plows the local administrator had sent him. Keita cut down and burned the branches of Dassiri, the sacred tree, protector of the village and the cultivated fields, at whose foot the dogs were sacrificed.

On the day when the little boys were to be circumcised and the little girls excised,† Sergeant Keita had leaped upon their teacher, the Gangour-

---

* A Senegalese pronunciation of *sergent*, the French for sergeant—Trans.
† Female circumcision—Ed.

ang, who was dancing and chanting. He tore off the porcupine quills the Gangourang wore upon his head, and the netting that hid his body. From the head of Papa Djombo, the venerable grandfather who taught the young girls, Keita had ripped the cone-shaped yellow headdress topped with *gri-gri* charms and ribbons. All this he called "the ways of savages." And yet he had been to Nice, and seen the carnival with the funny and frightening masks. The whites, the Toubabs, it is true, wore masks for fun and not in order to teach their children the wisdom of the ancients.

Sergeant Keita had unhooked the little bag hanging in his hut which held the Nyanaboli, the Keita family spirit, and had thrown it into the yard, where the skinny dogs nearly won it from the children before the chief could get there.

One morning he had gone into the sacred wood and broken the pots of boiled millet and sour milk. He had pushed over the little statues and pulled up the forked stakes tipped with hardened blood and chicken feathers. "The ways of savages," he called them. The sergeant, however, had been in churches. He had seen little statues there of saints and the Holy Virgin that people burned candles to. These statues, it is true, were covered with gilt and painted in bright colors—blues, reds, and yellows. Certainly they were more beautiful than the blackened pygmies with long arms and short legs carved of cailcedra or ebony that inhabited the sacred forest.

"You'll civilize them a bit," the local administrator had said. Sergeant Thiemokho Keita was going to "civilize" his people. It was necessary to break with tradition, do away with the beliefs upon which the village life, the existence of the families, the people's behavior had always rested. Superstition had to be eradicated. The ways of savages. Ways of savages, the hard treatment inflicted on the young initiates at circumcision to open their minds, form their character, and teach them that nowhere, at any moment of their lives, can they, will they ever be alone. A way of savages, the Kotéba, which forges real men on whom pain can hold no sway. The ways of savages, the sacrifices, the blood offered to the ancestors and the earth . . . the boiling of millet and curdled milk poured out to the wandering spirits and the protective genies . . . the ways of savages.

All this Sergeant Keita proclaimed to the young and old of the village, standing in the shade of the palaver tree.

It was nearly sunset when Thiemokho Keita went out of his mind. He was leaning against the palaver tree, talking, talking, talking, against the medicine man who had sacrificed some dogs that very morning, against the old who didn't want to hear him, against the young who still listened to the old. He was still speaking when suddenly he felt something like a prick on his left shoulder. He turned his head. When he looked at his listeners again, his eyes were no longer the same. A white, foamy spittle appeared at the corners of his mouth. He spoke, but it was no longer the same words that emerged from his lips. The spirits had taken his mind, and now they cried out their fear:

Black night! Black night!

He called at nightfall, and the women and children trembled in their huts:

Black night! Black night!

He cried at daybreak:

Black night! Black night!

He howled at high noon. Night and day the spirits and the genies and the ancestors made him speak, cry out and chant . . .

It was only at dawn that I was able to doze off in the hut where the dead lived. All night I had heard Sergeant Keita coming and going, howling, weeping, and singing:

> *Trumpeting elephants hoot*
> *In the darkening wood*
> *Above the cursèd drums,*
> *Black night, black night!*
>
> *Milk sours in the calabash*
> *Gruel hardens in the jar*
> *And fear stalks in the hut,*
> *Black night, black night!*
>
> *The torches throw*
> *Bodiless flames*
> *In the air*

And then, quietly, glarelessly
Smoke,
Black night, black night!

Restless spirits
Meander and moan
Muttering lost words,
Words that strike fear,
Black night, black night!

From the chickens' chilled bodies
Or the warm moving corpse
Not a drop of blood runs
Neither black blood nor red,
Black night, black night!
Trumpeting elephants hoot
Above the cursèd drums,
Black night, black night!

Orphaned, the river calls out
In fear for the people
Endlessly, fruitlessly wandering
Far from its desolate banks,
Black night, black night!

And in the savannah, forlorn
Deserted by ancestors' spirits
The trumpeting elephants hoot
Above the cursèd drums,
Black night, black night!

Sap freezes in the anxious trees
In trunks and leaves
That no longer can pray
To the ancestors haunting their feet,
Black night, black night!

Fear lurks in the hut
In the smoking torch
In the orphaned river
In the weary, soulless forest
In the anxious, faded trees

Trumpeting elephants hoot
In the darkening woods
Above the cursèd drums,
Black night, black night!

No one dared call him by his name anymore for the spirits and the ancestors had made another man of him. Thiemokho Keita was gone for the villagers. Only Sarzan was left, Sarzan-the-Mad.

—1961

Sembene Ousmane

(BORN 1923) SENEGAL

Although he is known internationally as Africa's most important filmmaker, Sembene Ousmane began his artistic career as a writer. At the beginning of World War II, he was drafted into the French Army. Following the war, after a brief return to Senegal, he lived for a number of years in Marseilles. His first novel, *Le docker noir (The Black Docker)*, published in 1956, was influenced by Claude McKay's *Banjo* (1929). Both novels are concerned with black stevedores living on the fringes of the white man's world.

Ousmane's most widely read novel, *Les bouts de bois de Dieu (God's Bits of Wood)*, was published in 1960. Events in the novel are based on the famous Dakar–Niger railway workers' strike in 1947, in which Ousmane participated. In the early 1950s, when Ousmane lived in France, he met other important Francophone writers, including those who had formulated the tenets of *négritude*, twenty years earlier. A decade later, Ousmane relocated again, to Russia, where he studied at the Moscow Film School.

Ousmane turned to film because of his realization that in Africa in the early 1960s his reading audience was limited by illiteracy; with the cinema, he could reach many more people. His first narrative film was based on the story published here, "Black Girl" ("Le Noir de . . ."), which originally appeared in *Voltaïque* (1962), a volume of the writer's early stories. *Black Girl* was followed by nearly a dozen films, widely shown across the African continent and in Europe. Because of their strong political content, some of these films have aroused the hostility of officials in Ousmane's native Senegal.

Yet he has continued to pursue controversial subjects in both his fiction and his films.

He has compared his role as filmmaker to that of the traditional African storyteller, remarking: "The artist must in many ways be the mouth and the ears of his people. In the modern sense, this corresponds to the role of the *griot* in traditional African culture. The artist is like a mirror. His work reflects and synthesizes the problems, the struggles and hopes of his people."

Besides the movie *Black Girl*, Sembene's later films include *Mandabi* (*The Money Order*), 1968; *Emitai*, 1971; *Xala*, 1974; *Ceddo*, 1976; and *Le Camp de Thiaroye*, 1988. He has continued to write novels and short stories. *Le Dernier de l'Empire* (*The Last of the Empire*), a two-volume novel about a fictitious Senegalese president, was published in 1981. Two earlier novellas, *Niiwan* and *Taaw*, were published in English translation in 1992.

Anny Wynchank, who has called Sembene the "voice of the voiceless," has stated: "Sembene's driving concern has been to denounce hypocrisy, stupidity and injustice, as well as to expose the consequences of ignorance, superstition, and fatalistic passivity. His goal has always been to restore a sense of honor and dignity in the poor and the exploited of Africa. . . ."

BLACK GIRL

Translated from the French by Ellen Conroy Kennedy

It was the morning of the 23rd of June in the year of Our Lord nineteen hundred fifty-eight. At Antibes, along the Riviera, neither the fate of the French Republic nor the future of Algeria nor the state of the colonial territories preoccupied those who swarmed across the beaches below La Croisette.

Above, on the road leading to the Hermitage, two old-style Citroëns, one behind the other, were moving up the mountain. They stopped and several men quickly got out, rushing down the gravel walk toward a house on which a worn sign spelled out VILLA OF GREEN HAPPINESS. The men were the police chief of the town of Grasse, a medical officer, and two police inspectors from Antibes, flanked by officers in uniform.

There was nothing green about the Villa of Green Happiness except its name. The garden was kept in the French manner, the walks covered with gravel, set off by a couple of palm trees with drooping fronds. The chief looked closely at the house, his eyes stopping at the third window, the broken glass, the ladder.

Inside were other inspectors and a photographer. Three people who seemed to be reporters were looking with rather absentminded interest at the African statues, masks, animal skins, and ostrich eggs set here and there. Entering the living room was like violating the privacy of a hunter's lair.

Two women were hunched together, sobbing. They looked very much alike, the same straight forehead, the same curved nose, the same dark circles about eyes reddened from crying. The one in the pale dress was speaking: "After my nap, I felt like taking a bath. The door was locked from the inside"—blowing her nose—"and I thought to myself, it's the maid taking her bath. I say 'the maid,' " she corrected, "but we never called her anything else but her name, Diouana. I waited for more than an hour, but didn't see her come out. I went back and called, knocking on the door. There was no answer. Then I phoned our neighbor, the Commodore . . ."

She stopped, wiped her nose, and began to cry again. Her sister, the younger of the two, hair cut in a boyish style, sat hanging her head.

"You're the one who discovered the body?" the chief asked the Commodore.

"Yes . . . that is, when Madame Pouchet called and told me that the black girl had locked herself in the bathroom, I thought it was a joke. I spent thirty-five years at sea, you know. I've roamed the seven seas. I'm retired from the Navy."

"Yes, yes, we know."

"Yes, well, when Madame Pouchet called I brought my ladder."

"You brought the ladder?"

"No. It was Mademoiselle Dubois, Madame's sister, who suggested the idea. And when I got to the window, I saw the black girl swimming in blood."

"Where is the key to the door?"

"Here it is, your honor," said the inspector.

"Just wanted to see it."

"I've checked the window," said the other inspector.

"I'm the one who opened it, after breaking the pane," said the retired Navy man.

"Which pane did you break?"

"Which pane?" he repeated. He was wearing white linen trousers and a blue jacket.

"Yes, I saw it, but I'd like to ask precisely."

"The second from the top," answered the sister.

At this, two stretcher-bearers came down, carrying a body wrapped in a blanket. Blood dripped on the steps. The magistrate lifted a corner of the blanket and frowned. A black girl lay dead on the stretcher, her throat cut from one ear to the other.

"It was with this knife. A kitchen knife," said another man, from the top of the stairs.

"Did you bring her from Africa, or did you hire her here?"

"We brought her back from Africa, in April. She came by boat. My husband is with aerial navigation in Dakar, but the company only pays air passage for the family. She worked for us in Dakar. For two and a half or three years."

"How old is she?"

"I don't know exactly."

"According to her passport, she was born in 1927."

"Oh! The natives don't know when they are born," offered the naval officer, plunging his hands in his pockets.

"I don't know why she killed herself. She was well treated here, she ate the same food, shared the same rooms as my children."

"And your husband, where is he?"

"He left for Paris the day before yesterday."

"Ah!" said the inspector, still looking at the knickknacks. "Why do you think it was suicide?"

"Why?" said the retired officer . . . "Oh! Who do you think would make an attempt on the life of a Negro girl? She never went out. She didn't know anyone, except for Madame's children."

The reporters were getting impatient. The suicide of a maid—even if she was black—didn't amount to a hill of beans. There was nothing newsworthy in it.

"It must have been homesickness. Because lately she'd been behaving very strangely. She wasn't the same."

The police magistrate went upstairs, accompanied by one of the inspectors. They examined the bathroom, the window.

"Some boomerang, this story," said the inspector.

The others waited in the living room.

"We'll let you know when the coroner is finished," said the inspector, on his way out with the police magistrate an hour after their arrival.

The cars and the reporters left. In the Villa of Green Happiness the two women and the retired naval officer remained silent.

Bit by bit, Madame Pouchet searched her memory. She thought back to Africa and her elegant villa on the road to Hann. She remembered Diouana pushing open the iron gate and signaling to the German shepherd to stop barking.

It was there, in Africa, that everything had started. Diouana had made the six-kilometer round trip on foot three times a week. For the last month she had made it gaily—enraptured, her heart beating as if she were in love for the first time. Beginning at the outskirts of Dakar, brand-new houses were scattered like jewels in a landscape of cactus, bougainvillea, and jasmine. The asphalt of the Avenue Gambetta stretched out like a long black ribbon. Joyous and happy as usual, the little maid had no complaints about the road or her employers. Though it was a long way, it had no longer seemed so far the past month, ever since Madame had announced she would take her to France. France! Diouana shouted the word in her head. Everything around her had become ugly, the magnificent villas she had so often admired seemed shabby.

In order to be able to travel, in order to go to France, since she was originally from the Casamance, she had needed an identity card. All her paltry savings went to get one. "So what?" she thought. "I'm on my way to France!"

"Is that you, Diouana?"

"*Viye*, Madame," came her answer in the Senegalese accent. She spoke from the vestibule, nicely dressed in her light-colored cotton, her hair neatly combed.

"Good! Monsieur is in town. Will you look after the children?"

"*Viye*, Madame," she agreed in her childish voice.

Though her identity card read "Born in 1927," Diouana was not yet thirty. But she must have been over twenty-one. She went to find the children. Every room was in the same condition. Parcels packed and tied with string, boxes piled here and there. After ten whole days of washing and ironing, there wasn't much left for Diouana to do. In the proper sense of her duties, she was a laundress. There was a cook, a houseboy, and herself. Three people. The servants.

"Diouana . . . Diouana," Madame called.

"Madame?" she answered, emerging from the children's room.

Madame was standing with a notebook in her hands, making an inventory of the baggage. The movers would be coming at any moment.

"Have you been to see your parents? Do you think they will be happy?"

"*Viye*, Madame. The whole family is agreed. I tell Mama for myself. Also tell Papa Boutoupa," she said.

Her face, which had been radiant with happiness, fixed on the empty walls, and began to fade. Her heartbeat slowed. She would be ill if Madame changed her mind. Diouana's ebony-black face grew gloomy; she lowered her eyes, ready to plead her case.

"You're not going to tell me at the last moment, on this very day, that you're leaving us in the lurch?"

"No, Madame, me go."

They were not speaking the same language. Diouana wanted to see France, this country whose beauty, richness, and joy of living everyone praised. She wanted to see it and make a triumphal return. This was where people got rich. Already, without having left African soil, she could see herself on the dock, returning from France, wealthy to the millions, with gifts of clothes for everyone. She dreamed of the freedom to go where she wished without having to work like a beast of burden. If Madame should change her mind, refuse to take her, it would truly make her ill.

As for Madame, she was remembering the last few holidays she had spent in France. Three of them. And then she had had only two children. In Africa, Madame had acquired bad habits when it came to servants. In France when she hired a maid not only was the salary higher but the maid demanded a day off to boot. Madame had had to let her go and hired another. The next one was no different from the first, if not worse. She answered Madame tit for tat. "Anyone who is capable of having children should take a turn with them herself. I can't live in. I have my own children to take care of and a husband, too," she declared.

Used to being waited on hand and foot, Madame had yielded to her wifely duties, and clumsily fulfilled the role of mother. As for a real vacation, she had hardly had any. She soon persuaded her husband to return to Africa.

On her return, grown thin and thoroughly exasperated, she had conceived a plan for her next vacation. She put want ads in all the newspapers. A hundred young girls answered. Her choice fell on Diouana, newly arrived from her native bush. Producing two more children during the three years that Diouana worked for her, between her last holiday and the one to come, Madame sang the praises of France. For three thousand francs a month, any young African girl would have followed her to the end of the earth. And to top it off, from time to time, especially lately, Madame would give Diouana little gifts of this and that, old clothes, shoes that could be mended.

This was the insurmountable moat that separated the maid and her employer.

"Did you give Monsieur your identity card?"

"*Viye*, Madame."

"You may go back to your work. Tell the cook to give the three of you a good meal."

"*Merci*, Madame," she answered, and went off to the kitchen.

Madame continued her inventory.

Monsieur returned on the stroke of noon, his arrival announced by the barking of the dog. Getting out of his Peugeot 403, he found his wife, indefatigable, pencil in hand.

"Haven't the baggage men come yet?" she said nervously.

"They'll be here at a quarter to two. Our bags will be on top. That way they'll be out first when we land in Marseilles. And what about Diouana? Diouana!"

The eldest of the children ran to fetch her. She was under the trees with the littlest one.

"*Viye*, Madame."

"It's Monsieur who was calling you."

"That's fine. Here are your ticket and your identity card."

Diouana held out a hand to take them.

"You keep the identity card, I'll take care of the ticket. The Duponts are returning on the same ship, they'll look after you. Are you glad to be going to France?"

"*Viye*, Monsieur."

"Good. Where are your bags?"

"At Rue Escarfait, Monsieur."

"After I've had lunch, we'll go fetch them in the car."

"Bring the children in, Diouana, it's time for their nap."

"*Viye*, Madame."

Diouana wasn't hungry. The cook's helper, two years younger than she, brought the plates and took the empty ones away noiselessly. The cook was sweating heavily. He wasn't happy. He was going to be out of work. This was how the departure affected him. And for this reason he was a bit resentful of the maid. Leaning out the wide window overlooking the sea, transported, Diouana watched the birds flying high above in the immense expanse of blue. In the distance she could barely make out the Island of Gorée. She was holding her identity card, turning it over and over, examining it and smiling quietly to herself. The picture was a gloomy one. She wasn't pleased with the pose or with the exposure. "What does it matter? I'm leaving!" she thought.

"Samba," said Monsieur, who had come to the kitchen, "the meal was excellent today. You outdid yourself. Madame is very pleased with you."

The cook's helper stood at attention. Samba, the cook, adjusted his tall white hat and made an effort to smile.

"Thank you very much, Monsieur," he said. "I too am happy, very happy, because Monsieur and Madame are happy. Monsieur very nice. My family big, unhappy. Monsieur leave, me no more work."

"We'll be back, my good man. And then, with your talent you'll soon find another job!"

Samba, the cook, wasn't so sure. The whites were stingy. And in a Dakar filled with country people each claiming to be a master cook, it wouldn't be easy to find a job.

"We'll be back, Samba. Maybe sooner than you think. The last time we stayed only two and a half months."

To these consoling words from Madame, who had joined her husband in the kitchen, Samba could only answer: "*Merci*, Madame. Madame very nice lady."

Madame was glad. She knew from experience what it meant to have a good reputation with the servants.

"You can go home this afternoon at four with Monsieur. I'll pack up the rest. When we come back I promise to hire you again. Are you pleased?"

"*Merci*, Madame."

Madame and Monsieur were gone. Samba gave Diouana a slap. She hit him back angrily.

"Hey! Careful. Careful. You're going away today. So we shouldn't fight."

"That hurt!" she said.

"And Monsieur, does he hurt you too?"

Samba suspected a secret liaison between the maid and her employer.

"They're calling for you, Diouana. I hear the car starting."

She left without even saying goodbye.

The car moved along the highway. Diouana didn't often have the privilege of being driven by Monsieur. Her very look invited the pedestrians' admiration, though she dared not wave a hand or shout while going past, "I'm on my way to France!" Yes, France! She was sure her happiness was plain to see. The subterranean sources of this tumultuous joy made her a bit shaky. When the car stopped in front of the house at Rue Escarfait, she was surprised. "Already?" she thought. Next door to her humble house, at the Gay Navigator Café, a few customers were seated at the tables and several were talking quietly on the sidewalk.

"Is it today you're leaving, little one?" asked Tive Correa. Already tipsy, he steadied himself, legs apart, holding his bottle by the neck. His clothes were rumpled.

Diouana would have nothing to do with the drunkard. She didn't listen to Tive Correa's advice. An old sailor, Tive Correa had come home from Europe after twenty years' absence. He had left, rich with youth, full of ambition, and come home a wreck. From having wanted everything, he had returned with nothing but an excessive love for the bottle. For Diouana he predicted nothing but misfortune. Once, when she had asked his advice, his opinion had been that she shouldn't go. In spite of his serious state of inebriety, he made a few steps toward Monsieur, bottle still in hand.

"Is it true that Diouana's leaving with you, Monsieur?"

Monsieur did not answer. He took out a cigarette and lit it, blew the smoke through the car door, and looked Tive Correa over from head to toe. What a bum he was, greasy clothes, stinking of palm wine.

Correa leaned over, putting a hand on the car door. "I was there. I lived in France for twenty years," he began, with a note of pride in his voice. "I, whom you see this way, ruin though I am today, I know France better than you do. During the war I lived in Toulon, and the Germans sent us with the other Africans to Aix-en-Provence, to the mines at Gardanne. I've been against her going."

"We haven't forced her to go! She wants to," Monsieur answered dryly.

"Certainly. What young African doesn't dream of going to France? Unfortunately, they confuse living in France with being a servant in France. I come from the village next to Diouana's, in Casamance. There, we don't say the way you do that it is the light that attracts the moth, but the other way round. In my country, Casamance, we say that the darkness pursues the moth."

In the meantime, Diouana returned, escorted by several women. They were chatting along, each begging for a little souvenir. Diouana promised happily; she was smiling, her white teeth gleaming.

"The others are at the dock," said one. "Don't forget my dress."

"For me, some shoes for the children. You've got the size in your suitcase. And remember the sewing machine."

"The petticoats, too."

"Write and tell me how much the hair-straightening irons cost and also the price of a red jacket with big buttons, size 44."

"Don't forget to send a little money to your mother in Boutoupa . . ."

Each one had something to tell her, some request to make of her; Diouana promised. Her face was radiant. Tive Correa took the suitcase, pushing it drunkenly but not roughly into the car.

"Let her go, girls. Do you think money grows on trees in France? She'll have something to say about that when she gets back."

Loud protests from the women.

"Goodbye, little cousin. Take care of yourself. You have the address of the cousin in Toulon. Write to him as soon as you get there, he will help you. Come, give me a kiss."

They all kissed each other goodbye. Monsieur was getting impatient. He started up the motor to indicate politely that he wished they'd be done with it.

The Peugeot was moving. Everyone waved.

At the dock it was the same—relatives, friends, little commissions. Everyone pressed around her. Always under the watchful eye of Monsieur. She embarked.

A week at sea. "No news," she would have written if she'd been keeping a diary, in which case she'd also have had to know how to read and write. Water in front, behind, to port, to starboard. Nothing but a sheet of liquid, and above it, the sky.

When the boat landed, Monsieur was there. After the formalities, they quickly made their way to the Côte d'Azur. She devoured everything with her eyes, marveling, astonished. She packed every detail into her head. It was beautiful. Africa seemed a sordid slum by comparison. Towns, buses, trains, trucks went by along the coastal highway. The heaviness of the traffic surprised her.

"Did you have a good crossing?"

"*Viye*, Monsieur," she would have answered, if Monsieur had asked the question.

After a two-hour drive, they were in Antibes.

Days, weeks, and the first month went by. The third month began. Diouana was no longer the joyous young girl with the ready laugh, full of life. Her eyes were beginning to look hollow, her glance was less alert, she no longer noticed details. She had a lot more work to do here than in Africa. At first her fretting was hardly noticeable. Of France, la Belle France, she had only a vague idea, a fleeting vision. French gardens, the hedges of the other villas, the crests of roofs appearing above the green trees, the palms. Everyone lived his own life, isolated, shut up in his own house. Monsieur and Madame went out a good deal, leaving her with the four children. The children quickly organized a mafia and persecuted her. "You've got to keep them happy," Madame would say. The oldest, a real scamp, recruited others of like inclination and they played explorer. Diouana was the "savage." The children pestered her. Once in a while the eldest got a good spanking. Having picked up phrases from the conversations of Mama, Papa, or the neighbors back in Africa—phrases in which notions of racial prejudice played a part— he made exaggerated remarks to his pals. Without the knowledge of his parents, they would turn up, chanting, "Black Girl, Black Girl. She's as black as midnight."

Perpetually harassed, Diouana began to waste away. In Dakar she had never had to think about the color of her skin. With the youngsters teasing, she began to question it. She understood that here she was alone. There was nothing that connected her with the others. And it aggravated her, poisoned her life, the very air she breathed.

Everything grew blunt—her old dreams, her contentment eroded. She did a lot of hard work. It was she who did all the cooking, laundry, baby-sitting, ironing. Madame's sister came to stay at the villa, making seven people to look after. At night, as soon as she went up to bed, Diouana slept like a log.

The venom was poisoning her heart. She had never hated anything. Everything became monotonous. Where was France? The beautiful cities she had seen at the movies in Dakar, the rare foods, the interesting crowds? The population of France reduced itself to these spiteful monsters, Monsieur, Madame, and Mademoiselle, who had become strangers to her. The country seemed limited to the immediate surroundings of the villa. Little by little she was drowning. The wide horizons of a short while ago stopped now at the color of her skin, which suddenly filled her with an invincible terror. Her skin. Her blackness. Timidly, she retreated into herself.

With no one from her universe to exchange ideas with, she held long moments of palaver with herself. A week ago, Monsieur and Madame had cleverly taken her along to visit their relatives in Cannes.

"Tomorrow we'll go to Cannes. My parents have never tasted African food. You'll do us African honor with your cooking," Madame had said. She was nearly bare, and getting bronzed from the sun.

"*Viye*, Madame."

"I've ordered some rice and two chickens . . . You'll be careful not to spice it too much?"

"*Viye*, Madame."

Answering this way, she felt her heart harden. It seemed the hundredth time that she'd been trailed from villa to villa. To this one's house and then to that one's. It was at the Commodore's—everyone called him the Commodore—that she had rebelled the first time. Some silly people, who followed her about, hanging on her heels in the kitchen, had been there for dinner. Their presence was an oppressive shadow on her slightest movement. She had the feeling of not knowing how to do anything. These strange, self-centered, sophisticated beings never stopped asking her idiotic questions about how African women do their cooking. She kept herself under control.

The three women were still chirping when she waited on them at the table, testing the first spoonful on the tip of their tongues, then gluttonously devouring the rest.

"This time, at my parents', you must outdo yourself."

"*Viye*, Madame."

Restored to her kitchen, she thought of Madame's former kindness. She detested it. Madame had been good to her, but in a self-seeking way. The only reason for her attentiveness had been to wind the strings around Diouana, the better to make her sweat. She loathed everything. Back in Dakar, Diouana used to gather Monsieur and Madame's leftovers to take home to Rue Escarfait. She had taken pride then in working for "important white people." Now she was so alone their meals made her sick to her stomach. The resentment spoiled her relations with her employers. She stood her ground, they stood theirs. They no longer exchanged any remarks but those of a business nature.

"Diouana, will you do the washing today?"

"*Viye*, Madame."

"Last time you didn't do a good job on my slips. The iron was too hot. And the collars of Monsieur's shirts were scorched. Do pay attention to what you're doing, will you?"

"*Viye*, Madame."

"Oh, I forgot. There are some buttons missing on Monsieur's shirts and his shorts."

Every little job was Diouana's. And then Madame started speaking to her in pidgin French, even in front of guests. And this was the only thing she did with honesty. In the end, no one in the house ever spoke to the maid anymore except in terms of "Missie," Senegalese pidgin talk. Bewildered by her inadequacies in French, Diouana closed herself into a sort of solitary confinement. After long, lonely moments of meditation she came to the conclusion first of all that she was nothing but a useful object, and furthermore that she was being put on exhibit like a trophy. At parties, when Monsieur or Madame made remarks about "native" psychology, Diouana was taken as an illustration. The neighbors would say: "It's the Pouchets' black girl . . ." She wasn't "the African girl" in her own right, but theirs. And that hurt.

The fourth month began. Things got worse. Her thoughts grew more lucid every day. She had work and work to spare. All week long. Sunday was Mademoiselle's favorite day for asking friends over. There were lots of them. The weeks began and ended with them.

Everything became clear. Why had Madame wanted her to come? Her generosities had been premeditated. Madame no longer took care of her children. She kissed them every morning, that was all. And where was la Belle France? These questions kept repeating themselves. "I am cook, nurse-maid, chambermaid; I do all the washing and ironing and for a mere three thousand francs a month. I do housework for six people. What am I doing here?"

Diouana gave way to her memories. She compared her "native bush" to these dead shrubs. How different from the forest of her home in Casamance. The memory of her village, of the community life, cut her off from the others even more. She bit her lip, sorry to have come. And on this film of the past, a thousand other details were projected.

As she returned to these surroundings, where she was doubly an outsider, her feelings hardened. She thought often of Tive Correa. His predictions had come cruelly true. She would have liked to write to him, but couldn't. Since arriving in France, she had had only two letters from her mother. She didn't have the time to answer, even though Madame had promised to write for her. Was it possible to tell Madame what she was thinking? She was angry with herself. Her ignorance made her mute. It was infuriating. And besides, Mademoiselle had made off with her stamps.

A pleasant idea crossed her mind, though, and raised a smile. This evening only Monsieur was at home, watching television. She decided to take advantage of the opportunity. Then, unexpectedly finding Madame there too, Diouana stopped abruptly and left the room.

"Sold, sold. Bought, bought," she repeated to herself. "They've bought me. For three thousand francs I do all this work. They lured me, tied me to them, and I'm stuck here like a slave." She was determined now. That night she opened her suitcase, looked at the objects in it, and wept. No one cared.

Yet she went through the same motions and remained as sealed off from the others as an oyster at low tide on the beach of her native Casamance.

"Douna"—it was Mademoiselle calling her. Why was it impossible for her to say Di-ou-a-na?

Her anger redoubled. Mademoiselle was even lazier than Madame: "Come take this away"—"There is such-and-such to be done, Douna"—"Why don't you do this, Douna?"—"Douna, now and then please rake the garden." For an answer Mademoiselle would receive an incendiary glance. Madame complained about her to Monsieur.

"What is the matter with you, Diouana? Are you ill or something?" he asked.

She no longer opened her mouth.

"You can tell me what's the matter. Perhaps you'd like to go to Toulon. I haven't had the time to go, but tomorrow I'll take you with me."

"Anyone would think we disgust her," said Madame.

Three days later Diouana took her bath.

Returning home after a morning of shopping, Madame Pouchet went in the bathroom and quickly emerged.

"Diouana! Diouana!" she called. "You *are* dirty, in spite of everything. You might have left the bathroom clean."

"No me, Madame. It was the children, *viye.*"

"The children! The children are tidy. It may be that you're fed up with them. But to find you telling lies, like a native, *that* I don't like. I don't like liars and you are a liar!"

Diouana kept silent, though her lips were trembling. She went upstairs to the bathroom and took her clothes off. It was there they found her, dead.

"Suicide," the investigators concluded. The case was closed.

The next day, in the newspaper, on page 4, column 6, hardly noticeable, was a small headline:

"Homesick African Girl Cuts Throat in Antibes."

—1965

Luís Bernardo Honwana

(BORN 1942) MOZAMBIQUE

Luís Bernardo Honwana, a journalist and newspaper editor in Beira, a major city in Mozambique, knew poverty as a child in a large family in Lourenço Marques, a village near the capital. His father was a translator for the Portuguese administration. While completing his studies, Honwana worked as a cartographer and subsequently as a reporter and editor. His first stories (including "Papa, Snake & I") were published in 1964 as *Nos Matámos o Cão-Tinhosa*. Later stories have appeared sporadically in international quarterlies and anthologies.

Honwana's story "Dina" ("Dinner") describes the oppressive condition of field workers for a Portuguese landowner. Although Donald E. Herdeck does not compare it to Kafka's "In the Penal Colony," his comments about the story imply a strong connection between the two works: "The story is not brutally told, but rather, it is about the almost unendurable work the peonized workers in the colony must perform, the power of violence exercised by the Portuguese overseers and the loss of self-respect by the Africans who are herded together for the long labors in the blazing-hot fields." The story was included in *African Writing Today* (1967), edited by the South African writer Es'kia Mphahlele (one of whose stories is included in the present anthology).

From 1964 to 1967, Luís Bernardo Honwana was imprisoned because of his nationalist ideas. At the time of his release, he stated that he intended to study law. He currently lives in South Africa.

PAPA, SNAKE & I

Translated from the Portuguese by Dorothy Guedes

As soon as Papa left the table to read the newspaper in the sitting room, I got up as well. I knew that Mama and the others would take a while longer, but I didn't feel like staying with them at all.

When I stood up, Mama looked at me and said, "Come here, let me look at your eyes."

I went toward her slowly, because when Mama calls us we never know whether she's cross or not. After she had lifted my lids with the index finger of her left hand to make a thorough examination, she looked down at her plate and I stood waiting for her to send me away or to say something. She finished chewing, swallowed, and picked up the bone in her fingers to peep through the cavity, shutting one eye.

Then she turned to me suddenly with a bewildered look on her face. "Your eyes are bloodshot, you're weak and you've lost your appetite."

The way she spoke made me feel obliged to say that none of this was my fault, or else that I didn't do it on purpose. All the others looked on very curiously to see what was going to happen.

Mama peered down the middle of the bone again. Then she began to suck it, shutting her eyes, and only stopped for a moment to say, "Tomorrow you're going to take a laxative."

As soon as the others heard this, they began eating again very quickly and noisily. Mama didn't seem to have anything else to say, so I went out into the yard.

It was hot everywhere, and I could see no one on the road. Over the back wall three oxen gazed at me. They must have come back from the water trough at the Administration and stayed to rest in the shade. Far away, over the oxen's horns, the gray tufts of the dusty thorn trees trembled like flames. Everything vibrated in the distance, and heat waves could even be seen rising from the stones in the road. Sartina was sitting on a straw mat in the shade of the house, eating her lunch. Chewing slowly, she looked around, and from time to time, with a careless gesture, she shooed away the fowls who came close to her, hoping for crumbs. Even so, every now and then one of the bolder ones would jump on to the edge of the plate and run off with a lump of mealie meal in its beak, only to be pursued by the others. In their wild dispute, the lump would become so broken up that in the end even the smallest chicken would get its bit to peck.

When she saw me coming near, Sartina pulled her *capulana* down over her legs, and even then kept her hand spread out in front of her knees, firmly convinced that I wanted to peep at something. When I looked away she still didn't move her hand.

Toto came walking along slowly with his tongue hanging out, and went to the place where Sartina was sitting. He sniffed the plate from afar and turned away, taking himself off to the shade of the wall, where he looked for a soft place to lie down. When he found one, he curled round with his nose almost on his tail, and only lay still when his stomach touched the ground. He gave a long yawn, and dropped his head between his paws. He wriggled a little, making sure that he was in the most comfortable position, then covered his ears with his paws.

When she had finished eating, Sartina looked at me insistently before removing her hand, which covered the space between her knees, and only when she was sure I was not looking did she spring to her feet with a jump. The plate was so clean that it shone, but after darting a last suspicious glance at me, she took it to the trough. She moved languidly, swaying from the waist as her hips rose and fell under her *capulana*. She bent over the trough, but the back of her legs was exposed in this position, so she went to the other side for me not to see.

Mama appeared at the kitchen door, still holding the bone in her hand, and before calling Sartina to clear the table, she looked around to see if everything was in order. "Don't forget to give Toto his food," she said in Ronga.

Sartina went inside, drying her hands on her *capulana*, and afterwards

came out with a huge pile of plates. When she came out the second time
she brought the tablecloth and shook it on the stairs. While the fowls were
skirmishing for the crumbs, pecking and squawking at each other, she folded
it in two, four, and eight, and then went back inside. When she came out
again she brought the aluminum plate with Toto's food, and put it on the
cement cover of the water meter. Toto didn't have to be called to eat, and
even before the plate was put down, he threw himself on his food. He
burrowed into the pile of rice with his nose, searching for the bits of meat,
which he gulped up greedily as he found them. When no meat was left, he
pushed the bones aside and ate some rice. The fowls were all around him,
but they didn't dare to come nearer because they knew very well what Toto
was like when he was eating.

When he had swallowed the rice, Toto pretended he didn't want any
more and went to sit in the shade of the sugarcane, waiting to see what the
fowls would do. They came nervously toward his food, and risked a peck
or two, very apprehensively. Toto watched this without making a single
movement. Encouraged by the passivity of the dog, the fowls converged on
the rice with great enthusiasm, creating an awful uproar. It was then that
Toto threw himself on the heap, pawing wildly in all directions and growling
like an angry lion. When the fowls disappeared, fleeing to all corners of the
yard, Toto went back to the shade of the sugarcane, waiting for them to
gather together again.

Before going to work Papa went to look at the chicken run with Mama.
They both appeared at the kitchen door, Mama already wearing her apron
and Papa with a toothpick in his mouth and his newspaper under his arm.
When they passed me Papa was saying, "It's impossible, it's impossible,
things can't go on like this."

I went after them, and when we entered the chicken run Mama turned
to me as if she wanted to say something, but then she changed her mind
and went toward the wire netting. There were all sorts of things piled up
behind the chicken run: pipes left over from the building of the windmill
on the farm, blocks which were bought when Papa was still thinking of
making outhouses of cement, boxes, pieces of wood, and who knows what
else. The fowls sometimes crept in among these things and laid their eggs
where Mama couldn't reach them. On one side of the run lay a dead fowl,
and Mama pointed to it and said, "Now there's this one, and I don't know
how many others have just died from one day to the next. The chickens

simply disappear, and the eggs, too. I had this one left here for you to see. I'm tired of talking to you about this, and you still don't take any notice."

"All right, all right, but what do you want me to do about it?"

"Listen, the fowls die suddenly, and the chickens disappear. No one goes into the chicken run at night, and we've never heard any strange noise. You must find out what's killing the fowls and chickens."

"What do you think it is?"

"The fowls are bitten and the chickens are eaten. It can only be the one thing you think it is—if there are any thoughts in your head."

"All right, tomorrow I'll get the snake killed. It's Sunday, and it will be easy to get people to do it. Tomorrow."

Papa was already going out of the chicken run when Mama said, now in Portuguese, "But tomorrow without fail, because I don't want any of my children bitten by a snake."

Papa had already disappeared behind the corner of the house on his way to work when Mama turned to me and said, "Haven't you ever been taught that when your father and mother are talking you shouldn't stay and listen! My children aren't usually so bad-mannered. Who do you take after?"

She turned on Sartina, who was leaning against the wire netting, listening. "What do you want? Did anyone call you? I'm talking to my son and it's none of your business."

Sartina couldn't have grasped all that because she didn't understand Portuguese very well, but she drew away from the netting, looking very embarrassed, and went to the trough again. Mama went on talking to me, "If you think you'll fool me and take the gun to go hunting you're making a big mistake. Heaven help you if you try to do a thing like that! I'll tan your backside for you! And if you think you'll stay here in the chicken run you're also mistaken. I don't feel like putting up with any of your nonsense, do you hear?"

Mama must have been very cross, because for the whole day I hadn't heard her laugh as she usually did. After talking to me she went out of the chicken run and I followed her. When she passed Sartina, she asked her in Ronga, "Is it very hot under your *capulana*? Who told you to come here and show your legs to everybody?"

Sartina said nothing, walked round the trough, and went on washing the plates, bending over the other side.

Mama went away and I went to sit where I had been before. When Sartina saw me she turned on me resentfully, threw me a furious glance, and went round the trough again. She began to sing a monotonous song, one of those songs of hers that she sometimes spent the whole afternoon singing over and over again when she was angry.

Toto was bored with playing with the fowls, and had already finished eating his rice. He was sleeping again with his paws over his ears. Now and then he rolled himself in the dust and lay on his back with his legs folded in the air.

It was stiflingly hot, and I didn't know whether I'd go hunting as I usually did every Saturday, or if I'd go to the chicken run to see the snake.

Madunana came into the yard with a pile of firewood on his back, and went to put it away in the corner where Sartina was washing the plates. When she saw him, she stopped singing and tried to manage an awkward smile.

After looking all around, Madunana pinched Sartina's bottom, and she gave an embarrassed giggle and responded with a sonorous slap on his arm. The two of them laughed happily together without looking at each other.

Just then, Nandito, Joãozinho, Nelita, and Gita ran out after a ball, and started kicking it around the yard with great enjoyment.

Mama came to the kitchen door, dressed up to go out. As soon as she appeared, Madunana bent down quickly to the ground, pretending to look for something, and Sartina bent over the trough.

"Sartina, see if you manage not to break any plates before you finish. Hurry up. You, Madunana, leave Sartina alone and mind your own business. I don't want any of that nonsense here. If you carry on like this I'll tell the boss."

"You, Ginho"—now she spoke in Portuguese—"look after the house and remember you're not a child anymore. Don't hit anybody and don't let the children go out of the yard. Tina and Lolota are inside clearing up— don't let them get up to mischief."

"Sartina"—in Ronga—"when you've finished with that, put the kettle on for the children's tea and tell Madunana to go and buy bread. Don't let the children finish the whole package of butter."

"Ginho"—now in Portuguese—"look after everything—I'm coming back just now. I'm going along to Auntie Lucia's for a little chat."

Mama straightened her dress and looked around to see if everything was in order, then went.

Senhor Castro's dog, Wolf, was watching Toto from the street. As soon as he saw Wolf, Toto ran toward him and they started to bark at each other.

All the dogs of the village were frightened of Toto, and even the biggest of them ran away when he showed his temper. Toto was small, but he had long white hair which bristled up like a cat's when he was angry, and this is what must have terrified the other dogs.

Usually he kept away from them, preferring to entertain himself with the fowls—even bitches he only tolerated at certain times. For me he was a dog with a "pedigree," or at least "pedigree" could only mean the qualities he possessed. He had an air of authority, and the only person he feared was Mama, although she had never hit him. Just to take him off a chair we had to call her because he snarled and showed his teeth even at Papa.

The two dogs were face-to-face, and Wolf had already started to retreat, full of fear. At this moment Dr. Reis's dog, Kiss, passed by, and Toto started to bark at him, too. Kiss fled at once, and Wolf pursued him, snapping at his hindquarters, only leaving him when he was whining with pain. When Wolf came back to Toto they immediately made friends and began playing together.

Nandito came and sat down next to me, and told me, without my asking, that he was tired of playing ball.

"So why have you come here?"

"Don't you want me to?"

"I didn't say that."

"Then I'll stay."

"Stay if you like."

I got up and he followed me. "Where are you going? Are you going hunting?"

"No."

"Well, then?"

"Stop pestering me. I don't like talking to kids."

"You're also a kid. Mama still hits you."

"Say that again and I'll bash your face in."

"All right, I won't say it again."

I went into the chicken run, and he came after me. The pipes were hot, and I had to move them with a cloth. The dust that rose was dense and suffocating.

"What are you looking for? Shall I help you?"

I began to move the blocks one by one and Nandito did the same. "Get away!"

He went to the other end of the run and began to cry.

When I had removed the last block of the pile I saw the snake. It was a mamba, very dark in color. When it realized it had been discovered, it wound itself up more tightly and lifted its triangular head. Its eyes shone vigilantly and its black forked tongue quivered menacingly.

I drew back against the fence, then sat down on the ground. "Don't cry, Nandito."

"You're nasty. You don't want to play with me."

"Don't cry anymore. I'll play with you just now. Don't cry."

We both sat quietly. The little head of the snake came slowly to rest on the topmost coil, and the rest of its body stopped trembling. But it continued to watch me attentively.

"Nandito, say something, talk to me."

"What do you want me to say?"

"Anything you like."

"I don't feel like saying anything."

Nandito was still rubbing his eyes and feeling resentful toward me.

"Have you ever seen a snake? Do you like snakes? Are you scared of them? Answer me!"

"Where are the snakes?" Nandito jumped up in terror, and looked around.

"In the bush. Sit down and talk."

"Aren't there any snakes here?"

"No. Talk. Talk to me about snakes."

Nandito sat down very close to me.

"I'm very frightened of snakes. Mama says it's dangerous to go out in the bush because of them. When we're walking in the grass we can step on one by mistake and get bitten. When a snake bites us we die. Sartina says that if a snake bites us and we don't want to die we must kill it, burn it till it's dry, then eat it. She says she's already eaten a snake, so she won't die even if she gets bitten."

"Have you ever seen a snake?"

"Yes, in Chico's house. The servant killed it in the chicken run."

"What was it like?"

"It was big and red, and it had a mouth like a frog."

"Would you like to see a snake now?"

Nandito got up and leaned against me fearfully. "Is there a snake in the chicken run? I'm scared—let's get out."

"If you want to get out, go away. I didn't call you to come in here."

"I'm frightened to go alone."

"Then sit here until I feel like going out."

The two of us stayed very quiet for a while.

Toto and Wolf were playing outside the fence. They were running from one post to another, going all the way round and starting again. At every post they raised a leg and urinated.

Then they came inside the chicken run and lay on their stomachs to rest. Wolf saw the snake immediately and began to bark. Toto barked as well, although he had his back turned toward it.

"Brother, are there always snakes in every chicken run?"

"No."

"Is there one in here?"

"Yes."

"Well then, why don't we go out. I'm scared!"

"Go out if you want to—go on!"

Wolf advanced toward the snake, barking more and more frenziedly. Toto turned his head, but still did not realize what was wrong.

Wolf's legs were trembling and he pawed the ground in anguish. Now and again he looked at me uncomprehendingly, unable to understand why I did not react to his hysterical alarm. His almost human eyes were filled with panic.

"Why is he barking like that?"

"Because he's seen the snake."

The mamba was curled up in the hollow between some blocks, and it unwound its body to give itself the most solid support possible. Its head and the raised neck remained poised in the air, unaffected by the movement of the rest of its body. Its eyes shone like fires.

Wolf's appeals were now horribly piercing, and his hair was standing up around his neck.

Leaning against the fence, Tina and Lolota and Madunana looked on curiously.

"Why don't you kill the snake?" Nandito's voice was very tearful and he was clutching me around the neck.

"Because I don't feel like it."

The distance between the snake and the dog was about five feet. However, the snake had inserted its tail in the angle formed between a block and the ground, and had raised its coils one by one, preparing for the strike. The triangular head drew back imperceptibly, and the base of the lifted neck came forward. Seeming to be aware of the proximity of his end, the dog began to bark even more frantically, without, however, trying to get away from the snake. From a little way behind, Toto, now on his feet as well, joined in the barking.

For a fraction of a second the neck of the snake curved while the head leaned back. Then, as if the tension of its pliant body had snapped a cord that fastened its head to the ground, it shot forward in a lightning movement impossible to follow. The dog had raised himself on his hind legs like a goat, and the snake struck him full on the chest. Free of support, the tail of the snake whipped through the air, reverberating with the movement of the last coil.

Wolf fell on his back with a suppressed whine, pawing convulsively. The mamba abandoned him immediately, and with a spring disappeared between the pipes.

"A *nhoka!*"* screamed Sartina.

Nandito threw me aside and ran out of the chicken run with a yell, collapsing into the arms of Madunana. As soon as he felt free of the snake, Wolf vanished in half a dozen leaps in the direction of Senhor Castro's house.

The children all started to cry without having understood what had happened. Sartina took Nandito to the house, carrying him in her arms. Only when the children disappeared behind Sartina did I call Madunana to help me kill the snake.

Madunana waited with a cloth held up high while I moved the pipes with the aid of a broomstick. As soon as the snake appeared Madunana threw the cloth over it, and I set to beating the heap with my stick.

When Papa came back from work Nandito had come round from the shock, and was weeping copiously. Mama, who had not yet been to see the snake, went with Papa to the chicken run. When I went there as well, I saw Papa turn the snake over onto its back with a stick.

"I don't like to think of what a snake like this could have done to one

---

* A snake.

of my children.'' Papa smiled. ''Or to anyone else. It was better this way. What hurts me is to think that these six feet of snake were attained at the expense of my chickens . . .''

At this point Senhor Castro's car drew up in front of our house. Papa walked up to him, and Mama went to talk to Sartina. I followed after Papa.

''Good afternoon, Senhor Castro . . .''

''Listen, Tchembene, I've just found out that my pointer is dead, and his chest's all swollen. My natives tell me that he came howling from your house before he died. I don't want any back-chat, and I'm just telling you— either you pay compensation or I'll make a complaint at the Administration. He was the best pointer I ever had.''

''I've just come back from work—I don't know anything . . .''

''I don't care a damn about that. Don't argue. Are you going to pay or aren't you?''

''But, Senhor Castro . . .''

''Senhor Castro nothing. It's 700 paus.* And it's better if the matter rests here.''

''As you like, Senhor Castro, but I don't have the money now . . .''

''We'll see about that later. I'll wait until the end of the month, and if you don't pay then, there'll be a row.''

''Senhor Castro, we've known each other such a long time, and there's never . . .''

''Don't try that with me. I know what you all need—a bloody good hiding is the only thing . . .''

Senhor Castro climbed into his car and pulled away. Papa watched while the car drove off. ''Son of a bitch . . .''

I went up to him and tugged at the sleeve of his coat. ''Papa, why didn't you say that to his face?''

He didn't answer.

We had hardly finished supper when Papa said, ''Mother, tell Sartina to clear the table quickly. My children, let us pray. Today we are not going to read the Bible. We will simply pray.''

Papa talked in Ronga, and for this reason I regretted having asked him that question a while ago.

* Slang for 700$00, about £8.

When Sartina finished clearing away the plates and folded the cloth, Papa began, "Tatana, ha ku dumba hosi ya tilo misaba . . ."*

When he finished, his eyes were red.

"Amen!"

"Amen!"

Mama got up and asked, as if it meant nothing. "But what did Senhor Castro want, after all?"

"It's nothing important."

"All right, tell me about it in our room. I'll go and set out the children's things. You, Ginho, wake up early tomorrow and take a laxative . . ."

When they had all gone away, I asked Papa, "Papa, why do you always pray when you are very angry?"

"Because He is the best counselor."

"And what counsel does He give you?"

"He gives me no counsel. He gives me strength to continue."

"Papa, do you believe a lot in Him?"

Papa looked at me as if he were seeing me for the first time, and then exploded. "My son, one must have a hope. When one comes to the end of a day, and one knows that tomorrow will be another day just like it, and that things will always be the same, we have got to find the strength to keep on smiling, and keep on saying, 'This is not important!' We ourselves have to allot our own reward for the heroism of every day. We have to establish a date for this reward, even if it's the day of our death! Even today you saw Senhor Castro humiliate me: this was only part of today's portion, because there were many things that happened that you didn't see. No, my son, there must be a hope! It must exist! Even if all this only denies Him, He must exist!"

Papa stopped suddenly, and forced himself to smile. Then he added, "Even a poor man has to have something. Even if it is only a hope! Even if it's a false hope!"

"Papa, I could have prevented the snake from biting Senhor Castro's dog . . ."

Papa looked at me with his eyes full of tenderness, and said under his breath, "It doesn't matter. It's a good thing that he got bitten."

Mama appeared at the door. "Are you going to let the child go to sleep or not?"

* Father, we put our trust in Thee, Lord of Heaven and earth.

I looked at Papa, and we remembered Senhor Castro and both of us burst out laughing. Mama didn't understand.

"Are you two going crazy?!"

"Yes, and it's about time we went crazy," said Papa with a smile.

Papa was already on the way to his room, but I must have talked too loud. Anyway, it was better that he heard, "Papa, I sometimes . . . I don't really know . . . but for some time . . . I have been thinking that I didn't love you all. I'm sorry . . ."

Mama didn't understand what we had been saying, so she became angry. "Stop all this, or else . . ."

"Do you know, my son"—Papa spoke ponderously, and gesticulated a lot before every word—"the most difficult thing to bear is that feeling of complete emptiness . . . and one suffers very much . . . very, very, very much. One grows with so much bottled up inside, but afterwards it is difficult to scream, you know."

"Papa, and when Senhor Castro comes? . . ."

Mama was going to object, but Papa clutched her shoulder firmly. "It's nothing, Mother, but, you know, our son believes that people don't mount wild horses, and that they only make use of the hungry, docile ones. Yet when a horse goes wild it gets shot down, and it's all finished. But tame horses die every day. Every day, do you hear? Day after day, after day—as long as they can stand on their feet."

Mama looked at him with her eyes popping out.

"Do you know, Mother, I'm afraid to believe that this is true, but I also can't bring myself to tell him that it's a lie . . . He sees, even today he saw . . . I only wish for the strength to make sure that my children know how to recognize other things . . ."

Papa and Mama were already in their room, so I couldn't hear any more, but even from there Mama yelled, "Tomorrow you'll take a laxative, that'll show you. I'm not like your father who lets himself get taken in . . ."

My bed was flooded in yellow moonlight, and it was pleasant to feel my naked skin quiver with its cold caress. For some unknown reason the warm sensation of Sartina's body flowed through my senses. I managed to cling to her almost physical presence for a few minutes, and I wanted to fall asleep with her so as not to dream of dogs and snakes.

—1969

Ngugi wa Thiong'o

(BORN 1938) KENYA

Ngugi wa Thiong'o is known as East Africa's most significant and popular literary figure. Born to a large family in Limuru, a short distance north of Nairobi, Ngugi had twenty-seven siblings—many of them half brothers and sisters. His university education began at Makerere University in Uganda and continued at Leeds in England. During his Makerere days, he began writing fiction. His first published novel, *Weep Not, Child* (1964), is his most widely read work. Njoroge, the hero of the story, goes through childhood and adolescence trying to establish his own personal loyalties to family, country, and friends. Much of the story is devoted to tracing Njoroge's education in the classroom (and his desire to acquire the white man's skills), but in the nearby forests the Mau Mau revolt has begun—the struggle that in time will lead to Kenya's independence.

Revolution and, to a lesser extent, education are two important themes of much of Ngugi's writing: these topics are of special importance in his novels *The River Between* (1965), *A Grain of Wheat* (1967), *Petals of Blood* (1977), and *Devil on the Cross* (1980), all written in English. The latter novel was formulated and sketched out on toilet paper during the author's year-long detention in prison in Kenya after a 1978 performance of *Ngaahika Ndeenda (I Will Marry When I Want)*, by workers and peasants. The drama marked Ngugi's shift to Gikuyu, the oral language of his people, the Kikuyu, and his language of choice for all subsequent creative works.

At the time of his detention, Ngugi was head of the Department of

Literature at Nairobi University, a position he lost after his release. He has remained a vocal critic of the abuse of power. Ngugi's initial writing attacked colonialism; when the colonial era ended, he continued his identification with workers and peasants, attacking neocolonialism, capitalism, and multinationalism. His remarks have not been ignored by his country's leaders, who have attempted to silence him by forcing him into exile. Since 1979, he has lived in England, the United States, and Sweden, holding a series of academic appointments.

Ngugi's beliefs about cultural nationalism can be found in *Homecoming* (1972) and *Detained: A Writer's Prison Diary* (1981), but they are also reflected in distilled form in a conversation between two characters in *Devil on the Cross*: "Let us now look about us. Where are our national languages now? Where are the books written in the alphabets of our national languages? Where is our own literature now? Where is the wisdom and knowledge of our fathers now? Where is the philosophy of our fathers now? The centers of wisdom that used to guard the entrance to our national homestead have been demolished; the fire of wisdom has been allowed to die; the seats around the fireside have been thrown onto a rubbish heap; the guard posts have been destroyed; and the youth of the nation has hung up its shields and spears. It is a tragedy that there is nowhere we can go to learn the history of our own country. A child without parents to counsel him—what is to prevent him from mistaking foreign shit for a delicious national dish?''

A MEETING IN THE DARK

His mother used to tell him stories. "Once upon a time there was a young girl who lived with her father and mother in a lonely house that was hidden by a hill. The house was old but strong. When the rains came and the winds blew, the house remained firm. Her father and mother liked her, but they quarreled sometimes and she would cry. Otherwise, she was happy. Nobody knew of the house. So nobody came to see them. Then one day a stranger came. He was tall and handsome. He had milk-white teeth. Her mother gave him food. Then he told them of a beautiful country beyond the hill. The girl wanted to go there. Secretly, she followed the man. They had not gone very far when the stranger turned into an Irimu. He became ugly and he had another mouth at the back which was hidden by his long hair. Occasionally, the hair was blown by the wind. Flies were taken in and the mouth would be shut. The girl ran back. The bad Irimu followed her. She ran hard, hard, and the Irimu could not catch her. But he was getting nearer her all the time. When she came close to her home, she found the Irimu had stopped running. But the house was no longer there. She had no home to go to and she could not go forward to the beautiful land, to see all the good things, because the Irimu was in the way."

How did the story end? John wondered. He thought: "I wish I were young again in our old home, then I would ask my mother about it." But now he was not young; not young anymore. And he was not a man yet!

He stood at the door of the hut and saw his old, frail, but energetic father coming along the village street, with a rather dirty bag made out of strong calico swinging by his side. His father always carried this bag. John knew what it contained: a Bible, a hymn book, and probably a notebook and a pen. His father was a preacher. It must have been he who had stopped his mother from telling him stories. His mother had stopped telling him stories long ago. She would say, "Now, don't ask for any more stories. Your father may come." So he feared his father. John went in and warned his mother of his father's coming. Then his father came in. John stood aside, then walked toward the door. He lingered there doubtfully; then he went out.

"John, hei, John!"

"Baba!"

"Come back."

He stood doubtfully in front of his father. His heart beat faster and an agitated voice within him seemed to ask: Does he know?

"Sit down. Where are you going?"

"For a walk, Father," he answered evasively.

"To the village?"

"Well—yes—no. I mean, nowhere in particular." John saw his father look at him hard, seeming to read his face. John sighed a very slow sigh. He did not like the way his father eyed him. He always looked at him as though John was a sinner, one who had to be watched all the time. "I am," his heart told him. John guiltily refused to meet the old man's gaze and looked past him and appealingly to his mother, who was quietly peeling potatoes. But she seemed to be oblivious of everything around her.

"Why do you look away? What have you done?"

John shrank within himself with fear. But his face remained expressionless. However, he could hear the loud beats of his heart. It was like an engine pumping water. He felt no doubt his father knew all about it. He thought: "Why does he torture me? Why does he not at once say he knows?" Then another voice told him: "No, he doesn't know, otherwise he would already have jumped at you." A consolation. He faced his thoughtful father with courage.

"When is the journey?"

Again John thought—why does he ask? I have told him many times.

Aloud, he said, "Next week, Tuesday."

"Right. Tomorrow we go to the shops, hear?"

"Yes, Father."

"Then be prepared."

* Cultural values

"Yes, Father."

"You can go."

"Thank you, Father." He began to move.

"John!"

"Yes?" John's heart almost stopped beating. That second, before his father's next words, was an age.

"You seem to be in a hurry. I don't want to hear of you loitering in the village. I know you young men, going to show off just because you are going away! I don't want to hear of trouble in the village."

Much relieved, John went out. He could guess what his father meant by not wanting trouble in the village. How did the story end? Funny, but he could not remember how his mother had ended it. It had been so long ago. Her home was not there. Where did she go? What did she do?

"Why do you persecute the boy so much?" Susan spoke for the first time. Apparently she had carefully listened to the whole drama without a word. Now was her time to speak. She looked at her tough old preacher who had been a companion for life. She had married him a long time ago. She could not tell the number of years. They had been happy. Then the man became a convert. And everything in the home put on a religious tone. He even made her stop telling stories to the child. "Tell him of Jesus. Jesus died for you. Jesus died for the child. He must know the Lord." She too had been converted. But she was never blind to the moral torture he inflicted on the boy (that's what she always called John), so that the boy had grown up mortally afraid of him. She always wondered if it was love for the son. Or could it be a resentment because, well, they two had "sinned" before marriage? John had been the result of that sin. But that had not been John's fault. It was the boy who ought to complain. She often wondered if the boy had . . . but no. The boy had been very small when they left Fort Hall. She looked at her husband. He remained mute, though his left hand did, rather irritably, feel about his face.

"It is as if he was not your son. Or do you . . ."

"Hm, sister." The voice was pleading. She was seeking a quarrel but he did not feel equal to one. Really, women could never understand. Women were women, whether saved or not. Their son had to be protected against all evil influences. He must be made to grow in the footsteps of the Lord. He looked at her, frowning a little. She had made him sin but that had been a long time ago. And he had been saved. John must not follow the same road.

"You ought to tell us to leave. You know I can go away. Go back to Fort Hall. And then everybody . . ."

"Look, sister." He hastily interrupted. He always called her sister. Sister-in-the-Lord, in full. But he sometimes wondered if she had been truly saved. In his heart, he prayed: Lord, be with our sister Susan. Aloud, he continued, "You know I want the boy to grow in the Lord."

"But you torture him so! You make him fear you!"

"Why! He should not fear me. I have really nothing against him."

"It is you. You. You have always been cruel to him . . ." She stood up. The peelings dropped from her dress and fell in a heap on the floor.

"Stanley!"

"Sister." He was startled by the vehemence in her voice. He had never seen her like this. Lord, take the devil out of her. Save her this minute. She did not say what she wanted to say. Stanley looked away from her. It was a surprise, but it seemed he feared his wife. If you had told people in the village about this, they would not have believed you. He took his Bible and began to read. On Sunday he would preach to a congregation of brethren and sisters.

Susan, a rather tall, thin woman who had once been beautiful, sat down again and went on with her work. She did not know what was troubling her son. Was it the coming journey?

Outside, John strolled aimlessly along the path that led from his home. He stood near the wattle tree which was a little way from his father's house, and surveyed the whole village. They lay before his eyes—crammed—rows and rows of mud and grass huts, ending in sharp sticks that pointed to heaven. Smoke was coming out of various huts, an indication that many women had already come from the *shambas*. Night would soon fall. To the west, the sun was hurrying home behind the misty hills. Again, John looked at the crammed rows and rows of huts that formed Makeno Village, one of the new mushroom "towns" that grew up all over the country during the Mau Mau War. It looked so ugly. A pang of pain rose in his heart and he felt like crying—I hate you, I hate you. You trapped me alive. Away from you, it would never have happened. He did not shout. He just watched.

A woman was coming toward where he stood. A path into the village was just near there. She was carrying a big load of *kuni*, which bent her into an Akamba-bow shape. She greeted him.

"Is it well with you, Njooni?"

"It is well with me, mother." There was no trace of bitterness in his voice. John was by nature polite. Everyone knew this. He was quite unlike the other proud, educated sons of the tribe—sons who came back from the other side of the waters with white or Negro wives who spoke English. And they behaved just like Europeans! John was a favorite, a model of humility and moral perfection. Everyone knew that, though a clergyman's son, John would never betray the tribe.

"When are you going to—to—"

"Makerere?"

"Makelele." She laughed. The way she pronounced the name was funny. And the way she laughed, too. She enjoyed it. But John felt hurt. So everyone knew of this.

"Next week."

"I wish you well."

"Thank you, mother."

She said quietly—as if trying to pronounce it better—"Makelele." She laughed at herself again but she was tired. The load was heavy.

"Stay well, son."

"Go well and in peace, mother."

And the woman, who all the time had stood, moved on, panting like a donkey, but obviously pleased with John's kindness.

John remained long looking at her. What made such a woman live on day to day, working hard, yet happy? Had she much faith in life? Or was her faith in the tribe? She and her kind, who had never been touched by the ways of the white man, looked as though they had something to cling to. As he watched her disappear, he felt proud that they should think well of him. He felt proud that he had a place in their esteem. And then came the pang. *Father will know. They will know.* He did not know what he feared most: the action his father would take when he knew, or the loss of the little faith the simple villagers had placed in him, when they knew.

He went down to the small local tea shop. He met many people who wished him well at the college. All of them knew that the Pastor's son had finished all the white man's learning in Kenya. He would now go to Uganda; they had read this in the *Baraza*, a Swahili weekly paper. John did not stay long at the shop. The sun had already gone to rest and now darkness was coming. The evening meal was ready. His tough father was still at the table reading his Bible. He did not look up when John entered. Strange silence settled in the hut.

"You look unhappy." His mother broke the silence first. John laughed. It was a nervous little laugh.

"No, Mother," he hastily replied, nervously looking at his father. He secretly hoped that Wamuhu had not blabbed.

"Then I am glad."

She did not know. He ate his dinner and went out to his hut. A man's hut. Every young man had his own hut. John was never allowed to bring any girl visitor in there. He did not want trouble. Even to be seen standing with one was a crime. His father could easily thrash him. He wished he had rebelled earlier, like all the other young educated men. He lit the lantern. He took it in his hand. The yellow light flickered dangerously and then went out. He knew his hands were shaking. He lit it again and hurriedly took his big coat and a huge *Kofia*, which were lying on the unmade bed. He left the lantern burning, so that his father would see it and think him in. John bit his lower lip spitefully. He hated himself for being so girlish. It was unnatural for a boy of his age.

Like a shadow, he stealthily crossed the courtyard and went on to the village street.

He met young men and women lining the streets. They were laughing, talking, whispering. They were obviously enjoying themselves. John thought, They are more free than I am. He envied their exuberance. They clearly stood outside or above the strict morality that the educated ones had to be judged by. Would he have gladly changed places with them? He wondered. At last, he came to the hut. It stood at the very heart of the village. How well he knew it—to his sorrow. He wondered what he would do! Wait for her outside? What if her mother came out instead? He decided to enter.

"*Hodi!*"

"Enter. We are in."

John pulled down his hat before he entered. Indeed, they were all there— all except she whom he wanted. The fire in the hearth was dying. Only a small flame from a lighted lantern vaguely illuminated the whole hut. The flame and the giant shadow created on the wall seemed to be mocking him. He prayed that Wamuhu's parents would not recognize him. He tried to be "thin," and to disguise his voice as he greeted them. They recognized him and made themselves busy on his account. To be visited by such an educated one who knew all about the white man's world and knowledge, and who would now go to another land beyond, was not such a frequent occurrence that it could be taken lightly. Who knew but he might be interested in their daughter? Stranger things had happened. After all, learning was not the only thing. Though Wamuhu had no learning, yet charms she had and she could be trusted to captivate any young man's heart with her looks and smiles.

"You will sit down. Take that stool."

"No!" He noticed with bitterness that he did not call her "mother."

"Where is Wamuhu?" The mother threw a triumphant glance at her husband. They exchanged a knowing look. John bit his lip again and felt like bolting. He controlled himself with difficulty.

"She has gone out to get some tea leaves. Please sit down. She will cook you some tea when she comes."

"I am afraid . . ." He muttered some inaudible words and went out. He almost collided with Wamuhu.

In the hut:

"Didn't I tell you? Trust a woman's eye!"

"You don't know these young men."

"But you see, John is different. Everyone speaks well of him and he is a clergyman's son."

"Y-e-e-s! A clergyman's son? You forgot your daughter is circumcised." The old man was remembering his own day. He had found for himself a good, virtuous woman, initiated in all the tribe's ways. And she had known no other man. He had married her. They were happy. Other men of his *Rika* had done the same. All their girls had been virgins, it being a taboo to touch a girl in that way, even if you slept in the same bed, as indeed so many young men and girls did. Then the white men had come, preaching a strange religion, strange ways, which all men followed. The tribe's code of behavior was broken. The new faith could not keep the tribe together. How could it? The men who followed the new faith would not let the girls be circumcised. And they would not let their sons marry circumcised girls. Puu! Look at what was happening. Their young men went away to the land of the white men. What did they bring? White women. Black women who spoke English. Aaa—bad. And the young men who were left just did not mind. They made unmarried girls their wives and then left them with fatherless children.

"What does it matter?" his wife was replying. "Is Wamuhu not as good as the best of them? Anyway, John is different."

"Different! different! Puu! They are all alike. Those coated with the white clay of the white man's ways are the worst. They have nothing inside.

[handwritten annotation] → Just as the whites found their culture odd, the Blacks felt the same way about the values of the white

Nothing—nothing here." He took a piece of wood and nervously poked the dying fire. A strange numbness came over him. He trembled. And he feared; he feared for the tribe. For now he said it was not only the educated men who were coated with strange ways, but the whole tribe. The tribe had followed a false Irimu like the girl in the story. For the old man trembled and cried inside, mourning for a tribe that had crumbled. The tribe had nowhere to go to. And it could not be what it was before. He stopped poking and looked hard at the ground.

"I wonder why he came. I wonder." Then he looked at his wife and said, "Have you seen strange behavior with your daughter?"

His wife did not answer. She was preoccupied with her own great hopes . . .

John and Wamuhu walked on in silence. The intricate streets and turns were well known to them both. Wamuhu walked with quick light steps; John knew she was in a happy mood. His steps were heavy and he avoided people even though it was dark. But why should he feel ashamed? The girl was beautiful, probably the most beautiful girl in the whole of Limuru. Yet he feared being seen with her. It was all wrong. He knew that he could have loved her, even then he wondered if he did not love her. Perhaps it was hard to tell but had he been one of the young men he had met, he would not have hesitated in his answer.

Outside the village he stopped. She, too, stopped. Neither had spoken a word all through. Perhaps the silence spoke louder than words. Each was only too conscious of the other.

"Do they know?" Silence. Wamuhu was probably considering the question. "Don't keep me waiting. Please answer me," he implored. He felt weary, very weary, like an old man who had suddenly reached his journey's end.

"No. You told me to give you one more week. A week is over today."

"Yes. That's why I came!" John whispered hoarsely.

Wamuhu did not speak. John looked at her. Darkness was now between them. He was not really seeing her; before him was the image of his father—haughtily religious and dominating. Again he thought: I John, a priest's son, respected by all and going to college, will fall, fall to the ground. He did not want to contemplate the fall.

"It was your fault." He found himself accusing her. In his heart he knew he was lying.

"Why do you keep on telling me that? Don't you want to marry me?"

He is afraid to imagine his life beyond what his father has set for him.

John sighed. He did not know what to do.

Once upon a time there was a young girl . . . She had no home to go to . . . She could not go forward to the beautiful land and see all the good things because the Irimu was the way . . .

"When will you tell them?"

"Tonight." He felt desperate. Next week he would go to the college. If he could persuade her to wait, he might be able to get away and come back when the storm and consternation had abated. But then the government might withdraw his bursary.

He was frightened and there was a sad note of appeal as he turned to her and said: "Look, Wamuhu, how long have you been pre—I mean like this?"

"I have told you over and over again. I have been pregnant for three months and Mother is being suspicious. Only yesterday she said I breathed like a woman with child."

"Do you think you could wait for three weeks more?" She laughed. Ah! the little witch! She knew his trick. Her laughter always aroused many emotions in him.

"All right. Give me just tomorrow. I'll think up something. Tomorrow I'll let you know all."

"I agree. Tomorrow. I cannot wait anymore unless you mean to marry me."

Why not marry her? She is beautiful! Why not marry her? And do I or don't I love her?

She left. John felt as if she was deliberately blackmailing him. His knees were weak and lost strength. He could not move but sank on the ground in a heap. Sweat poured profusely down his cheeks, as if he had been running hard under a strong sun. But this was cold sweat. He lay on the grass; he did not want to think. Oh! No! He could not possibly face his father. Or his mother. Or Reverend Thomas Carstone, who had had such faith in him. John realized that he was not more secure than anybody else, in spite of his education. He was no better than Wamuhu. *Then why don't you marry her?* He did not know. John had grown up under a Calvinistic father and learned under a Calvinistic headmaster—a missionary! John tried to pray. But to whom was he praying? To Carstone's God? It sounded false. It was as if he was blaspheming. Could he pray to the God of the tribe? His sense of guilt crushed him.

He woke up. Where was he? Then he understood. Wamuhu had left him. She had given him one day. He stood up; he felt good. Weakly, he began to walk back home. It was lucky that darkness blanketed the whole earth, and him in it. From the various huts, he could hear laughter, heated talks, or quarrels. Little fires could be seen flickering red through the open doors. Village stars, John thought. He raised up his eyes. The heavenly stars, cold and distant, looked down on him impersonally. Here and there, groups of boys and girls could be heard laughing and shouting. For them life seemed to go on as usual. John consoled himself by thinking that they, too, would come to face their day of trial.

John was shaky. Why! Why! Why could he not defy all expectations, all prospects of a future, and marry the girl? No. No. It was impossible. She was circumcised, and he knew that his father and the Church would never consent to such a marriage. She had no learning, or rather she had not gone beyond Standard 4. Marrying her would probably ruin his chances of ever going to a university . . .

He tried to move briskly. His strength had returned. His imagination and thought took flight. He was trying to explain his action before an accusing world—he had done so many times before, ever since he knew of this. He still wondered what he could have done. The girl had attracted him. She was graceful and her smile had been very bewitching. There was none who could equal her and no girl in the village had any pretense to any higher standard of education. Women's education was very low. Perhaps that was why so many Africans went "away" and came back married. He, too, wished he had gone with the others, especially in the last giant student airlift to America. If only Wamuhu had learning . . . and she was uncircumcised . . . then he might probably rebel . . .

The light still shone in his mother's hut. John wondered if he should go in for the night prayers. But he thought against it; he might not be strong enough to face his parents. In his hut, the light had gone out. He hoped his father had not noticed it . . .

John woke up early. He was frightened. He was normally not superstitious but still he did not like the dreams of the night. He dreamed of circumcision; he had just been initiated in the tribal manner. Somebody—he could not tell his face—came and led him because he took pity on him. They went, went into a strange land. Somehow, he found himself alone. The somebody had vanished. A ghost came. He recognized it as the ghost of the home he had left. It pulled him back; then another ghost came. It was the ghost of the land he had come to. It pulled him from the front. The two contested. Then came other ghosts from all sides and pulled him from all sides so that his body began to fall into pieces. And the ghosts were unsubstantial. He could not cling to any. Only they were pulling him, and he was becoming nothing, nothing . . . he was now standing a distance away. It had not been him. But he was looking at the girl, the girl in the story. She had nowhere to go. He thought he would go to help her; he would show her the way. But as he went to her, he lost his way . . . He was all alone . . . Something destructive was coming toward him, coming, coming . . . He woke up. He was sweating all over—

Dreams about circumcision were no good. They portended death. He dismissed the dream with a laugh. He opened the window only to find the whole country clouded in mist. It was perfect July weather in Limuru. The hills, ridges, valleys, and plains that surrounded the village were lost in the mist. It looked such a strange place. But there was almost a magic fascination in it. Limuru was a land of contrasts and evoked differing emotions at different times. Once, John would be fascinated and would yearn to touch the land, embrace it or just be on the grass. At another time he would feel repelled by the dust, the strong sun, and the potholed roads. If only his struggle were just against the dust, the mist, the sun and the rain, he might feel content. Content to live here. At least he thought he would never like to die and be buried anywhere else but at Limuru. But there was the human element whose vices and betrayal of other men were embodied as the new ugly villages. The last night's incident rushed into his mind like a flood, making him weak again. He came out of his blankets and went out. Today he would go to the shops. He was uneasy. An odd feeling was coming to him, in fact had been coming, that his relationship with his father was perhaps unnatural. But he dismissed the thought. Tonight would be the "day of reckoning." He shuddered to think of it. It was unfortunate that this scar had come into his life at this time when he was going to Makerere and it would have brought him closer to his father.

They went to the shops. All day long, John remained quiet as they moved from shop to shop, buying things from the lanky but wistful Indian traders. And all day long, John wondered why he feared his father so much. He had grown up fearing him, trembling whenever he spoke or gave commands. John was not alone in this.

Stanley was feared by all.

He preached with great vigor, defying the very gates of hell. Even during the Emergency, he had gone on preaching, scolding, judging, and condemning. All those who were not saved were destined for hell. Above all, Stanley was known for his great moral observances—a bit too strict, rather pharisaical in nature. None noticed this; certainly not the sheep he shepherded. If an elder broke any of the rules, he was liable to be expelled, or excommunicated. Young men and women, seen standing together "in a manner prejudicial to church and God's morality" (they were one anyway), were liable to be excommunicated. And so, many young men tried to serve two masters, by seeing their girls at night and going to church by day. The alternative was to give up churchgoing altogether . . .

Stanley took a fatherly attitude toward all the people in the village. You must be strict with what is yours. And because of all this, he wanted his house to be a good example. That is why he wanted his son to grow up right. But motives behind many human actions may be mixed. He could never forget that he had also fallen before his marriage. Stanley was also a product of the disintegration of the tribe due to the new influences.

The shopping took a long time. His father strictly observed the silences between them and neither by word nor by hint did he refer to last night. They reached home and John was thinking that all was well when his father called him.

"John."

"Yes, Father."

"Why did you not come for prayers last night?"

"I forgot—"

"Where were you?"

Why do you ask me? What right have you to know where I was? One day I am going to revolt against you. But immediately, John knew that this act of rebellion was something beyond him—not unless something happened to push him into it. It needed someone with something he lacked.

"I-I-I mean, I was—"

"You should not sleep so early before prayers. Remember to be there tonight."

"I will."

Something in the boy's voice made the father look up. John went away relieved. All was still well.

Evening came. John dressed like the night before and walked with faltering steps toward the fatal place. The night of reckoning had come. And he had not thought of anything. After this night, all would know. Even Reverend Thomas Carstone would hear of it. He remembered Mr. Carstone and the last words of blessing he had spoken to him. No! he did not want to remember. It was no good remembering these things; and yet the words came. They were clearly written in the air, or in the darkness of his mind. "You are going into the world. The world is waiting even like a hungry lion, to swallow you, to devour you. Therefore, beware of the world. Jesus said, Hold fast unto . . ." John felt a pain—a pain that wriggled through his flesh as he remembered these words. He contemplated the coming fall. Yes! He, John, would fall from the Gates of Heaven down through the open waiting gates of Hell. Ah! He could see it all, and what people would say. Everybody would shun his company, would give him oblique looks that told so much. The trouble with John was that his imagination magnified the fall from the heights of "goodness" out of proportion. And fear of people and consequences ranked high in the things that made him contemplate the fall with so much horror.

John devised all sorts of punishment for himself. And when it came to thinking of a way out, only fantastic and impossible ways of escape came into his head. He simply could not make up his mind. And because he could not and he feared father and people, and he did not know his true attitude toward the girl, he came to the agreed spot having nothing to tell the girl. Whatever he did looked fatal to him.

Then suddenly he said: "Look, Wamuhu. Let me give you money. You might then say that someone else was responsible. Lots of girls have done this. Then that man may marry you. For me, it is impossible. You know that."

"No. I cannot do that. How can you, you—"

"I will give you two hundred shillings."

"No!"

"Three hundred!"

"No!" She was almost crying. It pained her to see him so.

"Four hundred, five hundred, six hundred!" John had begun calmly but now his voice was running high. He was excited. He was becoming more desperate. Did he know what he was talking about? He spoke quickly, breathlessly, as if he was in a hurry. The figure was rapidly rising—nine thousand, ten thousand, twenty thousand . . . He is mad. He is foaming. He is quickly moving toward the girl in the dark. He has laid his hands on her shoulders and is madly imploring her in a hoarse voice. Deep inside him, something horrid that assumes the threatening anger of his father and the village seems to be pushing him. He is violently shaking Wamuhu, while his mind tells him that he is patting her gently. Yes. He is out of his mind. The figure has now reached fifty thousand shillings and is increasing. Wamuhu is afraid, extricates herself from him, the mad, educated son of a religious clergyman, and she runs. He runs after her and holds her, calling her by all sorts of endearing words. But he is shaking her, shake, shake, her, her—he tries to hug her by the neck, presses . . . She lets out one horrible scream and then falls on the ground. And so all of a sudden the struggle is over, the figures stop and John stands there trembling like the leaf of a tree on a windy day.

John, in the grip of fear, ran homeward. Soon everyone would know.

—1975

- John was caught in the middle of two cultural values. He did not know which ones to adapt to.

- He Had no character for himself.

Tayeb Salih

(BORN 1929) SUDAN

Tayeb Salih (Al-Tayeb Salih) was born in 1929, in al-Debba, a main village
in the Central Sudan, an area with which he continues to identify. "I still
live there. I spent my childhood there—until I passed the age of ten, and I
am still rooted there. . . . This village has many characteristics, because it
lies within the region that, in my opinion, represents the center of civilization
in the Sudan. I hope I am not just being prejudiced toward my region. It is
connected by caravan roads to the Western Sudan—and the Valley of Milik
flows into this area; because of that, it has characteristics of the stable society
of the Nile Valley. . . ."

Tayeb Salih's immediate background was agrarian and religious—farmers
and Islamic teachers, who shaped his early intention to work in agriculture
and become a teacher. He received his higher education at Khartoum University, followed by further work at British universities. He taught briefly
in the Sudan before he became head of the BBC's drama programming in
Arabic. His own writing began in 1953, though his first book, *The Wedding
of Zein and Other Stories*, a slim volume of three stories, was not published
until 1968. "A Handful of Dates" is from this volume.

Often described as one of the masterpieces of modern African fiction,
Season of Migration to the North, a novel, was published in English in 1969.
Donald E. Herdeck has described the story: "This work is a bizarre tale of
a sexually talented African scholar, abroad in a violent London full of women
who lust for exotic sensations. Both at home and abroad, the protagonist,

Mustafa Sa'eed, moves about in a dreamlike trance. The book is bitter and poetic. Every woman who wants Mustafa dies. In the end he is emotionally destroyed by the maddest of them all, a certain Jean Morris whom he labels 'the shore of destruction.' '' Other critics have described *Season of Migration to the North* as a Sudanese *Arabian Nights*.

Of the origins of his own writing career, Tayeb Salih has stated: ''[Writing] came by mere chance. I used to write when I was a student. I had linguistic ability. It was not an ambition. But sometimes a man discovers basic things which he should have done earlier, though he may discover these things by chance. The first story was written in 1953 in London—'Palm Tree on the Brook.' . . . Then, after a time, I wrote 'A Handful of Dates.' . . . Had I been in the Sudan, .perhaps I wouldn't have become a writer, because the society's values were against writing at that time. I would have experienced great psychological obstacles. . . . Moreover, the questions of art and literature did not command respect in the society of that time, because it believed in influence. I might have written but not published; or perhaps I might have written articles.''

A HANDFUL OF DATES

Translated from the Arabic by Denys Johnson-Davies

I must have been very young at the time. While I don't remember exactly how old I was, I do remember that when people saw me with my grandfather they would pat me on the head and give my cheek a pinch—things they didn't do to my grandfather. The strange thing was that I never used to go out with my father, rather it was my grandfather who would take me with him wherever he went, except for the mornings, when I would go to the mosque to learn the Koran. The mosque, the river, and the fields—these were the landmarks in our life. While most of the children of my age grumbled at having to go to the mosque to learn the Koran, I used to love it. The reason was, no doubt, that I was quick at learning by heart and the Sheikh always asked me to stand up and recite the *Chapter of the Merciful* whenever we had visitors, who would pat me on my head and cheek just as people did when they saw me with my grandfather.

Yes, I used to love the mosque, and I loved the river, too. Directly we finished our Koran reading in the morning I would throw down my wooden slate and dart off, quick as a genie, to my mother, hurriedly swallow down my breakfast, and run off for a plunge in the river. When tired of swimming about, I would sit on the bank and gaze at the strip of water that wound away eastwards, and hid behind a thick wood of acacia trees. I loved to give rein to my imagination and picture to myself a tribe of giants living behind that wood, a people tall and thin with white beards and sharp noses, like my grandfather. Before my grandfather ever replied to my many questions he would rub the tip of his nose with his forefinger; as for his beard, it was soft and luxuriant and as white as cotton wool—never in my life have I seen anything of a purer whiteness or greater beauty. My grandfather must also have been extremely tall, for I never saw anyone in the whole area address him without having to look up at him, nor did I see him enter a house without having to bend so low that I was put in mind of the way the river wound round behind the wood of acacia trees. I loved him and would imagine myself, when I grew to be a man, tall and slender like him, walking along with great strides.

I believe I was his favorite grandchild: no wonder, for my cousins were a stupid bunch and I—so they say—was an intelligent child. I used to know when my grandfather wanted me to laugh, when to be silent; also I would remember the times for his prayers and would bring him his prayer rug and fill the ewer for his ablutions without his having to ask me. When he had nothing else to do he enjoyed listening to me reciting to him from the Koran in a lilting voice, and I could tell from his face that he was moved.

One day I asked him about our neighbor Masood. I said to my grandfather: "I fancy you don't like our neighbor Masood?"

To which he answered, having rubbed the tip of his nose: "He's an indolent man and I don't like such people."

I said to him: "What's an indolent man?"

My grandfather lowered his head for a moment; then, looking across at the wide expanse of field, he said: "Do you see it stretching out from the edge of the desert up to the Nile bank? A hundred *feddans*. Do you see all those date palms? And those trees—*sant*, acacia, and *sayal*? All this fell into Masood's lap, was inherited by him from his father."

Taking advantage of the silence that had descended on my grandfather, I turned my gaze from him to the vast area defined by his words. "I don't care," I told myself, "who owns those date palms, those trees or this black, cracked earth—all I know is that it's the arena for my dreams and my playground."

My grandfather then continued: "Yes, my boy, forty years ago all this belonged to Masood—two-thirds of it is now mine."

This was news to me, for I had imagined that the land had belonged to my grandfather ever since God's Creation.

"I didn't own a single *feddan* when I first set foot in this village. Masood was then the owner of all these riches. The position has changed now, though, and I think that before Allah calls me to Him I shall have bought the remaining third as well."

I do not know why it was I felt fear at my grandfather's words—and pity for our neighbor Masood. How I wished my grandfather wouldn't do what he'd said! I remembered Masood's singing, his beautiful voice and powerful laugh that resembled the gurgling of water. My grandfather never laughed.

I asked my grandfather why Masood had sold his land.

"Women," and from the way my grandfather pronounced the word I felt that "women" was something terrible. "Masood, my boy, was a much-married man. Each time he married he sold me a *feddan* or two." I made the quick calculation that Masood must have married some ninety women. Then I remembered his three wives, his shabby appearance, his lame donkey and its dilapidated saddle, his *galabia* with the torn sleeves. I had all but rid my mind of the thoughts that jostled in it when I saw the man approaching us, and my grandfather and I exchanged glances.

"We'll be harvesting the dates today," said Masood. "Don't you want to be there?"

I felt, though, that he did not really want my grandfather to attend. My grandfather, however, jumped to his feet and I saw that his eyes sparkled momentarily with an intense brightness. He pulled me by the hand and we went off to the harvesting of Masood's dates.

Someone brought my grandfather a stool covered with an oxhide, while I remained standing. There were a vast number of people there, but though I knew them all, I found myself for some reason watching Masood: aloof from that great gathering of people he stood as though it were no concern of his, despite the fact that the date palms to be harvested were his own. Sometimes his attention would be caught by the sound of a huge clump of dates crashing down from on high. Once he shouted up at the boy perched on the very summit of the date palm who had begun hacking at a clump with his long, sharp sickle: "Be careful you don't cut the heart of the palm."

No one paid any attention to what he said and the boy seated at the very summit of the date palm continued, quickly and energetically, to work away at the branch with his sickle till the clump of dates began to drop like something descending from the heavens.

I, however, had begun to think about Masood's phrase "the heart of the palm." I pictured the palm tree as something with feeling, something possessed of a heart that throbbed. I remembered Masood's remark to me when he had once seen me playing with the branch of a young palm tree: "Palm trees, my boy, like humans, experience joy and suffering." And I had felt an inward and unreasoned embarrassment.

When I again looked at the expanse of ground stretching before me I saw my young companions swarming like ants around the trunks of the palm trees, gathering up dates and eating most of them. The dates were collected into high mounds. I saw people coming along and weighing them into measuring bins and pouring them into sacks, of which I counted thirty. The crowd of people broke up, except for Hussein the merchant, Mousa the owner of the field next to ours on the east, and two men I'd never seen before.

I heard a low whistling sound and saw that my grandfather had fallen asleep. Then I noticed that Masood had not changed his stance, except that he had placed a stalk in his mouth and was munching at it like someone sated with food who doesn't know what to do with the mouthful he still has.

Suddenly my grandfather woke up, jumped to his feet, and walked toward the sacks of dates. He was followed by Hussein the merchant, Mousa the owner of the field next to ours, and the two strangers. I glanced at Masood and saw that he was making his way toward us with extreme slowness, like a man who wants to retreat but whose feet insist on going forward. They formed a circle around the sacks of dates and began examining them, some taking a date or two to eat. My grandfather gave me a fistful, which I began munching. I saw Masood filling the palms of both hands with dates and bringing them up close to his nose, then returning them.

Then I saw them dividing up the sacks between them. Hussein the merchant took ten; each of the strangers took five. Mousa the owner of the field next to ours on the eastern side took five, and my grandfather took five. Understanding nothing, I looked at Masood and saw that his eyes were darting to left and right like two mice that have lost their way home.

"You're still fifty pounds in debt to me," said my grandfather to Masood. "We'll talk about it later."

Hussein called his assistants and they brought along donkeys, the two strangers produced camels, and the sacks of dates were loaded onto them. One of the donkeys let out a braying which set the camels frothing at the mouth and complaining noisily. I felt myself drawing close to Masood, felt my hand stretch out toward him as though I wanted to touch the hem of his garment. I heard him make a noise in his throat like the rasping of a lamb being slaughtered. For some unknown reason, I experienced a sharp sensation of pain in my chest.

I ran off into the distance. Hearing my grandfather call after me, I hesitated a little, then continued on my way. I felt at that moment that I hated him. Quickening my pace, it was as though I carried within me a secret I wanted to rid myself of. I reached the riverbank near the bend it made behind the wood of acacia trees. Then, without knowing why, I put my finger into my throat and spewed up the dates I'd eaten.

—1968

Es'kia Mphahlele

(BORN 1919) SOUTH AFRICA

In the depths of apartheid, at the same time that he wrote "Mrs. Plum," Es'kia Mphahlele noted in *Voices in the Whirlwind* (1972): "The black man is in the majority in South Africa. The agony of waiting for 'something' to happen here is of a different kind from the agony in the black American situation. The black American has to work toward the point where the white man will weaken, not out of any moral considerations but out of necessity. The black man in South Africa has to work toward breaking the white man. He needs to hate more than he is doing. Only after the revolution can he allow the civilized white to stay for the reconstruction."

In an earlier work called *The African Image* (1962), Mphahlele had remarked about the relationships between many Africans and Europeans: "This is a continent of servants—servants of all kinds. There are as many conceivable kinds of relationships between master and servant as the writer cares to explore; especially in the case of white master and black servant, the usual pattern in Africa."

Mphahlele has been a major force in African letters—literally across the continent. In 1950, he was one of the founding editors and writers of *Drum*, the South African journal. His autobiography, *Down Second Avenue* (1959), remains one of the major documents of growing up black under apartheid. That book and several of his other early works were banned in South Africa, forcing Mphahlele into exile for many years. *The African Image* codified black artistry from an African perspective at a time when most commentaries were Western.

Dr. Mphahlele (he earned a Ph.D. in English at the University of Denver) continued, in exile, to write short stories, novels, and criticism. His novel *The Wanderers* (1971) spoke eloquently about displacement for South Africans, though the exile was in West and East Africa. The narrator explores the problems of Pan-Africanism, asking at one point: "How can I make my children understand we have all wandered away from something—all of us blacks; that we are not in close contact with the spirit of Nature, although we may be with its forces, that growing up for us is no more the integrated process it was for our forebears, but that this is also a universal problem?"

Of the writer himself, Mphahlele remarked in *The African Image*: "I would like to think that the writer and the artist will be better able to delve deep down into a people's personality, a people's consciousness. . . . The best he can do is to make us aware of ourselves, know ourselves as we truly are and can be. The politician defines the social situation in terms of imperatives. The writer, as teacher and entertainer, in terms other than the politician's. And yet he arrives at something like a set of imperatives. That is the paradox he is."

Es'kia Mphahlele broke his exile in 1977 and returned to South Africa. He worked for two years as an educational inspector in Lebowa, where he had spent part of his childhood. In 1979, he was granted a Research Fellowship at Rhodes University, in the Institute for the Study of English in Africa. Later the same year, he was appointed Senior Research Fellow at the University of Witwatersrand, in Johannesburg. In 1983, he inaugurated the division of African Literature, at Witwatersrand, in the Department of Comparative Literature. Since that time, he has remained active as a writer, teacher, and editor/publisher of African literature.

MRS. PLUM

1

My madam's name was Mrs. Plum. She loved dogs and Africans and said that everyone must follow the law even if it hurt. These were three big things in Madam's life.

I came to work for Mrs. Plum in Greenside, not very far from the center of Johannesburg, after leaving two white families. The first white people I worked for as a cook and laundry woman were a man and his wife in Parktown North. They drank too much and always forgot to pay me. After five months I said to myself, No. I am going to leave these drunks. So that was it. That day I was as angry as a red-hot iron when it meets water. The second house I cooked and washed for had five children who were badly brought up. This was in Belgravia. Many times they called me You Black Girl and I kept quiet. Because their mother heard them and said nothing. Also I was only new from Phokeng, my home, far away near Rustenburg, I wanted to learn and know the white people before I knew how far to go with the others I would work for afterwards. The thing that drove me mad and made me pack and go was a man who came to visit them often. They said he was cousin or something like that. He came to the kitchen many times and tried to make me laugh. He patted me on the buttocks. I told the master. The man did it again and I asked the madam that very day to give me my money and let me go.

These were the first nine months after I had left Phokeng to work in

Johannesburg. There were many of us girls and young women from Phokeng, from Zeerust, from Shuping, from Kosten, and many other places who came to work in the cities. So the suburbs were full of blackness. Most of us had already passed Standard Six and so we learned more English where we worked. None of us liked to work for white farmers, because we know too much about them on the farms near our homes. They do not pay well and they are cruel people.

At Eastertime so many of us went home for a long weekend to see our people and to eat chicken and sour milk and *morogo*—wild spinach. We also took home sugar and condensed milk and tea and coffee and sweets and custard powder and tinned foods.

It was a home girl of mine, Chimane, who called me to take a job in Mrs. Plum's house, just next door to where she worked. This is the third year now. I have been quite happy with Mrs. Plum and her daughter Kate. By this I mean that my place as a servant in Greenside is not as bad as that of many others. Chimane, too, does not complain much. We are paid six pounds a month with free food and free servant's room. No one can ever say that they are well paid, so we go on complaining somehow. Whenever we meet on Thursday afternoons, which is time off for all of us black women in the suburbs, we talk and talk and talk: about our people at home and their letters; about their illnesses; about bad crops; about a sister who wanted a school uniform and books and school fees; about some of our madams and masters who are good, or stingy with money or food, or stupid or full of nonsense, or who kill themselves and each other, or who are dirty—and so many things I cannot count them all.

Thursday afternoons we go to town to look at the shops, to attend a woman's club, to see our boyfriends, to go to bioscope some of us. We turn up smart, to show others the clothes we bought from the black men who sell soft goods to servants in the suburbs. We take a number of things and they come round every month for a bit of money until we finish paying. Then we dress the way of many white madams and girls. I think we look really smart. Sometimes we catch the eyes of a white woman looking at us and we laugh and laugh until we nearly drop on the ground because we feel good inside ourselves.

2

What did the girl next door call you? Mrs. Plum asked me the first day I came to her. Jane, I replied. Was there not an African name? I said yes,

Karabo. All right, Madam said. We'll call you Karabo, she said. She spoke as if she knew a name is a big thing. I knew so many whites who did not care what they called black people as long as it was all right for their tongue. This pleased me, I mean Mrs. Plum's use of *Karabo*; because the only time I heard the name was when I was home or when my friends spoke to me. Then she showed me what to do: meals, mealtimes, washing, and where all the things were that I was going to use.

My daughter will be here in the evening, Madam said. She is at school. When the daughter came, she added, she would tell me some of the things she wanted me to do for her every day.

Chimane, my friend next door, had told me about the daughter Kate, how wild she seemed to be, and about Mr. Plum, who had killed himself with a gun in a house down the street. They had left the house and come to this one.

Madam is a tall woman. Not slender, not fat. She moves slowly, and speaks slowly. Her face looks very wise, her forehead seems to tell me she has a strong liver: she is not afraid of anything. Her eyes are always swollen at the lower eyelids like a white person who has not slept for many many nights or like a large frog. Perhaps it is because she smokes too much, like wet wood that will not know whether to go up in flames or stop burning. She looks me straight in the eyes when she talks to me, and I know she does this with other people, too. At first this made me fear her, now I am used to her. She is not a lazy woman, and she does many things outside, in the city and in the suburbs.

This was the first thing her daughter Kate told me when she came and we met. Don't mind Mother, Kate told me. She said, She is sometimes mad with people for very small things. She will soon be all right and speak nicely to you again.

Kate, I like her very much, and she likes me, too. She tells me many things a white woman does not tell a black servant. I mean things about what she likes and does not like, what her mother does or does not do, all these. At first I was unhappy and wanted to stop her, but now I do not mind.

Kate looks very much like her mother in the face. I think her shoulders will be just as round and strong-looking. She moves faster than Madam. I asked her why she was still at school when she was so big. She laughed. Then she tried to tell me that the school where she was was for big people who had finished with lower school. She was learning big things about cooking and food. She can explain better, me I cannot. She came home on weekends.

Since I came to work for Mrs. Plum, Kate has been teaching me plenty of cooking. I first learned from her and Madam the word *recipes*. When Kate was at the big school, Madam taught me how to read cookery books. I went on very slowly at first, slower than an ox-wagon. Now I know more. When Kate came home, she found I had read the recipe she left me. So we just cooked straightaway. Kate thinks I am fit to cook in a hotel. Madam thinks so, too. Never never! I thought. Cooking in a hotel is like feeding oxen. No one can say thank you to you. After a few months I could cook the Sunday lunch and later I could cook specials for Madam's or Kate's guests.

Madam did not only teach me cooking. She taught me how to look after guests. She praised me when I did very very well—not like the white people I had worked for before. I do not know what runs crooked in the heads of other people. Madam also had classes in the evenings for servants to teach them how to read and write. She and two other women in Greenside taught in a church hall.

As I say, Kate tells me plenty of things about Madam. She says to me she says, My mother goes to meetings many times. I ask her I say, What for? She says to me she says, For your people. I ask her I say, My people are in Phokeng far away. They have got mouths, I say. Why does she want to say something for them? Does she know what my mother and what my father want to say? They can speak when they want to. Kate raises her shoulders and drops them and says, How can I tell you, Karabo? I don't say your people—your family only. I mean all the black people in the country. I say, Oh! What do the black people want to say? Again she raises her shoulders and drops them, taking a deep breath.

I ask her I say, With whom is she in the meeting?

She says, With other people who think like her.

I ask her I say, Do you say there are people in the world who think the same things?

She nods her head.

I ask, What things?

So that a few of your people should one day be among those who rule this country, get more money for what they do for the white man, and—what did Kate say again? Yes, that Madam and those who think like her also wanted my people who have been to school to choose those who must speak for them in the—I think she said it looks like a *Kgotla* at home who rule the villages.

I say to Kate I say, Oh I see now. I say, Tell me, Kate, why is Madam always writing on the machine, all the time every day nearly?

She replies she says, Oh my mother is writing books.

I ask, You mean a book like those?—pointing at the books on the shelves. Yes, Kate says.

And she told me how Madam wrote books and other things for newspapers and she wrote for the newspapers and magazines to say things for the black people, who should be treated well, be paid more money, for the black people who can read and write many things to choose those who want to speak for them.

Kate also told me she said, My mother and other women who think like her put on black belts over their shoulders when they are sad and they want to show the white government they do not like the things being done by whites to blacks. My mother and the others go and stand where the people in government are going to enter or go out of a building.

I ask her I say, Does the government and the white people listen and stop their sins? She says No. But my mother is in another group of white people.

I ask, Do the people of the government give the women tea and cakes? Kate says, Karabo! How stupid; oh!

I say to her I say, Among my people if someone comes and stands in front of my house I tell him to come in and I give him food. You white people are wonderful. But they keep standing there and the government people do not give them anything.

She replies, You mean strange. How many times have I taught you not to say *wonderful* when you mean *strange*! Well, Kate says with a short heart and looking cross and she shouts, Well they do not stand there the whole day to ask for tea and cakes, stupid. Oh dear!

Always when Madam finished to read her newspapers she gave them to me to read to help me speak and write better English. When I had read she asked me to tell her some of the things in it. In this way, I did better and better and my mind was opening and opening and I was learning and learning many things about the black people inside and outside the towns which I did not know in the least. When I found words that were too difficult or I did not understand some of the things, I asked Madam. She always told me, You see this, you see that, eh? with a heart that can carry on a long way.

Yes, Madam writes many letters to the papers. She is always sore about the way the white police beat up black people; about the way black people who work for whites are made to sit at the Zoo Lake with their hearts hanging, because the white people say our people are making noise on Sunday afternoon when they want to rest in their houses and gardens; about many ugly things that happen when some white people meet black man on the pavement or street. So Madam writes to the papers to let others know, to ask the government to be kind to us.

In the first year Mrs. Plum wanted me to eat at table with her. It was very hard, one because I was not used to eating at table with a fork and knife, two because I heard of no other kitchen worker who was handled like this. I was afraid. Afraid of everybody, of Madam's guests if they found me doing this. Madam said I must not be silly. I must show that African servants can also eat at table. Number three, I could not eat some of the things I loved very much: mealie-meal porridge with sour milk or *morogo*, stamped mealies mixed with butter beans, sour porridge for breakfast, and other things. Also, except for morning porridge, our food is nice when you eat with the hand. So nice that it does not stop in the mouth or the throat to greet anyone before it passes smoothly down.

We often had lunch together with Chimane next door and our garden boy—Ha! I must remember never to say *boy* again when I talk about a man. This makes me think of a day during the first few weeks in Mrs. Plum's house. I was talking about Dick her garden man and I said "garden boy." And she says to me she says, Stop talking about a "boy," Karabo. Now listen here, she says, You Africans must learn to speak properly about each other. And she says, White people won't talk kindly about you if you look down upon each other.

I say to her I say, Madam, I learned the word from the white people I worked for, and all the kitchen maids say "boy."

She replies she says to me, Those are white people who know nothing, just low-class whites. I say to her I say, I thought white people know everything.

She said, You'll learn, my girl, and you must start in this house, hear? She left me there thinking, my mind mixed up.

I learned. I grew up.

3

If any woman or girl does not know the Black Crow Club in Bree Street, she does not know anything. I think nearly everything takes place inside and outside that house. It is just where the dirty part of the city begins, with factories and the market. After the market is the place where Indians and Coloured people live. It is also at the Black Crow that the buses turn round and go back to the black townships. Noise, noise, noise all the time. There are women who sell hot sweet potatoes and fruit and monkey nuts and boiled eggs in the winter, boiled mealies and the other things in the summer, all these on the pavements. The streets are always full of potato and fruit skins and monkey nut shells. There is always a strong smell of roast pork. I think it is because of Piel's cold storage down Bree Street.

Madam said she knew the black people who work in the Black Crow. She was happy that I was spending my afternoon on Thursday in such a club. You will learn sewing, knitting, she said, and other things that you like. Do you like to dance? I told her I said, Yes, I want to learn. She paid the two shillings fee for me each month.

We waited on the first floor, we the ones who were learning sewing; waiting for the teacher. We talked and laughed about madams and masters, and their children and their dogs and birds and whispered about our boyfriends.

Sies! My Madam you do not know—*mojuta oa'nete*—a real miser . . .

Jo—jo—jo! you should see our new dog. A big thing like this. People! Big in a foolish way . . .

What! Me, I take a master's bitch by the leg, me, and throw it away so that it keeps howling, *tjwe—tjwe! ngo—wu ngo—wu!* I don't play about with them, me . . .

Shame, poor thing! God sees you, true . . . !

They wanted me to take their dog out for a walk every afternoon and I told them I said, It is not my work, in other houses the garden man does it. I just said to myself I said, They can go to the chickens. Let them bite their elbows before I take out a dog, I am not so mad yet . . .

Hei! It is not like the child of my white people who keeps a big white rat and you know what? He puts it on his bed when he goes to school. And let the blankets just begin to smell of urine and all the nonsense and they tell me to wash them. *Hei*, people . . . !

Did you hear about Rebone, people? Her Madam put her out, because her master was always tapping her buttocks with his fingers. And yesterday the madam saw the master press Rebone against himself . . .

Jo—jo—jo! people . . . !

Dirty white man!

No, not dirty. The madam smells too old for him.

Hei! Go and wash your mouth with soap, this girl's mouth is dirty . . .

Jo, Rebone, daughter of the people! We must help her to find a job before she thinks of going back home.

The teacher came. A woman with strong legs, a strong face, and kind eyes. She had short hair and dressed in a simple but lovely floral frock. She stood well on her legs and hips. She had a black mark between the two top front teeth. She smiled as if we were her children. Our group began with games, and then Lilian Ngoyi took us for sewing. After this she gave a brief talk to all of us from the different classes.

I can never forget the things this woman said and how she put them to us. She told us that the time had passed for black girls and women in the suburbs to be satisfied with working, sending money to our people, and going to see them once a year. We were to learn, she said, that the world would never be safe for black people until they were in the government with the power to make laws. The power should be given by the Africans who were more than the whites.

We asked her questions and she answered them with wisdom. I shall put some of them down in my own words as I remember them.

Shall we take the place of the white people in the government?

Some yes. But we shall be more than they as we are more in the country. But also the people of all colors will come together and there are good white men we can choose and there are Africans some white people will choose to be in the government.

There are good madams and masters and bad ones. Should we take the good ones for friends?

A master and a servant can never be friends. Never, so put that out of your head, will you! You are not even sure if the ones you say are good are not like that because they cannot breathe or live without the work of your hands. As long as you need their money, face them with respect. But you must know that many sad things are happening in our country and you, all of you, must always be learning, adding to what you already know, and obey us when we ask you to help us.

At other times Lilian Ngoyi told us she said, Remember your poor people at home and the way in which the whites are moving them from place to place like sheep and cattle. And at other times again she told us she said, Remember that a hand cannot wash itself, it needs another to do it.

I always thought of Madam when Lilian Ngoyi spoke. I asked myself, What would she say if she knew that I was listening to such words. Words like: A white man is looked after by his black nanny and his mother when he is a baby. When he grows up the white government looks after him, sends him to school, makes it impossible for him to suffer from the great hunger, keeps a job ready and open for him as soon as he wants to leave school. Now Lilian Ngoyi asked she said, How many white people can be born in a white hospital, grow up in white streets, be clothed in lovely cotton, lie on white cushions; how many whites can live all their lives in a fenced place away from people of other colors and then, as men and women learn quickly the correct ways of thinking, learn quickly to ask questions in their minds, big questions that will throw over all the nice things of a white man's life? How many? Very, very few! For those whites who have not begun to ask, it is too late. For those who have begun and are joining us with both feet in our house, we can only say Welcome!

I was learning. I was growing up. Every time I thought of Madam, she became more and more like a dark forest which one fears to enter, and which one will never know. But there were several times when I thought, This woman is easy to understand, she is like all other white women. What else are they teaching you at the Black Crow, Karabo?

I tell her I say, Nothing, Madam. I ask her I say, Why does Madam ask?

You are changing.

What does Madam mean?

Well, you are changing.

But we are always changing, Madam.

And she left me standing in the kitchen. This was a few days after I had told her that I did not want to read more than one white paper a day. The only magazines I wanted to read, I said to her, were those from overseas, if she had them. I told her that white papers had pictures of white people most of the time. They talked mostly about white people and their gardens, dogs, weddings and parties. I asked her if she could buy me a Sunday paper that spoke about my people. Madam bought it for me. I did not think she would do it.

There were mornings when, after hanging the white people's washing on the line, Chimane and I stole a little time to stand at the fence and talk. We always stood where we could be hidden by our rooms.

Hei, Karabo, you know what? That was Chimane.

No—what? Before you start, tell me, has Timi come back to you?

Ach, I do not care. He is still angry. But boys are fools, they always come back dragging themselves on their empty bellies. *Hei*, you know what?

Yes?

The Thursday past I saw Moruti K.K. I laughed until I dropped on the ground. He is standing in front of the Black Crow. I believe his big stomach was crying from hunger. Now he has a small dog in his armpit, and is standing before a woman selling boiled eggs and—*hei* home girl!—tripe and intestines are boiling in a pot—oh—the smell! you could fill a hungry belly with it, the way it was good. I think Moruti K.K. is waiting for the woman to buy a boiled egg. I do not know what the woman was still doing. I am standing nearby. The dog keeps wriggling and pushing out its nose, looking at the boiling tripe. Moruti keeps patting it with his free hand, not so? Again the dog wants to spill out of Moruti's hand and it gives a few sounds through the nose. *Hei* man, home girl! One two three the dog spills out to catch some of the good meat! It misses falling into the hot gravy in which the tripe is swimming I do not know how. Moruti K.K. tries to chase it. It has tumbled onto the woman's eggs and potatoes and all are in the dust. She stands up and goes after K.K. She is shouting to him to pay, not so? Where am I at that time? I am nearly dead with laughter the tears are coming down so far.

I was myself holding tight on the fence so as not to fall through laughing. I held my stomach to keep back a pain in the side.

I ask her I say, Did Moruti K.K. come back to pay for the wasted food?

Yes, he paid.

The dog?

He caught it. That is a good African dog. A dog must look for its own food when it is not time for meals. Not these stupid spoiled angels the whites keep giving tea and biscuits.

Hmm.

Dick our garden man joined us, as he often did. When the story was repeated to him the man nearly rolled on the ground laughing.

He asks who is Reverend K.K.

I say he is the owner of the Black Crow.

Oh!

We reminded each other, Chimane and I, of the round minister. He would come into the club, look at us with a smooth smile on his smooth round face. He would look at each one of us, with that smile on all the time, as if he had forgotten that it was there. Perhaps he had, because as he looked at us, almost stripping us naked with his watery shining eyes— funny—he could have been a farmer looking at his ripe corn, thinking many things.

K.K. often spoke without shame about what he called ripe girls—*matji- tjana*—with good firm breasts. He said such girls were pure without any nonsense in their heads and bodies. Everybody talked a great deal about him and what they thought he must be doing in his office whenever he called in so-and-so.

The Reverend K.K. did not belong to any church. He baptized, married, and buried people for a fee—who had no church to do such things for them. They said he had been driven out of the Presbyterian Church. He had formed his own, but it did not go far. Then he later came and opened the Black Crow. He knew just how far to go with Lilian Ngoyi. She said although he used his club to teach us things that would help us in life, she could not go on if he was doing any wicked things with the girls in his office. Moruti K.K. feared her, and kept his place.

4

When I began to tell my story I thought I was going to tell you mostly about Mrs. Plum's two dogs. But I have been talking about people. I think Dick is right when he says, What is a dog! And there are so many dogs cats and parrots in Greenside and other places that Mrs. Plum's dogs do not look special. But there was something special in the dog business in Madam's house. The way in which she loved them, maybe.

Monty is a tiny animal with long hair and small black eyes and a face nearly like that of an old woman. The other, Malan, is a bit bigger, with brown and white colors. It has small hair and looks naked by the side of the friend. They sleep in two separate baskets which stay in Madam's bedroom. They are to be washed often and brushed and sprayed and they sleep on pink linen. Monty has a pink ribbon which stays on his neck most of the time. They both carry a cover on their backs. They make me fed up when I see them in their baskets, looking fat, and as if they knew all that was going on everywhere.

It was Dick's work to look after Monty and Malan, to feed them, and to do everything for them. He did this together with garden work and cleaning of the house. He came at the beginning of this year. He just came, as if from nowhere, and Madam gave him the job as she had chased away two before him, she told me. In both those cases, she said that they could not look after Monty and Malan.

Dick had a long heart, even although he told me and Chimane that European dogs were stupid, spoiled. He said, One day those white people will put earrings and toe rings and bangles on their dogs. That would be the day he would leave Mrs. Plum. For, he said, he was sure that she would want him to polish the rings and bangles with Brasso.

Although he had a long heart, Madam was still not sure of him. She often went to the dogs after a meal or after a cleaning and said to them, Did Dick give you food, sweethearts? Or, Did Dick wash you, sweethearts? Let me see. And I could see that Dick was blowing up like a balloon with anger. These things called white people! he said to me. Talking to dogs!

I say to him I say, People talk to oxen at home, do I not say so?

Yes, he says, but at home do you not know that a man speaks to an ox because he wants to make it pull the plow or the wagon or to stop or to stand still for a person to inspan it. No one simply goes to an ox looking at him with eyes far apart and speaks to it. Let me ask you, do you ever see a person where we come from take a cow and press it to his stomach or his cheek? Tell me!

And I say to Dick I say, We were talking about an ox, not a cow.

He laughed with his broad mouth until tears came out of his eyes. At a certain point I laughed aloud, too.

One day when you have time, Dick says to me he says, You should look into Madam's bedroom when she has put a notice outside her door.

Dick, what are you saying? I ask.

I do not talk, me. I know deep inside me.

Dick was about our age, I and Chimane. So we always said *moshiman'o* when we spoke about his tricks. Because he was not too big to be a boy to us. He also said to us *Hei, lona banyana kelona*— Hey you girls, you! His large mouth always seemed to be making ready to laugh. I think Madam did not like this. Many times she would say, What is there to make you laugh here? Or in the garden she would say, This is a flower and when it wants water that is not funny! Or again, if you did more work and stopped trying to water my plants with your smile you would be more useful. Even when

Dick did not mean to smile. What Madam did not get tired of saying was, If I left you to look after my dogs without anyone to look after you at the same time you would drown the poor things.

Dick smiled at Mrs. Plum. Dick hurt Mrs. Plum's dogs? Then cows can fly. He was really—really afraid of white people, Dick. I think he tried very hard not to feel afraid. For he was always showing me and Chimane in private how Mrs. Plum walked, and spoke. He took two bowls and pressed them to his chest, speaking softly to them as Madam speaks to Monty and Malan. Or he sat at Madam's table and acted the way she sits when writing. Now and again he looked back over his shoulder, pulled his face long like a horse's making as if he were looking over his glasses while telling me something to do. Then he would sit on one of the armchairs, cross his legs, and act the way Madam drank her tea; he held the cup he was thinking about between his thumb and the pointing finger, only letting their nails meet. And he laughed after every act. He did these things, of course, when Madam was not home. And where was I at such times? Almost flat on my stomach, laughing.

But oh how Dick trembled when Mrs. Plum scolded him! He did his housecleaning very well. Whatever mistake he made, it was mostly with the dogs; their linen, their food. One white man came into the house one afternoon to tell Madam that Dick had been very careless when taking the dogs out for a walk. His own dog was waiting on Madam's stoop. He repeated that he had been driving down our street, and Dick had let loose Monty and Malan to cross the street. The white man made plenty of noise about this and I think wanted to let Madam know how useful he had been. He kept on saying, Just one inch, *just* one inch. It was lucky I put on my brakes quick enough . . . But your boy kept on smiling— Why? Strange. My boy would only do it twice and only twice and then . . . ! His pass. The man moved his hand like one writing, to mean that he could sign his servant's pass for him to go and never come back. When he left, the white man said, Come on, Rusty, the boy is waiting to clean you. Dogs with names, men without, I thought.

Madam climbed on top of Dick for this, as we say.

Once one of the dogs, I don't know which—Malan or Monty—tore my stocking—brand-new, you hear—and tore it with its teeth and paws. When I told Madam about it, my anger as high as my throat, she gave me money to buy another pair. It happened again. This time she said she was not going to give me money because I must also keep my stockings where the two gentlemen would not reach them. Mrs. Plum did not want us ever to say *Voetsek* when we wanted the dogs to go away. Me I said this when they came sniffing at my legs or fingers. I hate it.

In my third year in Mrs. Plum's house, many things happened, most of them all bad for her. There was trouble with Kate; Chimane had big trouble; my heart was twisted by two loves; and Monty and Malan became real dogs for a few days.

Madam had a number of suppers and parties. She invited Africans to some of them. Kate told me the reasons for some of the parties. Like her mother's books when finished, a visitor from across the seas, and so on. I did not like the black people who came here to drink and eat. They spoke such difficult English like people who were full of all the books in the world. They looked at me as if I were right down there whom they thought little of—me a black person like them.

One day I heard Kate speak to her mother. She says I don't know why you ask so many Africans to the house. A few will do at a time. She said something about the government which I could not hear well. Madam replies she says to her, You know some of them do not meet white people often, so far away in their dark houses. And she says to Kate that they do not come because they want her as a friend but they just want drink for nothing.

I simply felt that I could not be the servant of white people and of blacks at the same time. At my home or in my room I could serve them without a feeling of shame. And now, if they were only coming to drink!

But one of the black men and his sister always came to the kitchen to talk to me. I must have looked unfriendly the first time, for Kate talked to me about it afterwards as she was in the kitchen when they came. I know that at that time I was not easy at all. I was ashamed and I felt that a white person's house was not the place for me to look happy in front of other black people while the white man looked on.

Another time it was easier. The man was alone. I shall never forget that night, as long as I live. He spoke kind words and I felt my heart grow big inside me. It caused me to tremble. There were several other visits. I knew that I loved him, I could never know what he really thought of me, I mean as a woman and he as a man. But I loved him, and I still think of him with a sore heart. Slowly I came to know the pain of it. Because he was a doctor and so full of knowledge and English I could not reach him. So I knew he could not stoop down to see me as someone who wanted him to love me.

Kate turned very wild. Mrs. Plum was very much worried. Suddenly it looked as if she were a new person, with new ways and new everything. I do not know what was wrong or right. She began to play the big gramophone aloud, as if the music were for the whole of Greenside. The music was wild and she twisted her waist all the time, with her mouth half-open. She did the same things in her room. She left the big school and every Saturday night now she went out. When I looked at her face, there was something deep and wild there on it, and when I thought she looked young she looked old, and when I thought she looked old she was young. We were both twenty-two years of age. I think that I could see the reason why her mother was so worried, why she was suffering.

Worse was to come.

They were now openly screaming at each other. They began in the sitting room and went upstairs together, speaking fast hot biting words, some of which I did not grasp. One day Madam comes to me and says, You know Kate loves an African, you know the doctor who comes to supper here often. She says he loves her, too, and they will leave the country and marry outside. Tell me, Karabo, what do your people think of this kind of thing between a white woman and a black man? It *cannot* be right, is it?

I reply and I say to her, We have never seen it happen before where I come from.

That's right, Karabo, it is just madness.

Madam left. She looked like a hunted person.

These white women, I say to myself I say, These white women, why do not they love their own men and leave us to love ours!

From that minute I knew that I would never want to speak to Kate. She appeared to me as a thief, as a fox that falls upon a flock of sheep at night. I hated her. To make it worse, he would never be allowed to come to the house again.

Whenever she was home there was silence between us. I no longer wanted to know anything about what she was doing, where or how.

I lay awake for hours on my bed. Lying like that, I seemed to feel parts of my body beat and throb inside me, the way I have seen big machines doing, pounding and pounding and pushing and pulling and pouring some water into one hole which came out at another end. I stretched myself so many times so as to feel tired and sleepy.

When I did sleep, my dreams were full of painful things.

One evening I made up my mind, after putting it off many times. I told my boyfriend that I did not want him any longer. He looked hurt, and that hurt me, too. He left.

The thought of the African doctor was still with me and it pained me to know that I should never see him again—unless I met him in the street on a Thursday afternoon. But he had a car. Even if I did meet him by luck, how could I make him see that I loved him? Ach, I do not believe he would even stop to think what kind of woman I am. Part of that winter was a time of longing and burning for me. I say part because there are always things to keep servants busy whose white people go to the sea for the winter.

To tell the truth, winter was the time for servants; not nannies, because they went with their madams so as to look after the children. Those like me stayed behind to look after the house and dogs. In winter so many families went away that the dogs remained the masters and madams. You could see them walk like white people in the streets. Silent but with plenty of power. And when you saw them you knew that they were full of more nonsense and fancies in the house.

There was so little work to do.

One week word was whispered round that a home boy of ours was going to hold a party in his room on Saturday. I think we all took it for a joke. How could the man be so bold and stupid? The police were always driving about at night looking for black people; and if the whites next door heard the party noise—*oho!* But still, we were full of joy and wanted to go. As for Dick, he opened his big mouth and nearly fainted when he heard of it and that I was really going.

During the day on the big Saturday Kate came.

She seemed a little less wild. But I was not ready to talk to her. I was surprised to hear myself answer her when she said to me, Mother says you do not like a marriage between a white girl and a black man, Karabo.

Then she was silent.

She says, But I want to help him, Karabo.

I ask her I say, You want to help him to do what?

To go higher and higher, to the top.

I knew I wanted to say so much that was boiling in my chest. I could not say it. I thought of Lilian Ngoyi at the Black Crow, what she said to us. But I was mixed up in my head and in my blood.

You still agree with my mother?

All I could say was, I said to your mother I had never seen a black man and a white woman marrying, you hear me? What I think about it is my business.

I remembered that I wanted to iron my party dress and so I left her. My mind was full of the party again and I was glad because Kate and the doctor would not worry my peace that day. And the next day the sun would shine for all of us, Kate or no Kate, doctor or no doctor.

The house where our home boy worked was hidden from the main road by a number of trees. But although we asked questions and counted many fingers of bad luck until we had no more hands for fingers, we put on our best pay-while-you-wear dresses and suits and clothes bought from boys who had stolen them, and went to our home boy's party. We whispered all the way while we climbed up to the house. Someone who knew told us that the white people next door were away for the winter. Oh, so that is the thing! we said.

We poured into the garden through the back and stood in front of his room laughing quietly. He came from the big house behind us, and were we not struck dumb when he told us to go into the white people's house! Was he mad? We walked in with slow footsteps that seemed to be sniffing at the floor, not sure of anything. Soon we were standing and sitting all over on the nice warm cushions and the heaters were on. Our home boy turned the lights low. I counted fifteen people inside. We saw how we loved one another's evening dress. The boys were smart, too.

Our home boy's girlfriend Naomi was busy in the kitchen preparing food. He took out glasses and cold drinks—fruit juice, tomato juice, ginger beers, and so many other kinds of soft drink. It was just too nice. The tarts, the biscuits, the snacks, the cakes, *woo*, that was a party, I tell you. I think I ate more ginger cake than I had ever done in my life. Naomi had baked some of the things. Our home boy came to me and said, I do not want the police to come here and have reason to arrest us, so I am not serving hot drinks, not even beer. There is no law that we cannot have parties, is there? So we can feel free. Our use of this house is the master's business. If I had asked him he would have thought me mad.

I say to him I say, You have a strong liver to do such a thing.

He laughed.

He played pennywhistle music on gramophone records—Miriam Makeba, Dorothy Masuka, and other African singers and players. We danced and the party became more and more noisy and more happy. *Hai*, those girls Miriam and Dorothy, they can sing, I tell you! We ate more and laughed more and told more stories. In the middle of the party, our home boy called us to listen to what he was going to say. Then he told us how he and a friend of his in Orlando collected money to bet on a horse for the July Handicap in Durban. They did this each year but lost. Now they had won two hundred pounds. We all clapped hands and cheered. Two hundred pounds, *woo!*

You should go and sit at home and just eat time, I say to him. He laughs and says, You have no understanding, not one little bit.

To all of us he says, Now my brothers and sisters enjoy yourselves. At home I should slaughter a goat for us to feast and thank our ancestors. But this is town life and we must thank them with tea and cake and all those sweet things. I know some people think I must be so bold that I could be midwife to a lion that is giving birth, but enjoy yourselves and have no fear.

Madam came back looking strong and fresh.

The very week she arrived the police had begun again to search servants' rooms. They were looking for what they called loafers and men without passes who they said were living with friends in the suburbs against the law. Our dog's-meat boys became scarce because of the police. A boy who had a girlfriend in the kitchens, as we say, always told his friends that he was coming for dog's meat when he meant he was visiting his girl. This was because we gave our boyfriends part of the meat the white people bought for the dogs and us.

One night a white and a black policeman entered Mrs. Plum's yard. They said they had come to search. She says no, they cannot. They say yes, they must do it. She answers no. They forced their way to the back, to Dick's room and mine. Mrs. Plum took the hose that was running in the front garden and quickly went round to the back. I cut across the floor to see what she was going to say to the men. They were talking to Dick, using dirty words. Mrs. Plum did not wait, she just pointed the hose at the two policemen. This seemed to surprise them. They turned round and she pointed it into their faces. Without their seeing me I went to the tap at the corner of the house and opened it more. I could see Dick, like me, was trying to keep down his laughter. They shouted and tried to wave the water away, but she kept the hose pointing at them, now moving it up and down. They turned and ran through the back gate, swearing the while.

That fixes them, Mrs. Plum said.

The next day the morning paper reported it.

They arrived in the afternoon—the two policemen—with another. They pointed out Mrs. Plum and she was led to the police station. They took her away to answer for stopping the police while they were doing their work.

She came back and said she had paid bail.

At the magistrate's court, Madam was told that she had done a bad thing. She would have to pay a fine or else go to prison for fourteen days. She said she would go to jail to show that she felt she was not in the wrong.

Kate came and tried to tell her that she was doing something silly, going to jail for a small thing like that. She tells Madam she says, This is not even a thing to take to the high court. Pay the money. What is £5?

Madam went to jail.

She looked very sad when she came out. I thought of what Lilian Ngoyi often said to us: You must be ready to go to jail for the things you believe are true and for which you are taken by the police. What did Mrs. Plum really believe about me, Chimane, Dick, and all the other black people? I asked myself. I did not know. But from all those things she was writing for the papers and all those meetings she was going to where white people talked about black people and the way they are treated by the government, from what those white women with black bands over their shoulders were doing standing where a white government man was going to pass, I said to myself I said, This woman, *hai*, I do not know she seems to think very much of us black people. But why was she so sad?

Kate came back home to stay after this. She still played the big gramophone loud-loud-loud and twisted her body at her waist until I thought it was going to break. Then I saw a young white man come often to see her. I watched them through the opening near the hinges of the door between the kitchen and the sitting room where they sat. I saw them kiss each other for a long time. I saw him lift up Kate's dress and her white-white legs begin to tremble, and—oh, I am afraid to say more, my heart was beating hard. She called him Jim. I thought it was funny because white people in the shops call black men Jim.

Kate had begun to play with Jim when I met a boy who loved me and I loved. He was much stronger than the one I sent away and I loved him more, much more. The face of the doctor came to my mind often, but it did not hurt me so anymore. I stopped looking at Kate and her Jim through openings. We spoke to each other, Kate and I, almost as freely as before but not quite. She and her mother were friends again.

Hallo, Karabo, I heard Chimane call me one morning as I was starching

my apron. I answered. I went to the line to hang it. I saw she was standing
at the fence, so I knew she had something to tell me. I went to her.

Hallo!

Hallo, Chimane!

O kae?

Ke teng. Wena?

At that moment a woman came out through the back door of the house
where Chimane was working.

I have not seen that one before, I say, pointing with my head.

Chimane looked back. Oh, that one. *Hei*, daughter-of-the-people, *Hei*,
you have not seen miracles. You know this is Madam's mother-in-law as
you see her there. Did I never tell you about her?

No, never.

White people, nonsense. You know what? That poor woman is here now
for two days. She has to cook for herself and I cook for the family.

On the same stove?

Yes. She comes after me when I have finished.

She has her own food to cook?

Yes, Karabo. White people have no heart no sense.

What will eat them up if they share their food?

Ask me, just ask me. God! She clapped her hands to show that only God
knew, and it was His business, not ours.

Chimane asks me she says, Have you heard from home?

I tell her I say, Oh daughter-of-the-people, more and more deaths. Something is finishing the people at home. My mother has written. She says they
are all right, my father, too, and my sisters, except for the people who have
died. Malebo, the one who lived alone in the house I showed you last year,
a white house, he is gone. Then teacher Sedimo. He was very thin and
looked sick all the time. He taught my sisters not me. His mother-in-law
you remember I told you died last year—no, the year before. Mother says
also there is a woman she does not think I remember because I last saw her
when I was a small girl, she passed away in Zeerust, she was my mother's
greatest friend when they were girls. She would have gone to her burial if
it was not because she has swollen feet.

How are the feet?

She says they are still giving her trouble. I ask Chimane, How are your
people at Nokaneng? They have not written?

She shook her head.

I could see from her eyes that her mind was on another thing and not her people at that moment.

Wait for me, Chimane eh, forgive me, I have scones in the oven, eh! I will just take them out and come back, eh!

When I came back to her, Chimane was wiping her eyes. They were wet.

Karabo, you know what?

E—e. I shook my head.

I am heavy with child.

Hau!

There was a moment of silence.

Who is it, Chimane?

Timi. He came back only to give me this.

But he loves you. What does he say, have you told him?

I told him yesterday. We met in town.

I remembered I had not seen her at the Black Crow.

Are you sure, Chimane? You have missed a month?

She nodded her head.

Timi himself—he did not use the thing?

I only saw after he finished, that he had not.

Why? What does he say?

He tells me he says I should not worry I can be his wife.

Timi is a good boy, Chimane. How many of these boys with town ways who know too much will even say Yes it is my child?

Hai, Karabo, you are telling me other things now. Do you not see that I have not worked long enough for my people? If I marry now who will look after them when I am the only child?

Hm. I hear your words. It is true. I tried to think of something soothing to say.

Then I say, You can talk it over with Timi. You can go home and when the child is born you look after it for three months and when you are married you come to town to work and can put your money together to help the old people while they are looking after the child.

What shall we be eating all the time I am at home? It is not like those days gone past when we had land and our mother could go to the fields until the child was ready to arrive.

The light goes out in my mind and I cannot think of the right answer.

How many times have I feared the same thing! Luck and the mercy of the
gods that is all I live by. That is all we live by—all of us.

Listen, Karabo. I must be going to make tea for Madam. It will soon
strike half-past ten.

I went back to the house. As Madam was not in yet, I threw myself on
the divan in the sitting room. Malan came sniffing at my legs. I put my foot
under its fat belly and shoved it up and away from me so that it cried
tjunk—tjunk—tjunk as it went out. I say to it I say, Go and tell your brother
what I have done to you and tell him to try it and see what I will do. Tell
your grandmother when she comes home, too.

When I lifted my eyes he was standing in the kitchen door, Dick. He says
to me he says *Hau!* now you have also begun to speak to dogs!

I did not reply, I just looked at him, his mouth ever stretched out like
the mouth of a bag, and I passed to my room.

I sat on my bed and looked at my face in the mirror. Since the morning
I had been feeling as if a black cloud were hanging over me, pressing on my
head and shoulders. I do not know how long I sat there. Then I smelled
Madam. What was it? Where was she? After a few moments I knew what
it was. My perfume and scent. I used the same cosmetics as Mrs. Plum's. I
should have been used to it by now. But this morning—why did I smell
Mrs. Plum like this? Then, without knowing why, I asked myself I said,
Why have I been using the same cosmetics as Madam? I wanted to throw
them all out. I stopped. And then I took all the things and threw them into
the dustbin. I was going to buy other kinds on Thursday; finished!

I could not sit down. I went out and into the white people's house. I
walked through and the smell of the house made me sick and seemed to fill
up my throat. I went to the bathroom without knowing why. It was full of
the smell of Madam. Dick was cleaning the bath. I stood at the door and
looked at him cleaning the dirt out of the bath, dirt from Madam's body.
Sies! I said aloud. To myself I said, Why cannot people wash the dirt of
their own bodies out of the bath? Before Dick knew I was near I went out.
Ach, I said again to myself, why should I think about it now when I have
been doing their washing for so long and cleaned the bath many times when
Dick was ill. I had held worse things from her body times without number . . .

I went out and stood midway between the house and my room, looking
into the next yard. The three-legged gray cat next door came to the fence
and our eyes met. I do not know how long we stood like that looking at

each other. I was thinking, Why don't you go and look at your grandmother like that? when it turned away and mewed hopping on the three legs. Just like someone who feels pity for you.

In my room I looked into the mirror on the chest of drawers. I thought, Is this Karabo, this?

Thursday came, and the afternoon off. At the Black Crow I did not see Chimane. I wondered about her. In the evening I found a note under my door. It told me if Chimane was not back that evening I should know that she was at 660 3rd Avenue, Alexandra Township. I was not to tell the white people.

I asked Dick if he could not go to Alexandra with me after I had washed the dishes. At first he was unwilling. But I said to him I said, Chimane will not believe that you refused to come with me when she sees me alone. He agreed.

On the bus Dick told me much about his younger sister whom he was helping with money to stay at school until she finished, so that she could become a nurse and a midwife. He was very fond of her, as far as I could find out. He said he prayed always that he should not lose his job, as he had done many times before, after staying a few weeks only at each job; because of this he had to borrow monies from people to pay his sister's school fees, to buy her clothes and books. He spoke of her as if she were his sweetheart. She was clever at school, pretty (she was this in the photo Dick had shown me before). She was in Orlando Township. She looked after his old people, although she was only thirteen years of age. He said to me he said, Today I still owe many people because I keep losing my job. You must try to stay with Mrs. Plum, I said.

I cannot say that I had all my mind on what Dick was telling me. I was thinking of Chimane: what could she be doing? Why that note?

We found her in bed. In that terrible township where night and day are full of knives and bicycle chains and guns and the barking of hungry dogs and of people in trouble. I even held my heart in my hands. She was in pain and her face, even in the candlelight, was gray. She turned her eyes at me. A fat woman was sitting in a chair. One arm rested on the other and held her chin in its palm. She had hardly opened the door for us after we had shouted our names when she was on her bench again as if there were nothing else to do.

She snorted, as if to let us know that she was going to speak. She said, There is your friend. There she is my own-own niece who comes from the womb of my own sister, my sister who was made to spit out my mother's breast to give way for me. Why does she go and do such an evil thing. *Ao!* you young girls of today you do not know children die so fast these days that you have to thank God for sowing a seed in your womb to grow into a child. If she had let the child be born I should have looked after it or my sister would have been so happy to hold a grandchild on her lap, but what does it help? She has allowed a worm to cut the roots, I don't know.

Then I saw that Chimane's aunt was crying. Not once did she mention her niece by her name, so sore her heart must have been. Chimane only moaned.

Her aunt continued to talk, as if she was never going to stop for breath, until her voice seemed to move behind me, not one of the things I was thinking: trying to remember signs, however small, that could tell me more about this moment in a dim little room in a cruel township without street-lights, near Chimane. Then I remembered the three-legged cat, its gray-green eyes, its *miau*. What was this shadow that seemed to walk about us but was not coming right in front of us?

I thanked the gods when Chimane came to work at the end of the week. She still looked weak, but that shadow was no longer there. I wondered Chimane had never told me about her aunt before. Even now I did not ask her.

I told her I told her white people that she was ill and had been fetched to Nokaneng by a brother. They would never try to find out. They seldom did, these people. Give them any lie, and it will do. For they seldom believe you whatever you say. And how can a black person work for white people and be afraid to tell them lies. They are always asking the questions, you are always the one to give the answers.

Chimane told me all about it. She had gone to a woman who did these things. Her way was to hold a sharp needle, cover the point with the finger, and guide it into the womb. She then fumbled in the womb until she found the egg and then pierced it. She gave you something to ease the bleeding. But the pain, spirits of our forefathers!

Mrs. Plum and Kate were talking about dogs one evening at dinner. Every time I brought something to table I tried to catch their words. Kate seemed to find it funny, because she laughed aloud. There was a word I could not hear well which began with *sem*—: whatever it was, it was to be for dogs. This I understood by putting a few words together. Mrs. Plum said it was something that was common in the big cities of America, like New York.

It was also something Mrs. Plum wanted and Kate laughed at the thought. Then later I was to hear that Monty and Malan could be sure of a nice burial.

Chimane's voice came up to me in my room the next morning, across the fence. When I come out she tells me she said, *Hei* child-of-my-father, here is something to tickle your ears. You know what? What? I say. She says, These white people can do things that make the gods angry. More godless people I have not seen. The madam of our house says the people of Greenside want to buy ground where they can bury their dogs. I heard them talk about it in the sitting room when I was giving them coffee last night. *Hei*, people, let our forefathers come and save us!

Yes, I say, I also heard the madam of our house talk about it with her daughter. I just heard it in pieces. By my mother one day these dogs will sit at table and use knife and fork. These things are to be treated like people now, like children who are never going to grow up.

Chimane sighed and she says, *Hela batho*, why do they not give me some of that money they will spend on the ground and on gravestones to buy stockings! I have nothing to put on, by my mother.

Over her shoulder I saw the cat with three legs. I pointed with my head. When Chimane looked back and saw it she said, *Hm*, even *they* live like kings. The mother-in-law found it on a chair and the madam said the woman should not drive it away. And there was no other chair, so the woman went to her room.

Hela!

I was going to leave when I remembered what I wanted to tell Chimane. It was that five of us had collected £1 each to lend her so that she could pay the woman of Alexandra for having done that thing for her. When Chimane's time came to receive money we collected each month and which we took in turns, she would pay us back. We were ten women and each gave £2 at a time. So one waited ten months to receive £20. Chimane thanked us for helping her.

I went to wake up Mrs. Plum as she had asked me. She was sleeping late this morning. I was going to knock at the door when I heard strange noises in the bedroom. What is the matter with Mrs. Plum? I asked myself. Should I call her, in case she is ill? No, the noises were not those of a sick person. They were happy noises but like those a person makes in a dream, the voice full of sleep. I bent a little to peep through the keyhole. What is this? I kept asking myself. Mrs. Plum! Malan! What is she doing this one? Her arm was round Malan's belly and pressing its back against her stomach at the navel, Mrs. Plum's body in a nightdress moving in jerks like someone in fits . . . her leg rising and falling . . . Malan silent like a thing to be owned without any choice it can make to belong to another.

The gods save me! I heard myself saying, the words sounding like wind rushing out of my mouth. So this is what Dick said I would find out for myself!

No one could say where it all started; who talked about it first; whether the police wanted to make a reason for taking people without passes and people living with servants and working in town or not working at all. But the story rushed through Johannesburg that servants were going to poison the white people's dogs. Because they were too much work for us: that was the reason. We heard that letters were sent to the newspapers by white people asking the police to watch over the dogs to stop any wicked things. Some said that we the servants were not really bad, we were being made to think of doing these things by evil people in town and in the locations. Others said the police should watch out lest we poison madams and masters because black people did not know right from wrong when they were angry. We were still children at heart, others said. Mrs. Plum said that she had also written to the papers.

Then it was the police came down on the suburbs like locusts on a cornfield. There were lines and lines of men who were arrested hour by hour in the day. They liked this very much, the police. Everybody they took, everybody who was working was asked, Where's the poison, eh? Where did you hide it? Who told you to poison the dogs, eh? If you tell us we'll leave you to go free, you hear? and so many other things.

Dick kept saying, It is wrong this thing they want to do to kill poor dogs. What have these things of God done to be killed for? Is it the dogs that make us carry passes? Is it dogs that make the laws that give us pain? People are just mad they do not know what they want, stupid! But when white policeman spoke to him, Dick trembled and lost his tongue and the things he thought. He just shook his head. A few moments after they had gone through his pockets he still held his arms stretched out, like the man of straw who frightens away birds in a field. Only when I hissed and gave him a sign did he drop his arms. He rushed to a corner of the garden to go on with his work.

Mrs. Plum had put Monty and Malan in the sitting room, next to her. She looked very much worried. She called me. She asked me she said,

Karabo, you think Dick is a boy we can trust? I did not know how to answer. I did not know whom she was talking about when she said *we*. Then I said I do not know, Madam. You know! she said. I looked at her. I said I do not know what Madam thinks. She said she did not think anything, that was why she asked. I nearly laughed because she was telling a lie this time and not I.

At another time I should have been angry if she lied to me, perhaps. She and I often told each other lies, as Kate and I also did. Like when she came back from jail, after that day when she turned a hose pipe on two policemen. She said life had been good in jail. And yet I could see she was ashamed to have been there. Not like our black people who are always being put in jail and only look at it as the white man's evil game. Lilian Ngoyi often told us this, and Mrs. Plum showed me how true those words are. I am sure that we have kept to each other by lying to each other.

There was something in Mrs. Plum's face as she was speaking which made me fear her and pity her at the same time. I had seen her when she had come from prison; I had seen her when she was shouting at Kate and the girl left the house; now there was this thing about dog poisoning. But never had I seen her face like this before. The eyes, the nostrils, the lips, the teeth seemed to be full of hate, tired, fixed on doing something bad; and yet there was something on that face that told me she wanted me on her side.

Dick is all right, Madam, I found myself saying. She took Malan and Monty in her arms and pressed them to herself, running her hands over their heads. They looked so safe, like a child in a mother's arm.

Mrs. Plum said, All right, you may go. She said, Do not tell anybody what I have asked about Dick, eh?

When I told Dick about it, he seemed worried.

It is nothing, I told him.

I had been thinking before that I did not stand with those who wanted to poison the dogs, Dick said. But the police have come out, I do not care what happens to the dumb things, now.

I asked him I said, Would you poison them if you were told by someone to do it?

No. But I do not care, he replied.

The police came again and again. They were having a good holiday, everyone could see that. A day later Mrs. Plum told Dick to go because she would not need his work anymore.

Dick was almost crying when he left. Is Madam so unsure of me? he asked. I never thought a white person could fear me! And he left.

Chimane shouted from the other yard. She said, *Hei ngoana'rona*, the boers are fire-hot, eh!

Mrs. Plum said she would hire a man after the trouble was over.

A letter came from my parents in Phokeng. In it they told me my uncle had passed away. He was my mother's brother. The letter also told me of other deaths. They said I would not remember some, I was sure to know the others. There were also names of sick people.

I went to Mrs. Plum to ask her if I could go home. She asks she says, When did he die? I answer I say, It is three days, Madam. She says, So that they have buried him? I reply, Yes, Madam. Why do you want to go home, then? Because my uncle loved me very much, Madam. But what are you going to do there? To take my tears and words of grief to his grave and to my old aunt, Madam. No, you cannot go, Karabo. You are working for me, you know? Yes, Madam. I, and not your people, pay you. I must go, Madam, that is how we do it among my people, Madam. She paused. She walked into the kitchen and came out again. If you want to go, Karabo, you must lose the money for the day you will be away. Lose my pay, Madam? Yes, Karabo.

The next day I went to Mrs. Plum and told her I was leaving for Phokeng and was not coming back to her. Could she give me a letter to say that I worked for her. She did, with her lips shut tight. I could feel that something between us was burning like raw chilies. The letter simply said that I had worked for Mrs. Plum for three years. Nothing more. The memory of Dick being sent away was still an open sore in my heart.

The night before the day I left, Chimane came to see me in my room. She had her own story to tell me. Timi, her boyfriend, had left her—for good. Why? Because I killed his baby. Had he not agreed that you should do it? No. Did he show he was worried when you told him you were heavy? He was worried, like me as you saw me, Karabo. Now he says if I kill one I shall eat all his children up when we are married. You think he means what he says? Yes, Karabo. He says his parents would have been very happy to know that the woman he was going to marry can make his seed grow.

Chimane was crying softly.

I tried to speak to her, to tell her that if Timi left her just like that, he had not wanted to marry her in the first place. But I could not, no, I could not. All I could say was, Do not cry, my sister, do not cry. I gave her my handkerchief.

Kate came back the morning I was leaving, from somewhere very far I cannot remember where. Her mother took no notice of what Kate said asking her to keep me, and I was not interested either.

One hour later I was on the Railway bus to Phokeng. During the early part of the journey I did not feel anything about the Greenside house I had worked in. I was not really myself, my thoughts dancing between Mrs. Plum, my uncle, my parents, and Phokeng, my home. I slept and woke up many times during the bus ride. Right through the ride I seemed to see, sometimes in sleep, sometimes between sleep and waking, a red car passing our bus, then running behind us. Each time I looked out it was not there.

Dreams came and passed. He tells me he says, You have killed my seed. I wanted my mother to know you are a woman in whom my seed can grow . . . Before you make the police take you to jail make sure that it is for something big you should go to jail for, otherwise you will come out with a heart and mind that will bleed inside you and poison you . . .

The bus stopped for a short while, which made me wake up.

The Black Crow, the club women . . . *Hei*, listen! I lie to the madam of our house and I say I had a telegram from my mother telling me she is very very sick. I show her a telegram my sister sent me as if Mother were writing. So I went home for a nice weekend . . .

The laughter of the women woke me up, just in time for me to stop a line of saliva coming out over my lower lip. The bus was making plenty of dust now as it was running over part of the road they were digging up. I was sure the red car was just behind us, but it was not there when I woke.

Any one of you here who wants to be baptized or has a relative without a church who needs to be can come and see me in the office . . . A round man with a fat tummy and sharp hungry eyes, a smile that goes a long, long way . . .

The bus was going uphill, heavily and noisily.

I kick a white man's dog, me, or throw it there if it has not been told the black people's law . . . This is Mister Monty and this is Mister Malan. Now get up you lazy boys and meet Mister Kate. Hold out your hands and say hallo to him . . . Karabo, bring two glasses there . . . Wait a bit— What will you chew, boys, while Mister Kate and I have a drink? Nothing? Sure?

We were now going nicely on a straight tarred road and the trees rushed back. Mister Kate. What nonsense, I thought.

Look, Karabo, Madam's dogs are dead. What? Poison. I killed them. She drove me out of a job, did she not? For nothing. Now I want her to feel she drove me out for something. I came back when you were in your room and took the things and poisoned them . . . And you know what? She has buried them in clean pink sheets in the garden. *Ao*, clean clean good sheets. I am going to dig them out and take one sheet, do you want the other one? Yes, give me the other one I will send it to my mother . . . *Hei*, Karabo, see here they come. Monty and Malan. The bloody fools they do not want to stay in their hole. Go back, you silly fools. Oh you do not want to move, eh? Come here, now I am going to throw you in the big pool. No, Dick! No Dick! no, no! Dick! They cannot speak do not kill things that cannot speak. Madam can speak for them she always does. No! Dick . . . !

I woke up with a jump after I had screamed Dick's name, almost hitting the window. My forehead was full of sweat. The red car also shot out of my sleep and was gone. I remembered a friend of ours who told us how she and the garden man had saved two white sheets in which their white master had buried their two dogs. They went to throw the dogs in a dam.

When I told my parents my story Father says to me he says, So long as you are in good health, my child, it is good. The worker dies, work does not. There is always work. I know when I was a boy a strong sound body and a good mind were the biggest things in life. Work was always there, and the lazy man could never say there was no work. But today people see work as something bigger than everything else, bigger than health, because of money.

I reply I say, Those days are gone, Papa. I must go back to the city after resting a little to look for work. I must look after you. Today people are too poor to be able to help you.

I knew when I left Greenside that I was going to return to Johannesburg to work. Money was little, but life was full and it was better than sitting in Phokeng and watching the sun rise and set. So I told Chimane to keep her eyes and ears open for a job.

I had been at Phokeng for one week when a red car arrived. Somebody was sitting in front with the driver, a white woman. At once I knew it to be Mrs. Plum. The man sitting beside her was showing her the way, for he pointed toward our house in front of which I was sitting. My heart missed a few beats. Both came out of the car. The white woman said Thank you to the man after he had spoken a few words to me.

I did not know what to do and how to look at her as she spoke to me. So I looked at the piece of cloth I was sewing pictures on. There was a tired but soft smile on her face. Then I remembered that she might want to sit. I went inside to fetch a low bench for her. When I remembered it afterwards, the thought came to me that there are things I never think white people can want to do at our homes when they visit for the first time: like sitting, drinking water, or entering the house. This is how I thought when the white priest came to see us. One year at Easter Kate drove me home as she was going to the north. In the same way I was at a loss what to do for a few minutes.

Then Mrs. Plum says, I have come to ask you to come back to me, Karabo. Would you like to?

I say I do not know, I must think about it first.

She says, Can you think about it today? I can sleep at the town hotel and come back tomorrow morning, and if you want to, you can return with me.

I wanted her to say she was sorry to have sent me away, I did not know how to make her say it because I know white people find it too much for them to say Sorry to a black person. As she was not saying it, I thought of two things to make it hard for her to get me back and maybe even lose me in the end.

I say, You must ask my father first, I do not know, should I call him?

Mrs. Plum says, Yes.

I fetched both Father and Mother. They greeted her while I brought benches. Then I told them what she wanted.

Father asks Mother and Mother asks Father. Father asks me. I say if they agree, I will think about it and tell her the next day.

Father says, It goes by what you feel, my child.

I tell Mrs. Plum I say, If you want me to think about it I must know if you will want to put my wages up from £6 because it is too little.

She asks me, How much will you want?

Up by £4.

She looked down for a few moments.

And then I want two weeks at Easter and not just the weekend. I thought if she really wanted me she would want to pay for it. This would also show how sorry she was to lose me.

Mrs. Plum says, I can give you one week. You see you already have something like a rest when I am in Durban in the winter.

I tell her I say I shall think about it.

She left.

The next day she found me packed and ready to return with her. She was very much pleased and looked kinder than I had ever known her. And me, I felt sure of myself, more than I had ever done.

Mrs. Plum says to me, You will not find Monty and Malan.

Oh?

Yes, they were stolen the day after you left. The police have not found them yet. I think they are dead myself.

I thought of Dick . . . my dream. Could he? And she . . . did this woman come to ask me to return because she had lost two animals she loved?

Mrs. Plum says to me she says, You know, I like your people, Karabo, the Africans.

And Dick and me? I wondered.

—1967

Grace Ogot

(BORN 1930) KENYA

According to Lee Nichols in *African Writers at the Microphone*, Grace Ogot has "managed boutiques in Nairobi, conducted her own radio program and engaged in other activities. . . ." One of these other activities was serving as Assistant Minister in the Kenyan Government. She has also written for the BBC, worked as a Public Relations Officer and as a Community Development Officer, been a midwifery tutor as well as the Headmistress of the Kisumu Homecraft Training Center, taught at Makerere University College in Uganda, and served as a delegate to the United Nations. And she is a writer. Of the last, she mentions her daughter's remark to her brothers: "Hey, you guys, keep quiet, Mommy's writing."

Besides numerous journalistic pieces, Grace Ogot has published many short stories which have been reprinted in international publications. Her collected stories appeared as *Land without Thunder* (1968); a Swahili translation of the volume was published in 1979. Her novels include *The Other Woman* (1976), *The Island of Tears* (1980), and *The Strange Bride* (1989). The last was originally written and published as *Miaha*, in Dholuo, her first language, in 1983.

Luo mythology is at the center of *The Strange Bride*, which begins: "In the distant ancestral days, our god, Were Nyakalaga, lived on the earth with his own people. But no one could see him because he was a mysterious being whose essence spread all over the surface of the earth.

"However, even though people could not see Were Nyakalaga, they were aware of his closeness to them. They saw his hand in lightning and heard his voice in thunder and the winds that blew around them.

"People believed that Were Nyakalaga liked to live in the mountains. They therefore built him a small shrine—with a roof thatched with the *buoywe* grass—at the peak of Got Owaga. From there, they believed, Were Nyakalaga was able to look after all his people who lived in the big village that surrounded the mountain."

Much of Grace Ogot's writing career has involved a successful attempt to straddle the question of language: African or European? She confesses: "I love writing for myself. I read them [my stories], I cry over them sometimes."

TEKAYO

The period of short rains was just starting in a semi-arid part of the Sudan. The early-morning mist had cleared, and faint blue smoke rose from the ground as the hot sun touched the surface of the wet earth.

"People in the underworld are cooking.

"People in the underworld are cooking!"

The children shouted, as they pelted one another with wet sand.

"Come on, Opija," Tekayo shouted to his son. "Give me a hand, I must get the cows to the river before it is too hot."

Opija hit his younger brother with his last handful of sand, and then ran to help his father. The cows were soon out of the village and Tekayo picked up the leather pouch containing his lunch and followed them.

They had not gone far from home when Tekayo saw an eagle flying above his head with a large piece of meat in its claws. The eagle was flying low, searching for a suitable spot to have its meal. Tekayo promptly threw his stick at the bird. He hit the meat and it dropped to the ground. It was a large piece of liver, and fresh blood was still oozing from it. Tekayo nearly threw the meat away, but he changed his mind. What was the use of robbing the eagle of its food only to throw it away? The meat looked good: it would supplement his vegetable lunch wonderfully. He wrapped the meat in a leaf and pushed it into his pouch.

They reached a place where there was plenty of grass. Tekayo allowed the cows to graze while he sat under an *ober* tree watching the sky. It was not yet lunchtime, but Tekayo could not wait. The desire to taste that meat was burning within him. He took out the meat and roasted it on a log fire under the *ober* tree. When the meat was cooked he ate it greedily with millet bread which his wife had made the previous night.

"My, what delicious meat!" Tekayo exclaimed. He licked the fat juice that stained his fingers, and longed for a little more. He threw away the bitter herbs that were the rest of his lunch. The meat was so good, and the herbs would merely spoil its taste.

The sun was getting very hot, but the cows showed no desire to go to the river to drink. One by one they lay down in the shade, chewing the cud. Tekayo also became overpowered by the afternoon heat. He rested against the trunk and slept.

While asleep, Tekayo had a dream. He was sitting before a log fire roasting a large piece of liver like the one he had eaten earlier. His mouth watered as he watched rich fat from the roasting meat dropping into the fire. He could not wait, and although the meat was not completely done, he removed it from the fire and cut it up with his hunting knife. But just as he was about to take the first bite, he woke up.

Tekayo looked around him, wondering what had happened to the meat. Could it be that he was dreaming? "No, no, no," he cried. "It was too vivid to be a dream!" He sat upright and had another look around, as if by some miracle he might see a piece of liver roasting on the log fire beside him. But there was nothing. All he saw were large roots of the old tree protruding above the earth's surface like sweet potatoes in the sandy soil.

The cattle had wandered a long way off. Tekayo got up and followed them. They reached the riverbank, and the thirsty cows ran to the river. While the cows drank, Tekayo sat on a white stone cooling his feet and gazing lazily at the swollen river as it flowed mightily toward the plain.

Beyond the river stood the great Ghost Jungle. A strong desire for the rich meat came back to Tekayo, and he whispered, "The animal with that delicious liver must surely be in that jungle." He sat there for a while, thinking. The temptation to start hunting for the animal nagged him. But he managed to suppress it. The afternoon was far spent and they were a long way from home.

The next morning Tekayo left home earlier than usual. When his wife begged him to wait for his lunch, he refused. He hurried from home, taking his hunting spears with him.

Tekayo made it impossible for the cows to graze. He rushed them along, lashing at any cow that lingered in one spot for long. They reached the edge of the Ghost Jungle and there he left the cows grazing unattended.

Tekayo could not see any path or trail leading into the Ghost Jungle. The whole place was a mass of thick bush and long grass covered with the morning dew. And except for the sounds of mating birds, there was a weird silence in the jungle that frightened him. But the vehement desire within him blindly drove him on, through the thick wet grass.

After walking for some time, he stood and listened. Something was racing toward him. He turned round to look, and sure enough a big impala was running frantically toward him. Warm blood rushed through Tekayo's body, and he raised his spear to kill the animal. But the spear never landed. He came face-to-face with a big leopardess that was chasing the impala. The leopardess roared at Tekayo several times, challenging him, as it were, to a duel. But Tekayo looked away, clutching the spear in his trembling hand. There was no one to fight and the beast went away after her prey.

"What a bad start," Tekayo said slowly and quietly when his heart beat normally again. "That wildcat will not leave me alone now."

He started to walk back toward the plain, following the trail he had made. The roaring leopardess had taken the life out of him.

He saw another trail that cut across the forest. He hesitated a little, and then decided to follow it, leaving his own. The trail got bigger and bigger, and without any warning Tekayo suddenly came upon a baby wildebeest which was following a large flock grazing at the foot of a hill. He killed it without any difficulty. He skinned the animal and extracted its liver, leaving the rest of the carcass.

Tekayo returned to the herd, and he sat down to roast the meat on a log fire. When the meat was cooked he took a bite and chewed it hurriedly. But he did not swallow it: he spat it all out! The liver was as bitter as the strong green herbs given to constipated children. The back of his tongue was stinging as if it had been burned. Tekayo threw the rest of the meat away and took his cows home.

He arrived home tired and disappointed; and when his young wife set food before him, he refused to eat. He pretended that he had stomachache and did not feel like eating. That night Tekayo was depressed and in low spirits. He did not even desire his young wife, who slept by his side. At dawn the young wife returned to her hut disappointed, wondering why the old man had not desired her.

The doors of all the huts were still closed when Tekayo looked out through his door. A cold east wind hit his face, and he quickly shut himself in again.

It was getting rather late and the calves were calling. But it was pouring with rain so much that he could not start milking. He sat on the hard bed looking at the dead ashes in the fireplace. He longed to get out to start hunting.

When the rain stopped, Tekayo milked the cows in a great hurry. Then he picked up the lunch that had been left near his hut for him, and left the village. His disappointed wife of the previous night watched him till he disappeared at the gate.

When he reached the Ghost Jungle, it was drizzling again. The forest looked so lonely and wet. He left the cows grazing as usual, and entered the bush, stealing his way through the dripping leaves. He turned to the left to avoid the thick part of the jungle. Luck was with him. He spotted a family of antelope grazing not far from him. He crawled on his knees till he was quite close to them, and then threw his spear, killing one animal instantly. After skinning it, he extracted its liver, and also took some delicate parts for the family.

When he sat down under the tree to roast the meat, Tekayo was quite sure that he had been successful. But when he tasted the meat, he shook his head. The meat was tender, but it was not what he was looking for.

They reached the riverbank. The cows continued to graze after drinking, and Tekayo, without realizing it, wandered a long way from his herd, still determined to discover the owner of that wonderful liver. When he suddenly looked round, the herd was nowhere to be seen. The sun was sinking behind Mt. Pajulu, and Tekayo started to run, looking for his cows.

The cows, heavy with milk, had gone home without Tekayo. For one day when Tekayo's children got lost in the forest, the cows had gone home without them, following the old trail they knew well. On that day the whole village came out in search of the children in fear that the wild animals might harm them.

It was getting dark when Tekayo arrived home. They started to milk and Odipo remarked, "Why, Father, you are late coming home today."

"It is true," said Tekayo thoughtfully. "See that black bull there? He went to another herd across the river. I didn't miss him until it was time to come home. One of these days, we shall have to castrate him—he is such a nuisance."

They milked in silence until one of the little girls came to fetch some milk for preparing vegetables.

At suppertime the male members of the family sat around the log fire waiting and talking. One by one, baskets of millet meal and earthen dishes of meat and vegetables arrived from different huts. There was fish, dried meat, fried white ants, and herbs. A little food was thrown to the ground, to the ancestors, and then they started eating. They compared and contrasted the deliciousness of the various dishes they were having. But Tekayo kept quiet. All the food he tasted that evening was bitter as bile.

When the meal was over, the adults told stories of war and the clans to the children, who listened attentively. But Tekayo was not with them: he was not listening. He watched the smoky clouds as they raced across the sky.

"Behind those clouds, behind those clouds, rests Okenyu, my great-grandfather. Please! Please!" Tekayo beseeched him. "Please, Father, take this longing away from me. Give me back my manhood that I may desire my wives. For what is a man without this desire!" ~~Questioning his manhood.~~

A large cloud covered the moon, giving the earth temporary darkness. Tears stung Tekayo's eyes, and he dismissed the family to sleep. As he entered his own hut, a woman was throwing small logs on the fire.

He offered many secret prayers to the departed spirits, but the craving for the mysterious liver never left him. Day after day he left home in the morning, taking his cows with him. And on reaching the jungle, he left them unattended while he hunted. The rough and disappointed life that he led soon became apparent to the family. He suddenly became old and disinterested in life. He had nothing to tell his sons around the evening fire, and he did not desire his wives. The sons of Tekayo went to Lakech and told her, "Mother, speak to Father—he is sick. He does not talk to us, and he does not eat. We don't know how to approach him."

Though Lakech had passed the age of child-bearing and no longer went to Tekayo's hut at night, she was his first wife, and he loved her. She therefore went and asked him, "Man, what ails you?" Tekayo looked at Lakech, but he could not look into her eyes. He looked at her long neck, and instead of answering her question he asked her, "Would you like to get free from those heavy brass rings around your neck?"

"Why?" Lakech replied, surprised.

"Because they look so tight."

- when he questions about the rings he loses his understanding of human values.
- Due to this lack of understanding he is now questioning the rings.

"But they are not tight," Lakech said softly. "I would feel naked without them."

And Tekayo looked away from his wife. He was longing to tell Lakech everything, and to share with her this maddening craving that was tearing his body to pieces. But he checked himself. Lakech must not know: she would not understand. Then he lied to her.

"It is my old indigestion. I have had it for weeks now. It will soon pass."

A mocking smile played on Lakech's lips, and Tekayo knew that she was not convinced. Some visitors arrived, and Lakech left her husband.

Tekayo hunted for many months, but he did not succeed in finding the animal with the delicious liver.

One night, as he lay awake, he asked himself where else he could hunt. And what animal would he be looking for? He had killed all the different animals in the Ghost Jungle. He had risked his life when he killed and ate the liver of a lion, a leopard, and a hyena, all of which were tabooed by his clan.

A little sleep came to Tekayo's heavy eyes and he was grateful. But then Apii stood beside his bed, calling: "Grandpa, Grandpa, it is me." Tekayo sat up, but the little girl was not there. He went back to sleep again. And Apii was there calling him: "Can't you hear me, Grandpa?"

Tekayo woke up a second time, but nobody was there. He lay down without closing his eyes. Again the child's fingers touched his drooping hand, and the playful voice of a child tickled the skin of the old man. Tekayo sat up a third time, and looked round the room. But he was alone. The cock crowed a third time, and it was morning.

And Lakech died without knowing her husband's secret, and was buried in the middle of the village, being the first wife. Tekayo sat at his wife's grave morning and evening for a long time, and his grief for her appeased his hunger for the unknown animal's liver. He wept, but peacefully, as if his craving for the liver was buried with his wife.

It was during this time of grief that Tekayo decided never to go hunting again. He sat at home and looked after his many grandchildren, while the younger members of the family went out to work daily in the fields.

And then one day as Tekayo sat warming himself in the early-morning sun near the granary, he felt slightly sick from the smell of grain sprouting inside the dark store. The shouting and singing of his grandchildren attracted his attention. As he watched them playing, the craving for the liver of the unknown animal returned powerfully to him.

Now, among the children playing was a pretty little girl called Apii, the daughter of Tekayo's eldest son. Tekayo sent the other children away to play, and as they were going, he called Apii and told her, "Come, my little one, run to your mother's hut and bring me a calabash of water."

Apii ran to her mother's hut to get water for her grandfather. And while she was fumbling in a dark corner of the house looking for a clean calabash, strong hands gripped her neck and strangled her. She gave a weak cry as she struggled for the breath of life. But it was too much for her. Her eyes closed in everlasting sleep, never to see the beauty of the shining moon again.

The limp body of the child slipped from Tekayo's hands and fell on the floor with a thud. He looked at the body at his feet and felt sick and faint. His ears were buzzing. He picked up the body, and as he staggered out with it, the air seemed black, and the birds of the air screamed ominously at him. But Tekayo had to eat his meal. He buried the body of Apii in a nearby anthill in a shallow grave.

The other children were still playing in the field when Tekayo returned with the liver in his bag. He roasted it in his hut hastily and ate it greedily. And alas! it was what he had been looking for for many years. He sat lazily resting his back on the granary, belching and picking his teeth. The hungry children, back from their play in the fields, sat in the shade eating sweet potatoes and drinking sour milk.

The older people came back in the evening, and the children ran to meet their parents. But Apii was not among them. In great desperation they asked the grandfather about the child. But Tekayo replied, "Ask the children— they should know where Apii is. They were playing together in the fields."

It was already pitch-dark. Apii's younger brothers and sisters sat in front of the fire weeping with their mother. It was then that they remembered their grandfather sending Apii to fetch water for him. The desperate parents repeated this information to the old man, asking him if Apii had brought water for him that morning.

"She did," Tekayo replied, "and then ran away after the others. I watched her go with my own eyes. When they came back, I was asleep."

The grief-stricken family sat near the fireplace, their heads in their hands. They neither ate nor drank. Outside, the little crickets sang in chorus as if they had a secret to tell.

For many days Apii's parents looked for their child, searching every corner and every nook. But there was no trace of her. Apii was gone. Months went by, and people talked no more about the disappearance of Apii. Only her mother thought of her. She did not lose hope of finding her child alive one day.

Tekayo forgot his deed. And when he killed a second child in the same way to satisfy his savage appetite, he was not even conscious of what he was doing. And when the worried parents asked the old man about the child, Tekayo wept, saying, "How could I know? The children play out in the fields—I stay here at home."

It was after this that Tekayo's sons said among themselves, "Who steals our children? Which animal can it be? Could it be a hyena? Or a leopard? But these animals only hunt at night. Could it be an eagle, because it hunts during the day? But no! Father would have seen the eagle—he would have heard the child screaming." After some thought, Aganda told his brother, "Perhaps it is a malicious animal brought upon us by the evil spirits."

"Then my father is too old to watch the children," put in Osogo. "Yes, Father is too old, he is in danger," the rest agreed.

And from that time onward the sons kept watch secretly on the father and the children. They watched for many months, but nothing threatened the man and the children.

The sons were almost giving up the watch. But one day when it was the turn of Apii's father to keep watch, he saw Tekayo sending away the children to play in the field—all except one. He sent this child to fetch him a pipe from his hut. As the child ran to the hut, Tekayo followed him. He clasped the frightened child and dragged him toward the fireplace. As Tekayo was struggling with the child, a heavy blow landed on his old back. He turned round sharply, his hands still holding the child's neck. He was facing Aganda, his eldest son. The child broke loose from the limp hands of Tekayo and grabbed Aganda's knees, as if he had just escaped from the teeth of a crocodile. "Father!" Aganda shouted.

Seeing that the child was not hurt, Aganda pushed him aside, saying, "Go to your mother's hut and lie down."

He then got hold of the old man and dragged him toward the little windowless hut built for goats and sheep. As he was being dragged away, the old man kept on crying, *"Atimo ang'o? Atimo ang'o?"?*—What have I done? What have I done?

Aganda pushed the old man into the little hut and barred the door behind him, as you would to the animals. He went to the child, who was still sobbing.

The rest of the family returned from the fields, and when Apii's father broke the news to them, they were appalled. The family wore mourning garments and went without food.

"Tho! Tho!" they spat toward the sun, which, although setting on them, was rising on the ancestors.

"Great-grandfathers, cleanse us," they all cried.

And they lit the biggest fire that had ever been lit in that village. Tekayo's eldest son took the old greasy drum hanging above the fireplace in his father's hut and beat it. The drum throbbed out sorrowful tunes to warn the clan that there was sad news in Tekayo's home. The people who heard the drum left whatever they were doing and ran to Tekayo's village, following the sound of the drum. Within a short time the village was teeming with anxious-looking relatives.

"What news? What news?" they asked in trembling voices.

"And where is Tekayo?" another old man asked.

"Is he in good health?" asked another.

There was confusion and panic.

"Death of death, who will give us medicine for death? Death knocks at your door, and before you can tell him to come in, he is in the house with you."

"Listen!" Someone touched the old woman who was mourning death.

Aganda spoke to the people. "Men of my clan. We have not called you here for nothing. Listen to me and let our sorrow be yours. Weep with us! For several months we have been losing our children when we go to work on the fields. Apii, my own child, was the first one to disappear." Sobbing broke out among the women at the mention of the children's names.

"My people," Aganda continued, "the children in this clan get sick and die. But ours disappear unburied. It was our idea to keep watch over our children that we may catch whoever steals them. For months we have been watching secretly. We were almost giving up because we thought it was probably the wrath of our ancestors that was upon us. But today I caught him."

"What man? What man?" the people demanded angrily.

"And from what clan is he?" others asked.

"We must declare war on his clan, we must we must!"

Aganda stopped for a while, and told them in a quavering voice, "The man is in that little hut. The man is none often than my father."

"*Mayo!*" the women shouted. There was a scuffle and the women and children screamed as if Tekayo was around the fire and they were afraid of him. But the men kept quiet.

When the commotion died down, an old man asked, "Do you speak the truth, man?"

The son nodded. Men and women now shouted, "Where is the man? Kill him! He is not one of us. He is not one of us. He is an animal!"

There was nothing said outside that Tekayo did not hear. And there in the hut the children he had killed haunted him. He laid his head on the rough wall of the hut and wept.

Outside the hut the angry villagers continued with their demand, shouting, "Stone him now! Stone him now! Let his blood be upon his own head!"

But one of the old men got up and calmed the people. "We cannot stone him now. It is the custom of the clan that a wicked man should be stoned in broad daylight, outside the village. We cannot depart from this custom."

"Stone me now, stone me now," Tekayo whispered. "Take me away quickly from this torture and shame. Let me die and be finished with."

Tekayo knew by the angry shouting of the men and the shrill cries of frightened women and children that he was banished from society, nay, from life itself. He fumbled in his leather bag suspended around his waist to find his hunting knife, but it was not there. It had been taken away from him.

The muttering and shouting continued outside. There was weeping, too. But Tekayo was now hearing them from afar as if a powerful wave were carrying him farther and farther away from his people.

At dawn the villagers got up from the fireplace to gather stones from nearby fields. The sun was not up yet, but it was just light enough to see. Everyone in the clan must throw a stone at the murderer. It was bad not to throw a stone, for it was claimed that the murderer's wicked spirit would rest upon the man who did not help to drive him away.

When the first rays of the sun appeared, the villagers had gathered enough stones to cover several bodies. They returned to the village to fetch Tekayo from the hut, and to lead him to his own garden outside the village. They surrounded the hut and stood in silence, waiting to jeer and spit at him when he came out.

Aganda and three old men tore the papyrus door open and called Tekayo to come out. But there was no reply. They rushed into the hut to drag him out to the people who were now demanding, "Come out, come out!"

At first it was too dark to see. But soon their eyes got used to the darkness. Then they saw the body of Tekayo, hanged on a short rope that he had unwound from the thatched roof.

The men came out shaking their heads. The crowd peered into the hut in turn until all of them had seen the dangling body of Tekayo—the man they were preparing to stone. No one spoke. Such a man, they knew, would have to be buried outside the village. They knew, too, that no newborn child would ever be named after him.

—1968

Ama Ata Aidoo

(BORN 1942) GHANA

In her major drama, *The Dilemma of a Ghost* (1965), Ama Ata Aidoo examines the quixotic relationship that sometimes exists between Africans and African Americans. Ato Yawson, a Ghanaian student educated in America, returns home with his Harlem-born wife, Eulalie Rush. The play deftly probes the question of heritage at a time when many black Americans were confronting Pan-Africanism because of their firsthand experiences of living on the continent. Perhaps the most interesting character in Aidoo's play is Nana, Ato's mother, who wrestles with the issues of fertility and procreation from her traditional animist perspective. As Karen C. Chapman has noted of *The Dilemma of a Ghost*, "the ancestors . . . are not only alive and in possession of great wisdom, but they are also, from time to time, rather intimidating as they hover protectively over the heads of those still on earth."

Aidoo's own background is cosmopolitan. She attended the University of Ghana at Legon, graduating in 1964; in the summer of 1966, she participated in the Harvard International Seminar at Harvard University. She has taught at the University of Nairobi, and at University College, Cape Coast, Ghana, as well as at a number of American universities. She has spoken out eloquently on issues of cultural hegemony.

Writing about her compatriot Ayi Kwei Armah's *The Beautyful Ones Are Not Yet Born*, Ms. Aidoo had this to say about Ghanaian women: ". . . especially in the area of what exactly the African woman is, the assumption on the part of most Westerners [has been] that the poor African woman was a downtrodden wretch until the European missionary brought her Christianity, civilization and emancipation. This may apply in certain areas of Africa, but certainly, for most Ghanaian women, the question of their emancipation is not really a problem to discuss since it has always been ensured by the system anyway. Nor is this an idealized view. It is there for anyone to see who is prepared to observe a society instead of imposing on it his own prejudices. . . .''

Ama Ata Aidoo's lengthy writing career bridges the genres of fiction, poetry, drama, and criticism. ''Two Sisters'' is from her short-story collection, *No Sweetness Here* (1970). Her two published novels are *Our Sister Killjoy* (1977) and *Changes* (1992).

TWO SISTERS

As she shakes out the typewriter cover and covers the machine with it, the thought of the bus she has to hurry to catch goes through her like a pain. It is her luck, she thinks. Everything is just her luck. Why, if she had one of those graduates for a boyfriend, wouldn't he come and take her home every evening? And she knows that a girl does not herself have to be a graduate to get one of those boys. Certainly, Joe is dying to do exactly that—with his taxi. And he is as handsome as anything, and a good man, but you know . . . Besides, there are cars and there are cars. As for the possibility of the other actually coming to fetch her—oh well. She has to admit it will take some time before she can bring herself to make demands of that sort on *him*. She has also to admit that the temptation is extremely strong. Would it really be so dangerously indiscreet? Doesn't one government car look like another? The hugeness of it? Its shaded glass? The uniformed chauffeur? She can already see herself stepping out to greet the dead-with-envy glances of the other girls. To begin with, she will insist on a little discretion. The driver can drop her under the *neem* trees in the morning and pick her up from there in the evening . . . anyway, she will have to wait a little while for that and it is all her luck.

There are other ways, surely. One of these, for some reason, she has sworn to have nothing of. Her boss has a car and does not look bad. In fact, the man is all right. But she keeps telling herself that she does not fancy having some old and dried-out housewife walking into the office one afternoon to tear her hair out and make a row . . . Mm, so for the meantime it is going to continue to be the municipal bus with its grimy seats, its common passengers and impudent conductors . . . Jesus! She doesn't wish herself dead or anything as stupidly final as that. Oh no. She just wishes she could sleep deep and only wake up on the morning of her glory.

The new pair of black shoes are more realistic than their owner, though. As she walks down the corridor, they sing:

> *Count, Mercy, count your blessings*
> *Count, Mercy, count your blessings*
> *Count, count, count your blessings.*

They sing along the corridor, into the avenue, across the road, and into the bus. And they resume their song along the gravel path as she opens the front gate and crosses the cemented courtyard to the door.

"Sissie!" she called.

"*Hei* Mercy." And the door opened to show the face of Connie, big sister, six years or more older and now heavy with her second child. Mercy collapsed into the nearest chair.

"Welcome home. How was the office today?"

"Sister, don't ask. Look at my hands. My fingers are dead with typing. Oh God, I don't know what to do."

"Why, what is wrong?"

"You tell me what is right. Why should I be a typist?"

"What else would you be?"

"What a strange question. Is typing the only thing one can do in this world? You are a teacher, are you not?"

"But . . . but . . ."

"But what? Or you want me to know that if I had done better in the exams, I could have trained to be a teacher too, eh, sister? Or even a proper secretary?"

"Mercy, what is the matter? What have I done? What have I done? Why have you come home so angry?"

Mercy broke into tears.

"Oh I am sorry. I am sorry, Sissie. It's just that I am sick of everything. The office, living with you and your husband. I want a husband of my own, children. I want . . . I want . . ."

"But you are so beautiful."

"Thank you. But so are you."

"You are young and beautiful. As for marriage, it's you who are postponing it. Look at all these people who are running after you."

"Sissie, I don't like what you are doing. So stop it."

'Okay, okay, okay."

And there was a silence.

"Which of them could I marry? Joe is—mm, fine—but, but I just don't like him."

"You mean . . ."

"Oh, Sissie!"

"Little sister, you and I can be truthful with one another."

"Oh yes."

"What I would like to say is that I am not that old or wise. But still I could advise you a little. Joe drives someone's car now. Well, you never know. Lots of taxi drivers come to own their taxis, sometimes fleets of cars."

"Of course. But it's a pity you are married already. Or I could be a go-between for you and Joe!"

And the two of them burst out laughing. It was when she rose to go to the bedroom that Connie noticed the new shoes.

"*Ei*, those are beautiful shoes. Are they new?"

From the other room, Mercy's voice came interrupted by the motions of her body as she undressed and then dressed again. However, the uncertainty in it was due to something entirely different.

"Oh, I forgot to tell you about them. In fact, I was going to show them to you. I think it was on Tuesday I bought them. Or was it Wednesday? When I came home from the office, you and James had taken Akosua out. And later I forgot all about them."

"I see. But they are very pretty. Were they expensive?"

"No, not really." This reply was too hurriedly said.

And she said only last week that she didn't have a penny on her. And I believed her because I know what they pay her is just not enough to last anyone through any month, even minus rent . . . I have been thinking she manages very well. But these shoes. And she is not the type who would borrow money just to buy a pair of shoes, when she could have gone on wearing her old pairs until things get better. Oh, I wish I knew what to do. I mean, I am not her mother. And I wonder how James will see these problems.

"Sissie, you look worried."

"Hmm, when don't I? With the baby due in a couple of months and the government's new ruling on salaries and all. On top of everything, I have reliable information that James is running after a new girl."

Mercy laughed. "Oh, Sissie. You always get reliable information on these things."

"But yes. And I don't know why."

"Sissie, men are like that."

"They are selfish."

"No, it's just that women allow them to behave the way they do instead of seizing some freedom themselves."

"But I am sure that even if we were free to carry on in the same way, I wouldn't make use of it."

"But why not?"

"Because I love James. I love James and I am not interested in any other man." Her voice was full of tears.

But Mercy was amused. "Oh God. Now listen to that. It's women like you who keep all of us down."

"Well, I am sorry but it's how the good God created me."

"Mm. I am sure that I can love several men at the same time."

"Mercy!"

They burst out laughing again. And yet they are sad. But laughter is always best.

Mercy complained of hunger and so they went to the kitchen to heat up some food and eat. The two sisters alone. It is no use waiting for James. And this evening a friend of Connie's has come to take out the baby girl, Akosua, and had threatened to keep her until her bedtime.

"Sissie, I am going to see a film." This from Mercy.

"Where?"

"The Globe."

"Are you going with Joe?"

"No."

"Are you going alone?"

"No."

Careful Connie.

"Whom are you going with?"

Careful Connie, please. Little sister's nostrils are widening dangerously. Look at the sudden creasing up of her mouth and between her brows.

Connie, a sister is a good thing. Even a younger sister. Especially when you have no mother or father.

"Mercy, whom are you going out with?"

"Well, I had food in my mouth! And I had to swallow it down before I could answer you, no?"

"I am sorry." How softly said.

"And anyway, do I have to tell you everything?"

"Oh no. It's just that I didn't think it was a question I should not have asked."

There was more silence. Then Mercy sucked her teeth with irritation and Connie cleared her throat with fear.

"I am going out with Mensar-Arthur."

As Connie asked the next question, she wondered if the words were leaving her lips. "Mensar-Arthur?"

"Yes."

"Which one?"

"How many do you know?"

Her fingers were too numb to pick up the food. She put the plate down. Something jumped in her chest and she wondered what it was. Perhaps it was the baby.

"Do you mean that Member of Parliament?"

"Yes."

"But, Mercy . . ."

Little sister only sits and chews her food.

"But, Mercy . . ."

Chew, chew, chew.

"But, Mercy . . ."

"What?"

She startled Connie.

"He is so old."

Chew, chew, chew.

"Perhaps, I mean, perhaps that really doesn't matter, does it? Not very much anyway. But they say he has so many wives and girlfriends."

Please little sister. I am not trying to interfere in your private life. You said yourself a little while ago that you wanted a man of your own. That man belongs to so many women already . . .

That silence again. Then there was only Mercy's footsteps as she went to put her plate in the kitchen sink, running water as she washed her plate and her hands. She drank some water and coughed. Then, as tears streamed down her sister's averted face, there was the sound of her footsteps as she left the kitchen. At the end of it all, she banged a door. Connie only said something like, "O Lord, O Lord," and continued sitting in the kitchen. She had hardly eaten anything at all. Very soon Mercy went to have a bath. Then Connie heard her getting ready to leave the house. The shoes. Then she was gone. She needn't have carried on like that, eh? Because Connie had not meant to probe or bring on a quarrel. What use is there in this old world for a sister, if you can't have a chat with her? What's more, things like this never happen to people like Mercy. Their parents were good Presbyterians. They feared God. Mama had not managed to give them all the rules of life before she died. But Connie knows that running around with an old and depraved public man would have been considered an abomination by the parents.

A big car with a super-smooth engine purred into the drive. It actually purrs, this huge machine from the white man's land. Indeed, its well-mannered protest as the tires slid onto the gravel seemed like a lullaby compared to the loud thumping of the girl's stiletto shoes. When Mensar-Arthur saw Mercy, he stretched his arm and opened the door to the passenger seat. She sat down and the door closed with a civilized thud. The engine hummed into motion and the car sailed away.

After a distance of a mile or so from the house, the man started a conversation.

"And how is my darling today?"

"I am well," and only the words did not imply tragedy.

"You look solemn today, why?"

She remained silent and still.

"My dear, what is the matter?"

"Nothing."

"Oh . . ." He cleared his throat again. "Eh, and how were the shoes?"

"Very nice. In fact, I am wearing them now. They pinch a little but then all new shoes are like that."

"And the handbag?"

"I like it very much, too . . . My sister noticed them. I mean the shoes." The tragedy was announced.

"Did she ask you where you got them from?"

"No."

He cleared his throat again. "Where did we agree to go tonight?"

"The Globe, but I don't want to see a film."

"Is that so? Mm, I am glad because people always notice things."

"But they won't be too surprised."

"What are you saying, my dear?"

"Nothing."

"Okay, so what shall we do?"

"I don't know."

"Shall I drive to the Seaway?"

"Oh yes."

He drove to the Seaway. To a section of the beach they knew very well. She loves it here. This wide expanse of sand and the old sea. She has often wished she could do what she fancied: one thing she fancies. Which is to drive very near to the end of the sands until the tires of the car touched the water. Of course it is a very foolish idea, as he pointed out sharply to her the first time she thought aloud about it. It was in his occasional I-am-more-than-old-enough-to-be-your-father tone. There are always disadvantages. Things could be different. Like if one had a younger lover. Handsome, maybe not rich like this man here, but well off, sufficiently well off to be able to afford a sports car. A little something very much like those in the films driven by the white racing drivers. With tires that can do everything . . . and they would drive to exactly where the sea and the sand meet.

"We are here."

"Don't let's get out. Let's just sit inside and talk."

"Talk?"

"Yes."

"Okay. But what is it, my darling?"

"I have told my sister about you."

"Good God. Why?"

"But I had to. I couldn't keep it to myself any longer."

"Childish. It was not necessary at all. She is not your mother."

"No. But she is all I have. And she has been very good to me."

"Well, it was her duty."

"Then it is my duty to tell her about something like this. I may get into trouble."

"Don't be silly," he said. "I normally take good care of my girlfriends."

"I see," she said, and for the first time in the one month since she agreed to be this man's lover, the tears which suddenly rose into her eyes were not forced.

"And you promised you wouldn't tell her." It was Father's voice now.

"Don't be angry. After all, people talk so much, as you said a little while ago. She was bound to hear it one day."

"My darling, you are too wise. What did she say?"

"She was pained."

"Don't worry. Find out something she wants very much but cannot get in this country because of the import restrictions."

"I know for sure she wants an electric motor for her sewing machine."

"Is that all?"

"That's what I know of."

"Mm. I am going to London next week on some delegation, so if you bring me the details on the make of the machine, I shall get her the motor."

"Thank you."

"What else is worrying my Black Beauty?"

"Nothing."

"And by the way, let me know as soon as you want to leave your sister's place. I have got you one of the government estate houses."

"Oh . . . oh," she said, pleased, contented for the first time since this typically ghastly day had begun, at half past six in the morning.

Dear little child came back from the playground with her toe bruised. Shall we just blow cold air from our mouth on it or put on a salve? Nothing matters really. Just see that she does not feel unattended. And the old sea roars on. This is a calm sea, generally. Too calm in fact, this Gulf of Guinea. The natives sacrifice to him on Tuesdays and once a year celebrate him. They might save their chickens, their eggs, and their yams. And as for the feast once a year, he doesn't pay much attention to it either. They are always celebrating one thing or another and they surely don't need him for an excuse to celebrate one day more. He has seen things happen along these beaches. Different things. Contradictory things. Or just repetitions of old patterns. He never interferes in their affairs. Why should he? Except in places like Keta, where he eats houses away because they leave him no choice. Otherwise, he never allows them to see his passions. People are worms, and even the God who created them is immensely bored with their antics. Here is a fifty-year-old "big man" who thinks he is somebody. And a twenty-three-year-old child who chooses a silly way to conquer unconquerable problems. Well, what did one expect of human beings? And so, as those two settled on the back seat of the car to play with each other's bodies, he, the Gulf of Guinea, shut his eyes with boredom. It is right. He could sleep, no?

He spread himself and moved farther ashore. But the car was parked at a very safe distance and the rising tides could not wet its tires.

James has come home late. But then he has been coming back late for the past few weeks. Connie is crying and he knows it as soon as he enters the bedroom. He hates tears, for, like so many men, he knows it is one of the most potent weapons in women's bitchy and inexhaustible arsenal. She speaks first.

"James."

"Oh, are you still awake?" He always tries to deal with these nightly funeral parlor doings by pretending not to know what they are about.

"I couldn't sleep."

"What is wrong?"

"Nothing."

So he moves quickly and sits beside her. "Connie, what is the matter? You have been crying again."

"You are very late again."

"Is that why you are crying? Or is there something else?"

"Yes."

"Yes to what?"

"James, where were you?"

"Connie, I have warned you about what I shall do if you don't stop examining me, as though I were your prisoner, every time I am a little late."

She sat up. "A little late! It is nearly two o'clock."

"Anyway, you won't believe me if I told you the truth, so why do you want me to waste my breath?"

"Oh well." She lies down again and turns her face to the wall. He stands up but does not walk away. He looks down at her. So she remembers every night: they have agreed, after many arguments, that she should sleep like this. During her first pregnancy, he kept saying after the third month or so that the sight of her tummy the last thing before he slept always gave him nightmares. Now he regrets all this. The bed creaks as he throws himself down by her.

"James."

"Yes."

"There is something much more serious."

"You have heard about my newest affair?"

"Yes, but that is not what I am referring to."

"Jesus, is it possible that there is anything more important than that?"

And as they laugh they know that something has happened. One of those things which, with luck, will keep them together for some time to come.

"He teases me on top of everything."

"What else can one do to you but tease when you are in this state?"

"James! How profane!"

"It is your dirty mind which gave my statement its shocking meaning."

"Okay! But what shall I do?"

"About what?"

"Mercy. Listen, she is having an affair with Mensar-Arthur."

"Wonderful."

She sits up and he sits up.

"James, we must do something about it. It is very serious."

"Is that why you were crying?"

"Of course."

"Why shouldn't she?"

"But it is wrong. And she is ruining herself."

"Since every other girl she knows has ruined herself prosperously, why shouldn't she? Just forget for once that you are a teacher. Or at least remember she is not your pupil."

"I don't like your answers."

"What would you like me to say? Every morning her friends who don't earn any more than she does wear new dresses, shoes, wigs, and what-have-you to work. What would you have her do?"

"The fact that other girls do it does not mean that Mercy should do it, too."

"You are being very silly. If I were Mercy, I am sure that's exactly what I would do. And you know I mean it, too."

James is cruel. He is terrible and mean. Connie breaks into fresh tears and James comforts her. There is one point he must drive home, though.

"In fact, encourage her. He may be able to intercede with the Ministry for you so that after the baby is born they will not transfer you from here for some time."

"James, you want me to use my sister!"

"She is using herself, remember."

"James, you are wicked."

"And maybe he would even agree to get us a new car from abroad. I shall pay for everything. That would be better than paying a fortune for that old thing I was thinking of buying. Think of that."

"You will ride in it alone."

"Well . . ."

That was a few months before the coup. Mensar-Arthur did go to London for a conference and bought something for all his wives and girlfriends, including Mercy. He even remembered the motor for Connie's machine. When Mercy took it to her she was quite confused. She had wanted this thing for a long time, and it would make everything so much easier, like the clothes for the new baby. And yet one side of her said that accepting it was a betrayal. Of what, she wasn't even sure. She and Mercy could never bring the whole business into the open and discuss it. And there was always James supporting Mercy, to Connie's bewilderment. She took the motor with thanks and sold even her right to dissent. In a short while, Mercy left the house to go and live in the estate house Mensar-Arthur had procured for her. Then, a couple of weeks later, the coup. Mercy left her new place before anyone could evict her. James never got his car. Connie's new baby was born. Of the three, the one who greeted the new order with undisguised relief was Connie. She is not really a demonstrative person but it was obvious from her eyes that she was happy. As far as she was concerned, the old order as symbolized by Mensar-Arthur was a threat to her sister and therefore to her own peace of mind. With it gone, things could return to normal. Mercy would move back to the house, perhaps start to date someone more—ordinary, let's say. Eventually, she would get married and then the nightmare of those past weeks would be forgotten. God being so good, he brought the coup early before the news of the affair could spread and brand her sister . . .

The arrival of the new baby has magically waved away the difficulties between James and Connie. He is that kind of man, and she that kind of woman. Mercy has not been seen for many days. Connie is beginning to get worried . . .

James heard the baby yelling—a familiar noise, by now—the moment he opened the front gate. He ran in, clutching to his chest the few things he had bought on his way home.

"We are in here."

"I certainly could hear you. If there is anything people of this country have, it is a big mouth."

"Don't I agree? But on the whole, we are well. He is eating normally and everything. You?"

"Nothing new. Same routine. More stories about the overthrown politicians."

"What do you mean, nothing new? Look at the excellent job the soldiers have done, cleaning up the country of all that dirt. I feel free already and I am dying to get out and enjoy it."

James laughed mirthlessly. "All I know is that Mensar-Arthur is in jail. No use. And I am not getting my car. Rough deal."

"I never took you seriously on that car business."

"Honestly, if this were in the ancient days, I could brand you a witch. You don't want me, your husband, to prosper?"

"Not out of my sister's ruin."

"Ruin, ruin, ruin! Christ! See, Connie, the funny thing is that I am sure you are the only person who thought it was a disaster to have a sister who was the girlfriend of a big man."

"Okay; now all is over, and don't let's quarrel."

"I bet the coup could have succeeded on your prayers alone."

And Connie wondered why he said that with so much bitterness. She wondered if . . .

"Has Mercy been here?"

"Not yet, later, maybe. Mm. I had hoped she would move back here and start all over again."

"I am not surprised she hasn't. In fact, if I were her, I wouldn't come back here either. Not to your nagging, no thank you, big sister."

And as the argument progressed, as always, each was forced into a more aggressive defensive stand.

"Well, just say what pleases you, I am very glad about the soldiers. Mercy is my only sister, brother; everything. I can't sit and see her life going wrong without feeling it. I am grateful to whatever forces there are which put a stop to that. What pains me now is that she should be so vague about where she is living at the moment. She makes mention of a girlfriend but I am not sure that I know her."

"If I were you, I would stop worrying because it seems Mercy can look after herself quite well."

"Hmm" was all she tried to say.

Who heard something like the sound of a car pulling into the drive? Ah, but the footsteps were unmistakably Mercy's. Are those shoes the old pair which were new a couple of months ago? Or are they the newest pair? And here she is herself, the pretty one. A gay Mercy.

"Hello, hello, my clan!" And she makes a lot of her nephew. "Dow-dah-dee-day! And how is my dear young man today? My lord, grow up fast and come to take care of Auntie Mercy."

Both Connie and James cannot take their eyes off her. Connie says, "He says to Auntie Mercy he is fine."

Still they watch her, horrified, fascinated, and wondering what it's all about. Because they both know it is about something.

"Listen, people, I brought a friend to meet you. A man."

"Where is he?" from James.

"Bring him in," from Connie.

"You know, Sissie, you are a new mother. I thought I'd come and ask you if it's all right."

"Of course," say James and Connie, and for some reason they are both very nervous.

"He is Captain Ashley."

"Which one?"

"*How many do you know?*"

James still thinks it is impossible. "Eh . . . do you mean the officer who has been appointed the . . . the . . ."

"Yes."

"Wasn't there a picture in *The Crystal* over the weekend of his daughter's wedding? And another one of him with his wife and children and grand-children?"

"Yes."

"And he is heading a commission to investigate something or other?"

"Yes."

Connie just sits there with her mouth open that wide . . .

—1970

Chinua Achebe

(BORN 1930) NIGERIA

Chinua Achebe is not only the most widely read African writer of the twentieth century but also the most admired and respected. His first novel, *Things Fall Apart* (1958), has sold more than two million copies in the United States. Six million additional copies have been sold worldwide in fifty different languages. The archetypal African novel, *Things Fall Apart* chronicles the fall in the 1890s of a strong man named Okonkwo, who is brought down in large part because of upheavals within his own traditional Ibo world— caused, most notably, by the arrival of English missionaries and colonial officials. Yet Achebe also makes it clear that Ibo traditional life had its own built-in weaknesses and was ripe for historic change. Commenting specifically about Okonkwo's dilemma some years after the publication of the novel, Achebe stated: ". . . My sympathies were not entirely with Okonkwo. . . . Life just has to go on and if you refuse to accept changes, then, tragic though it may be, you are swept aside."

Things Fall Apart was followed by a sequel, *No Longer at Ease*, published in 1960. Achebe's second novel jumps ahead to the 1950s and focuses on Okonkwo's grandson, Obi, who must confront more contemporary issues within his country on the verge of independence. Subsequent works include the novels *Arrow of God* (1964), *A Man of the People* (1966), and *Anthills of the Savannah* (1987); a volume of poems, *Beware Soul Brother* (1971), and a collection of short stories, *Girls at War and Other Stories* (1972); as well as political commentary, *The Trouble with Nigeria* (1983), and critical essays, *Morning Yet on Creation Day* (1975).

Achebe has remained throughout his career both a critic and a defender of his people—not simply the Ibos of his own ethnic group, but his fellow Nigerians as well as Africans as a whole. In the celebrated essay "The Novelist as Teacher" (from *Morning Yet on Creation Day*), he wrote: "Writing of the kind I do is relatively new in my part of the world and it is too soon to try and describe in detail the complex of relationships between us and our readers. . . . The writer cannot expect to be excused from the task of reeducation and regeneration that must be done. In fact, he should march right in front. . . . I would be quite satisfied if my novels (especially the ones I set in the past) did no more than teach my readers that their past— with all its imperfections—was not one long night of savagery from which the first Europeans acting on God's behalf delivered them. Perhaps what I write is applied art as distinct from pure. But who cares? Art is important but so is education of the kind I have in mind. And I don't see that the two need be mutually exclusive."

Away from the domain of art, more recently Achebe has written of a different kind of cleavage: "The trouble with Nigeria is simply and squarely a failure of leadership. There is nothing basically wrong with the Nigerian character. There is nothing wrong with the Nigerian land or climate or water or anything else. The Nigerian problem is the unwillingness or inability of its leaders to rise to the responsibility, to the challenge of personal example which are the hallmarks of true leadership."

Since 1991, Chinua Achebe has taught at Bard College, in Annondale, New York.

GIRLS AT WAR

The first time their paths crossed, nothing happened. That was in the first heady days of warlike preparation, when thousands of young men (and sometimes women, too) were daily turned away from enlistment centers because far too many of them were coming forward burning with readiness to bear arms in defense of the exciting new nation.

The second time they met was at a checkpoint at Awka. Then the war had started and was slowly moving southwards from the distant northern sector. He was driving from Onitsha to Enugu and was in a hurry. Although intellectually he approved of thorough searches at roadblocks, emotionally he was always offended whenever he had to submit to them. He would probably not admit it but the feeling people got was that if you were put through a search then you could not really be one of the big people. Generally he got away without a search by pronouncing in his deep, authoritative voice: "Reginald Nwankwo, Ministry of Justice." That almost always did it. But sometimes either through ignorance or sheer cussedness the crowd at the odd checkpoint would refuse to be impressed. As happened now at Awka. Two constables carrying heavy Mark 4 rifles were watching distantly from the roadside, leaving the actual searching to local vigilantes.

"I am in a hurry," he said to the girl who now came up to his car. "My name is Reginald Nwankwo, Ministry of Justice."

"Good afternoon, sir. I want to see your boot."

"Oh Christ! What do you think is in the boot?"

"I don't know, sir."

He got out of the car in suppressed rage, stalked to the back, opened the boot, and holding the lid up with his left hand he motioned with the right as if to say: After you!

"Are you satisfied?" he demanded.

"Yes, sir. Can I see your pigeonhole?"

"Christ Almighty!"

"Sorry to delay you, sir. But you people gave us this job to do."

"Never mind. You are damn right. It's just that I happen to be in a hurry. But never mind. That's the glove box. Nothing there as you can see."

"All right, sir, close it." Then she opened the rear door and bent down to inspect under the seats. It was then he took the first real look at her, starting from behind. She was a beautiful girl in a breasty blue jersey, khaki jeans, and canvas shoes with the new-style hair plait which gave a girl a defiant look and which they called—for reasons of their own—"air force base"; and she looked vaguely familiar.

"I am all right, sir," she said at last, meaning she was through with her task. "You don't recognize me?"

"No. Should I?"

"You gave me a lift to Enugu that time I left my school to go and join the militia."

"Ah, yes, you were the girl. I told you, didn't I, to go back to school because girls were not required in the militia. What happened?"

"They told me to go back to my school or join the Red Cross."

"You see, I was right. So, what are you doing now?"

"Just patching up with Civil Defense."

"Well, good luck to you. Believe me, you are a great girl."

That was the day he finally believed there might be something in this talk about revolution. He had seen plenty of girls and women marching and demonstrating before now. But somehow he had never been able to give it much thought. He didn't doubt that the girls and the women took themselves seriously, they obviously did. But so did the little kids who marched up and down the streets at the time, drilling with sticks and wearing their mothers' soup bowls for steel helmets. The prime joke of the time among his friends was the contingent of girls from a local secondary school marching behind a banner: WE ARE IMPREGNABLE!

But after that encounter at the Awka checkpoint he simply could not sneer at the girls again, nor at the talk of revolution, for he had seen it in action in that young woman whose devotion had simply and without self-righteousness convicted him of gross levity. What were her words? We are doing the work you asked us to do. She wasn't going to make an exception even for one who once did her a favor. He was sure she would have searched her own father just as rigorously.

When their paths crossed a third time, at least eighteen months later, things had got very bad. Death and starvation, having long chased out the headiness of the early days, now left in some places blank resignation, in others a rock-like, even suicidal, defiance. But surprisingly enough there were many at this time who had no other desire than to corner whatever good things were still going and to enjoy themselves to the limit. For such people a strange normalcy had returned to the world. All those nervous checkpoints disappeared. Girls became girls once more and boys boys. It was a tight, blockaded, and desperate world but nonetheless a world—with some goodness and some badness and plenty of heroism, which, however, happened most times far, far below the eye level of the people in this story— in out-of-the-way refugee camps, in the damp tatters, in the hungry and barehanded courage of the first line of fire.

Reginald Nwankwo lived in Owerri then. But that day he had gone to Nkwerri in search of relief. He had got from Caritas in Owerri a few heads of stockfish, some tinned meat, and the dreadful American stuff called Formula Two which he felt certain was some kind of animal feed. But he always had a vague suspicion that not being a Catholic put one at a disadvantage with Caritas. So he went now to see an old friend who ran the WCC depot at Nkwerri to get other items like rice, beans, and that excellent cereal commonly called *Gabon gari*.

He left Owerri at six in the morning so as to catch his friend at the depot, where he was known never to linger beyond 8:30 for fear of air raids. Nwankwo was very fortunate that day. The depot had received on the previous day large supplies of new stock as a result of an unusual number of plane landings a few nights earlier. As his driver loaded tins and bags and cartons into his car the starved crowds that perpetually hung around relief centers made crude, ungracious remarks like "War Can Continue!" meaning the WCC! Somebody else shouted "*Irevolu!*" and his friends replied "*shum!*" "*Irevolu!*" "*shum!*" "*Isofeli?*" "*shum*" "*Isofeli?*" "*Mba!*"

Nwankwo was deeply embarrassed not by the jeers of this scarecrow crowd of rags and floating ribs but by the independent accusation of their wasted bodies and sunken eyes. Indeed, he would probably have felt much worse had they said nothing, simply looked on in silence, as his boot was loaded with milk, and powdered egg and oats and tinned meat and stockfish. By nature such singular good fortune in the midst of a general desolation was certain to embarrass him. But what could a man do? He had a wife and four children living in the remote village of Ogbu and completely dependent on what relief he could find and send them. He couldn't abandon them to kwashiorkor. The best he could do—and did do, as a matter of fact—was to make sure that whenever he got sizable supplies like now he made over some of it to his driver, Johnson, with a wife and six, or was it seven, children and a salary of ten pounds a month when *gari* in the market was climbing to one pound per cigarette cup. In such a situation one could do nothing at all for crowds; at best one could try to be of some use to one's immediate neighbors. That was all.

On his way back to Owerri, a very attractive girl by the roadside waved for a lift. He ordered the driver to stop. Scores of pedestrians, dusty and exhausted, some military, some civilian, swooped down on the car from all directions.

"No, no, no," said Nwankwo firmly. "It's the young woman I stopped for. I have a bad tire and can only take one person. Sorry."

"My son, please," cried one old woman in despair, gripping the door handle.

"Old woman, you want to be killed?" shouted the driver as he pulled away, shaking her off. Nwankwo had already opened a book and sunk his eyes there.

For at least a mile after that he did not even look at the girl until she, finding, perhaps, the silence too heavy, said: "You've saved me today. Thank you."

"Not at all. Where are you going?"

"To Owerri. You don't recognize me?"

"Oh yes, of course. What a fool I am . . . You are . . ."

"Gladys."

"That's right, the militia girl. You've changed, Gladys. You were always beautiful, of course, but now you are a beauty queen. What do you do these days?"

"I am in the Fuel Directorate."

"That's wonderful."

It was wonderful, he thought, but even more it was tragic. She wore a high-tinted wig and a very expensive skirt and low-cut blouse. Her shoes, obviously from Gabon, must have cost a fortune. In short, thought Nwankwo, she had to be in the keep of some well-placed gentleman, one of those piling up money out of the war.

"I broke my rule today to give you a lift. I never give lifts these days."

"Why?"

"How many people can you carry? It is better not to try at all. Look at that old woman."

"I thought you would take her."

He said nothing to that and after another spell of silence Gladys thought maybe he was offended and so added: "Thank you for breaking your rule for me." She was scanning his face, turned slightly away.

He smiled, turned, and tapped her on the lap. "What are you going to Owerri to do?"

"I am going to visit my girlfriend."

"Girlfriend? You sure?"

"Why not? . . . If you drop me at her house you can see her. Only I pray God she hasn't gone on weekend today; it will be serious."

"Why?"

"Because if she is not at home I will sleep on the road today."

"I pray to God that she is not at home."

"Why?"

"Because if she is not at home I will offer you bed and breakfast . . . What is that?" he asked the driver, who had brought the car to an abrupt stop. There was no need for an answer. The small crowd ahead was looking upwards. The three scrambled out of the car and stumbled for the bush, necks twisted in a backward search of the sky. But the alarm was false. The sky was silent and clear except for two high-flying vultures. A humorist in the crowd called them Fighter and Bomber and everyone laughed in relief. The three climbed into their car again and continued their journey.

"It is much too early for raids," he said to Gladys, who had both her palms on her breast as though to still a thumping heart. "They rarely come before ten o'clock."

But she remained tongue-tied from her recent fright. Nwankwo saw an opportunity there and took it at once.

"Where does your friend live?"

"250 Douglas Road."

"Ah; that's the very center of town—a terrible place. No bunkers, nothing. I won't advise you to go there before 6 p.m.; it's not safe. If you don't mind I will take you to my place, where there is a good bunker, and then as soon as it is safe, around six, I shall drive you to your friend. How's that?''

"It's all right," she said lifelessly. "I am so frightened of this thing. That's why I refused to work in Owerri. I don't even know who asked me to come out today."

"You'll be all right. We are used to it."

"But your family is not there with you?"

"No," he said. "Nobody has his family there. We like to say it is because of air raids but I can assure you there is more to it. Owerri is a real swinging place now, and we live the life of gay bachelors."

"That is what I have heard."

"You will not just hear it; you will see it today. I shall take you to a real swinging party. A friend of mine, a lieutenant colonel, is having a birthday party. He's hired the Sound Smashers to play. I'm sure you'll enjoy it."

He was immediately and thoroughly ashamed of himself. He hated the parties and frivolities to which his friends clung like drowning men. And to talk so approvingly of them because he wanted to take a girl home! And this particular girl, too, who had once had such beautiful faith in the struggle and was betrayed (no doubt about it) by some man like him out for a good time. He shook his head sadly.

"What is it?" asked Gladys.

"Nothing. Just my thoughts."

They made the rest of the journey to Owerri practically in silence.

She made herself at home very quickly as if she was a regular girlfriend of his. She changed into a housedress and put away her auburn wig.

"That is a lovely hairdo. Why do you hide it with a wig?"

"Thank you," she said, leaving his question unanswered for a while. Then she said: "Men are funny."

"Why do you say that?"

" 'Now you are a beauty queen,' " she mimicked.

"Oh, that! I meant every word of it." He pulled her to him and kissed her. She neither refused nor yielded fully, which he liked for a start. Too many girls were simply too easy those days. War sickness, some called it.

He drove off a little later to look in at the office and she busied herself in the kitchen helping his boy with lunch. It must have been literally a look-in, for he was back within half an hour, rubbing his hands and saying he could not stay away too long from his beauty queen.

As they sat down to lunch, she said: "You have nothing in your fridge."

"Like what?" he asked, half offended.

"Like meat," she replied, undaunted.

"Do you still eat meat?" he challenged.

"Who am I? But other big men like you eat."

"I don't know which big men you have in mind. But they are not like me. I don't make money trading with the enemy or selling relief or . . ."

"Augusta's boyfriend doesn't do that. He just gets foreign exchange."

"How does he get it? He swindles the government—that's how he gets foreign exchange, whoever he is. Who is Augusta, by the way?"

"My girlfriend."

"I see."

"She gave me three dollars last time which I changed to forty-five pounds. The man gave her fifty dollars."

"Well, my dear girl, I don't traffic in foreign exchange and I don't have meat in my fridge. We are fighting a war and I happen to know that some young boys at the front drink *gari* and water once in three days."

"It is true," she said simply. "Monkey de work, baboon de chop."

"It is not even that; it is worse," he said, his voice beginning to shake. "People are dying every day. As we talk now somebody is dying."

"It is true," she said again.

"Plane!" screamed his boy from the kitchen.

"My mother!" screamed Gladys. As they scuttled toward the bunker of palm stems and red earth, covering their heads with their hands and stooping slightly in their flight, the entire sky was exploding with the clamor of jets and the huge noise of homemade antiaircraft rockets.

Inside the bunker she clung to him even after the plane had gone and the guns, late to start and also to end, had all died down again.

"It was only passing," he told her, his voice a little shaky. "It didn't drop anything. From its direction I should say it was going to the war front. Perhaps our people are pressing them. That's what they always do. Whenever our boys press them, they send an SOS to the Russians and Egyptians to bring the planes." He drew a long breath.

She said nothing, just clung to him. They could hear his boy telling the servant from the next house that there were two of them and one dived like this and the other dived like that.

"I see dem well well," said the other with equal excitement. "If no to say de ting de kill porson e for sweet for eye. To God."

"Imagine!" said Gladys, finding her voice at last. She had a way, he thought, of conveying with a few words or even a single word whole layers of meaning. Now it was at once her astonishment as well as reproof, tinged perhaps with grudging admiration for people who could be so lighthearted about these bringers of death.

"Don't be so scared," he said. She moved closer and he began to kiss her and squeeze her breasts. She yielded more and more and then fully. The bunker was dark and unswept and might harbor crawling things. He thought of bringing a mat from the main house but reluctantly decided against it. Another plane might pass and send a neighbor or simply a chance passerby crashing into them. That would be only slightly better than a certain gentleman in another air raid who was seen in broad daylight fleeing his bedroom for his bunker stark-naked, pursued by a woman in a similar state!

Just as Gladys had feared, her friend was not in town. It would seem her powerful boyfriend had wangled for her a flight to Libreville to shop. So her neighbors thought, anyway.

"Great!" said Nwankwo as they drove away. "She will come back on an arms plane loaded with shoes, wigs, pants, bras, cosmetics, and what have you, which she will then sell and make thousands of pounds. You girls are really at war, aren't you?"

She said nothing and he thought he had got through at last to her. Then suddenly she said, "That is what you men want us to do."

"Well," he said, "here is one man who doesn't want you to do that. Do you remember that girl in khaki jeans who searched me without mercy at the checkpoint?"

She began to laugh.

"That is the girl I want you to become again. Do you remember her? No wig. I don't even think she had any earrings . . ."

"Ah, na lie-o. I had earrings."

"All right. But you know what I mean."

"That time done pass. Now everybody want survival. They call it number six. You put your number six; I put my number six. Everything all right."

The lieutenant colonel's party turned into something quite unexpected. But before it did, things had been going well enough. There was goat meat, some chicken and rice, and plenty of homemade spirits. There was one fiery brand nicknamed "tracer" which indeed sent a flame down your gullet. The funny thing was, looked at in the bottle, it had the innocent appearance of an orange drink. But the thing that caused the greatest stir was the bread— one little roll for each person! It was the size of a golf ball and about the same consistency, too! But it was real bread. The band was good, too, and there were many girls. And to improve matters even further two white Red Cross people soon arrived with a bottle of Courvoisier and a bottle of Scotch! The party gave them a standing ovation and then scrambled to get a drop. It soon turned out from his general behavior, however, that one of the white men had probably drunk too much already. And the reason, it would seem, was that a pilot he knew well had been killed in a crash at the airport the night before, flying in relief in awful weather.

Few people at the party had heard of the crash by then. So there was an immediate damping of the air. Some dancing couples went back to their seats and the band stopped. Then for some strange reason the drunken Red Cross man just exploded.

"Why should a man, a decent man, throw away his life. For nothing! Charley didn't need to die. Not for this stinking place. Yes, everything stinks here. Even these girls who come here all dolled up and smiling, what are they worth? Don't I know? A head of stockfish, that's all, or one American dollar and they are ready to tumble into bed."

In the threatening silence following the explosion one of the young officers walked up to him and gave him three thundering slaps—right! left! right!— pulled him up from his seat and (there were things like tears in his eyes) shoved him outside. His friend, who had tried in vain to shut him up, followed him out and the silenced party heard them drive off. The officer who did the job returned, dusting his palms.

"Fucking beast!" said he with an impressive coolness. And all the girls showed with their eyes that they rated him a man and a hero.

"Do you know him?" Gladys asked Nwankwo.

He didn't answer her. Instead, he spoke generally to the party. "The fellow was clearly drunk," he said.

"I don't care," said the officer. "It is when a man is drunk that he speaks what is on his mind."

"So you beat him for what was on his mind," said the host. "That is the spirit, Joe."

"Thank you, sir," said Joe, saluting.

"His name is Joe," Gladys and the girl on her left said in unison, turning to each other.

At the same time Nwankwo and a friend on the other side of him were saying quietly, very quietly, that although the man had been rude and offensive what he had said about the girls was unfortunately the bitter truth, only he was the wrong man to say it.

When the dancing resumed Captain Joe came to Gladys for a dance. She sprang to her feet even before the word was out of his mouth. Then she remembered immediately and turned round to take permission from Nwankwo. At the same time the captain also turned to him and said, "Excuse me."

"Go ahead," said Nwankwo, looking somewhere between the two.

It was a long dance and he followed them with his eyes without appearing to do so. Occasionally a relief plane passed overhead and somebody immediately switched off the lights, saying it might be the Intruder. But it was only an excuse to dance in the dark and make the girls giggle, for the sound of the Intruder was well known.

Gladys came back feeling very self-conscious and asked Nwankwo to dance with her. But he wouldn't. "Don't bother about me," he said. "I am enjoying myself perfectly sitting here and watching those of you who dance."

"Then let's go," she said, "if you won't dance."

"But I never dance, believe me. So please enjoy yourself."

She danced next with the lieutenant colonel and again with Captain Joe, and then Nwankwo agreed to take her home.

"I am sorry I didn't dance," he said as they drove away. "But I swore never to dance as long as this war lasts."

She said nothing.

"When I think of somebody like that pilot who got killed last night. And he had no hand whatever in the quarrel. All his concern was to bring us food . . ."

"I hope that his friend is not like him," said Gladys.

"The man was just upset by his friend's death. But what I am saying is that with people like that getting killed and our own boys suffering and dying at the war fronts I don't see why we should sit around throwing parties and dancing."

"You took me there," said she in final revolt. "They are your friends. I don't know them before."

"Look, my dear, I am not blaming you. I am merely telling you why I personally refuse to dance. Anyway, let's change the subject . . . Do you still say you want to go back tomorrow? My driver can take you early enough on Monday morning for you to go to work. No? All right, just as you wish. You are the boss.''

She gave him a shock by the readiness with which she followed him to bed and by her language.

''You want to shell?'' she asked. And without waiting for an answer said, ''Go ahead but don't pour in troops!''

He didn't want to pour in troops either and so it was all right. But she wanted visual assurance and so he showed her.

One of the ingenious economies taught by the war was that a rubber condom could be used over and over again. All you had to do was wash it out, dry it, and shake a lot of talcum powder over it to prevent its sticking; and it was as good as new. It had to be the real British thing, though, not some of the cheap stuff they brought in from Lisbon, which was about as strong as a dry *cocoyam* leaf in the *harmattan*.

He had his pleasure but wrote the girl off. He might just as well have slept with a prostitute, he thought. It was clear as daylight to him now that she was kept by some army officer. What a terrible transformation in the short period of less than two years! Wasn't it a miracle that she still had memories of the other life, that she even remembered her name? If the affair of the drunken Red Cross man should happen again now, he said to himself, he would stand up beside the fellow and tell the party that here was a man of truth. What a terrible fate to befall a whole generation! The mothers of tomorrow!

By morning he was feeling a little better and more generous in his judgments. Gladys, he thought, was just a mirror reflecting a society that had gone completely rotten and maggoty at the center. The mirror itself was intact; a lot of smudge but no more. All that was needed was a clean duster. ''I have a duty to her,'' he told himself, ''the little girl that once revealed to me our situation. Now she is in danger, under some terrible influence.''

He wanted to get to the bottom of this deadly influence. It was clearly not just her good-time girlfriend, Augusta, or whatever her name was. There must be some man at the center of it, perhaps one of these heartless attack traders who traffic in foreign currencies and make their hundreds of thousands by sending young men to hazard their lives bartering looted goods for cigarettes behind enemy lines, or one of those contractors who receive piles of money daily for food they never deliver to the army. Or perhaps some vulgar and cowardly army officer full of filthy barrack talk and fictitious stories of heroism. He decided he had to find out. Last night he had thought of sending his driver alone to take her home. But no, he must go and see for himself where she lived. Something was bound to reveal itself there. Something on which he could anchor his rescue operation. As he prepared for the trip his feeling toward her softened with every passing minute. He assembled for her half of the food he had received at the relief center the day before. Difficult as things were, he thought, a girl who had something to eat would be spared, not all, but some of the temptation. He would arrange with his friend at the WCC to deliver something to her every fortnight.

Tears came to Gladys's eyes when she saw the gifts. Nwankwo didn't have too much cash on him but he got together twenty pounds and handed it over to her.

"I don't have foreign exchange, and I know this won't go far at all, but . . ."

She just came and threw herself at him, sobbing. He kissed her lips and eyes and mumbled something about victims of circumstances, which went over her head. In deference to him, he thought with exultation, she had put away her high-tinted wig in her bag.

"I want you to promise me something," he said.

"What?"

"Never use that expression about shelling again."

She smiled with tears in her eyes. "You don't like it? That's what all the girls call it."

"Well, you are different from all the girls. Will you promise?"

"O.K."

Naturally their departure had become a little delayed. And when they got into the car it refused to start. After poking around the engine the driver decided that the battery was flat. Nwankwo was aghast. He had that very week paid thirty-four pounds to change two of the cells and the mechanic who performed it had promised him six months' service. A new battery, which was then running at two hundred and fifty pounds, was simply out of the question. The driver must have been careless with something, he thought.

"It must be because of last night," said the driver.

"What happened last night?" asked Nwankwo sharply, wondering what insolence was on the way. But none was intended.

"Because we use the headlight."

"Am I supposed not to use my light, then? Go and get some people and try pushing it." He got out again with Gladys and returned to the house while the driver went over to neighboring houses to seek the help of other servants.

After at least half an hour of pushing it up and down the street, and a lot of noisy advice from the pushers, the car finally spluttered to life, shooting out enormous clouds of black smoke from the exhaust.

It was eight-thirty by his watch when they set out. A few miles away a disabled soldier waved for a lift.

"Stop!" screamed Nwankwo. The driver jammed his foot on the brakes and then turned his head toward his master in bewilderment.

"Don't you see the soldier waving? Reverse and pick him up!"

"Sorry, sir," said the driver. "I don't know Master want to pick him."

"If you don't know you should ask. Reverse back."

The soldier, a mere boy, in filthy khaki drenched in sweat, lacked his right leg from the knee down. He seemed not only grateful that a car should stop for him but greatly surprised. He first handed in his crude wooden crutches, which the driver arranged between the two front seats, then painfully he levered himself in.

"Thanks, sir," he said, turning to look at the back and completely out of breath.

"I am very grateful. Madame, thank you."

"The pleasure is ours," said Nwankwo. "Where did you get your wound?"

"At Azumini, sir. On tenth of January."

"Never mind. Everything will be all right. We are proud of you boys and will make sure you receive your due reward when it is all over."

"I pray God, sir."

They drove on in silence for the next half hour or so. Then as the car sped down a slope toward a bridge somebody screamed—perhaps the driver, perhaps the soldier—"They have come!" The screech of the brakes merged into the scream and the shattering of the sky overhead. The doors flew open even before the car had come to a stop and they were fleeing blindly to the bush. Gladys was a little ahead of Nwankwo when they heard through the drowning tumult the soldier's voice crying: "Please come and open for me!" Vaguely he saw Gladys stop; he pushed past her, shouting to her at the same time to come on. Then a high whistle descended like a spear through the chaos and exploded in a vast noise and motion that smashed up everything. A tree he had embraced flung him away through the bush. Then another terrible whistle starting high up and ending again in a monumental crash of the world; and then another, and Nwankwo heard no more.

He woke up to human noises and weeping and the smell and smoke of a charred world. He dragged himself up and staggered toward the source of the sounds.

From afar he saw his driver running toward him in tears and blood. He saw the remains of his car smoking and the entangled remains of the girl and the soldier. And he let out a piercing cry and fell down again.

—1972

Bessie Head

(1937–86) SOUTH AFRICA / BOTSWANA

When critics discuss African women writers, they inevitably mention Bessie Head, often placing her name at the top of the list. Bessie Head had to overcome incredible obstacles to become a writer. She was born in Pietermaritzburg, South Africa, in 1937. The name on her birth certificate was Bessie Amelia Emery. Her mother was white, her father African. Head lived her entire life unaware that she had two older siblings, half brothers who were white. One of them died tragically as a child, and her mother was institutionalized for mental instability several times. Under the rigid South African apartheid laws, she was considered insane because of her affair with a black man.

Bessie herself suffered emotionally because of her mixed racial identity. Though initially listed as white as a child, she was subsequently reclassified as Coloured. For many years, she knew little, if anything, about her birth mother, assuming that her foster parents (named Heathcote) were her biological parents. She was an excellent student. At age thirteen, she began attending St. Monica's Home for Coloured girls, an Anglican school. Afterwards, from 1956 to 1958, she taught briefly in Durban. Soon, she stopped teaching and began working as a reporter in Cape Town and later in Johannesburg.

She made several early attempts at suicide. A sudden marriage to Harold Head (who was Coloured) led to the birth of her only child, Howard. When Howard was two years old, Bessie left South Africa with the child on an exit permit and moved to Botswana. Gillian Stead Eilersen, Head's biographer, states that although she had fled to Botswana in order to teach, "she was not a very successful teacher." She had, in fact, brought too much emotional baggage along with her.

In Serowe, where she lived much of the rest of her life, Bessie Head became a writer of fiction. *When Rain Clouds Gather* (1968) was followed by *Maru* (1971), both set in Botswana. These novels were widely read and praised, but with *A Question of Power* (1973) critics were initially hostile because of the novel's inaccessibility. That novel, now usually regarded as Head's masterpiece, had been taken from the raw material of her childhood—her years under apartheid, the source of many of the emotional scars she wrestled with for much of her adult life. Head herself was institutionalized for "insanity," one of the major themes of *A Question of Power*.

Other works followed, including a collection of short stories, *The Collector of Treasures* (1977), and *Serowe: Village of the Rain Wind* (1981). The latter is Head's lyrical homage to her adopted village, where she lived in relative isolation, tending to her writing and her garden. Excessive drinking hastened her death in 1986. Several volumes of previously unpublished writings have subsequently been published.

Toward the end of her life, *Libération*, the French newspaper, requested that Bessie Head and other international writers explain why they write. Her random thoughts included the following statements:

"I write because I have authority from life to do so."

"Friends walk through my life, talk, smile and shake hands but no one is near me."

"I am building a stairway to the stars. I have the authority to take the whole of mankind up there with me. That is why I write."

THE PRISONER
WHO WORE GLASSES

Scarcely a breath of wind disturbed the stillness of the day and the long rows of cabbages were bright green in the sunlight. Large white clouds drifted slowly across the deep blue sky. Now and then they obscured the sun and caused a chill on the backs of the prisoners who had to work all day long in the cabbage field. This trick the clouds were playing with the sun eventually caused one of the prisoners who wore glasses to stop work, straighten up, and peer shortsightedly at them. He was a thin little fellow with a hollowed-out chest and comic knobbly knees. He also had a lot of fanciful ideas because he smiled at the clouds.

"Perhaps they want me to send a message to the children," he thought tenderly, noting that the clouds were drifting in the direction of his home some hundred miles away. But before he could frame the message, the warder in charge of his work detail shouted: "Hey, what you tink you're doing, Brille?"

The prisoner swung round, blinking rapidly, yet at the same time sizing up the enemy. He was a new warder, named Jacobus Stephanus Hannetjie. His eyes were the color of the sky but they were frightening. A simple, primitive, brutal soul gazed out of them.

The prisoner bent down quickly and a message was quietly passed down the line: "We're in for trouble this time, comrades."

"Why?" rippled back up the line.

"Because he's not human," the reply rippled down and yet only the crunching of the spades as they turned over the earth disturbed the stillness.

This particular work detail was known as Span One. It was composed of ten men and they were all political prisoners. They were grouped together for convenience, as it was one of the prison regulations that no black warder should be in charge of a political prisoner lest this prisoner convert him to his views. It never seemed to occur to the authorities that this very reasoning was the strength of Span One and a clue to the strange terror they aroused in the warders. As political prisoners they were unlike the other prisoners in the sense that they felt no guilt nor were they outcasts of society. All guilty men instinctively cower, which was why it was the kind of prison where men got knocked out cold with a blow at the back of the head from an iron bar. Up until the arrival of Warder Hannetjie, no warder had dared beat any member of Span One and no warder had lasted more than a week with them. The battle was entirely psychological. Span One was assertive and it was beyond the scope of white warders to handle assertive black men. Thus, Span One had got out of control. They were the best thieves and liars in the camp. They lived all day on raw cabbages. They chatted and smoked tobacco. And since they moved, thought, and acted as one, they had perfected every technique of group concealment.

Trouble began that very day between Span One and Warder Hannetjie. It was because of the shortsightedness of Brille. That was the nickname he was given in prison and is the Afrikaans word for someone who wears glasses. Brille could never judge the approach of the prison gates and on several previous occasions he had munched on cabbages and dropped them almost at the feet of the warder, and all previous warders had overlooked this. Not so Warder Hannetjie.

"Who dropped that cabbage?" he thundered.

Brille stepped out of line. "I did," he said meekly.

"All right," said Hannetjie. "The whole Span goes three meals off."

"But I told you I did it," Brille protested.

The blood rushed to Warder Hannetjie's face. "Look 'ere," he said. "I don't take orders from a kaffir. I don't know what kind of kaffir you tink you are. Why don't you say Baas. I'm your Baas. Why don't you say Baas, hey?"

Brille blinked his eyes rapidly but by contrast his voice was strangely calm. "I'm twenty years older than you," he said.

It was the first thing that came to mind but the comrades seemed to think it a huge joke. A titter swept up the line. The next thing, Warder Hannetjie whipped out a knobkerrie and gave Brille several blows about the head. What surprised his comrades was the speed with which Brille had removed his glasses or else they would have been smashed to pieces on the ground.

That evening in the cell Brille was very apologetic. "I'm sorry, comrades," he said. "I've put you into a hell of a mess."

"Never mind, brother," they said. "What happens to one of us happens to all."

"I'll try to make up for it, comrades," he said. "I'll steal something so that you don't go hungry."

Privately, Brille was very philosophical about his head wounds. It was the first time an act of violence had been perpetrated against him but he had long been a witness of extreme, almost unbelievable human brutality. He had twelve children and his mind traveled back that evening through the sixteen years of bedlam in which he had lived. It had all happened in a small drab little three-bedroom house in a small drab little street in the Eastern Cape and the children kept coming year after year because neither he nor Martha managed the contraceptives the right way and a teacher's salary never allowed moving to a bigger house and he was always taking exams to improve this salary only to have it all eaten up by hungry mouths. Everything was pretty horrible, especially the way the children fought. They'd get hold of each other's heads and give them a good bashing against the wall. Martha gave up somewhere along the line, so they worked out a thing between them. The bashings, biting, and blood were to operate in full swing until he came home. He was to be the bogeyman and when it worked he never failed to have a sense of godhead at the way in which his presence could change savages into fairly reasonable human beings.

Yet somehow it was this chaos and mismanagement at the center of his life that drove him into politics. It was really an ordered beautiful world with just a few basic slogans to learn along with the rights of mankind. At one stage, before things became very bad, there were conferences to attend, all very far away from home.

"Let's face it," he thought ruefully. "I'm only learning right now what it means to be a politician. All this while I've been running away from Martha and the kids."

And the pain in his head brought a hard lump to his throat. That was what the children did to each other daily and Martha wasn't managing and if Warder Hannetjie had not interrupted him that morning he would have sent the following message: "Be good comrades, my children. Cooperate, then life will run smoothly."

The next day Warder Hannetjie caught this old man with twelve children stealing grapes from the farm shed. They were an enormous quantity of grapes in a ten-gallon tin and for this misdeed the old man spent a week in the isolation cell. In fact, Span One as a whole was in constant trouble. Warder Hannetjie seemed to have eyes at the back of his head. He uncovered the trick about the cabbages, how they were split in two with the spade and immediately covered with earth and then unearthed again and eaten with split-second timing. He found out how tobacco smoke was beaten into the ground and he found out how conversations were whispered down the wind.

For about two weeks Span One lived in acute misery. The cabbages, tobacco, and conversations had been the pivot of jail life to them. Then one evening they noticed that their good old comrade who wore the glasses was looking rather pleased with himself. He pulled out a four-ounce packet of tobacco by way of explanation and the comrades fell upon it with great greed. Brille merely smiled. After all, he was the father of many children. But when the last shred had disappeared, it occurred to the comrades that they ought to be puzzled.

Someone said: "I say, brother. We're watched like hawks these days. Where did you get the tobacco?"

"Hannetjie gave it to me," said Brille.

There was a long silence. Into it dropped a quiet bombshell. "I saw Hannetjie in the shed today"—and the failing eyesight blinked rapidly. "I caught him in the act of stealing five bags of fertilizer and he bribed me to keep my mouth shut."

There was another long silence.

"Prison is an evil life," Brille continued, apparently discussing some irrelevant matter. "It makes a man contemplate all kinds of evil deeds."

He held out his hand and closed it. "You know, comrades," he said. "I've got Hannetjie. I'll betray him tomorrow."

Everyone began talking at once.

"Forget it, brother. You'll get shot."

Brille laughed.

"I won't," he said. "That is what I mean about evil. I am a father of children and I saw today that Hannetjie is just a child and stupidly truthful. I'm going to punish him severely because we need a good warder."

The following day, with Brille as witness, Hannetjie confessed to the theft of the fertilizer and was fined a large sum of money. From then on, Span One did very much as they pleased while Warder Hannetjie stood by and said nothing. But it was Brille who carried this to extremes.

One day, at the close of work Warder Hannetjie said: "Brille, pick up my jacket and carry it back to the camp."

"But nothing in the regulations says I'm your servant, Hannetjie," Brille replied coolly.

"I've told you not to call me Hannetjie. You must say, Baas," but Warder Hannetjie's voice lacked conviction.

In turn, Brille squinted up at him. "I'll tell you something about this Baas business, Hannetjie," he said. "One of these days we are going to run the country. You are going to clean my car. Now, I have a fifteen-year-old son and I'd die of shame if you had to tell him that I ever called you Baas."

Warder Hannetjie went red in the face and picked up his coat.

On another occasion Brille was seen to be walking about the prison yard, openly smoking tobacco. On being taken before the prison commander, he claimed to have received the tobacco from Warder Hannetjie. All throughout the tirade from his chief, Warder Hannetjie failed to defend himself, but his nerve broke completely.

He called Brille to one side. "Brille," he said. "This thing between you and me must end. You may not know it but I have a wife and children and you're driving me to suicide."

"Why, don't you like your own medicine, Hannetjie?" Brille asked quietly.

"I can give you anything you want," Warder Hannetjie said in desperation.

"It's not only me but the whole of Span One," said Brille cunningly. "The whole of Span One wants something from you."

Warder Hannetjie brightened with relief. "I tink I can manage if it's tobacco you want," he said.

Brille looked at him, for the first time struck with pity and guilt. He wondered if he had carried the whole business too far. The man was really a child.

"It's not tobacco we want, but you," he said. "We want you on our side. We want a good warder because without a good warder we won't be able to manage the long stretch ahead."

Warder Hannetjie interpreted this request in his own fashion and his interpretation of what was good and human often left the prisoners of Span

One speechless with surprise. He had a way of slipping off his revolver and picking up a spade and digging alongside Span One. He had a way of producing unheard-of luxuries like boiled eggs from his farm nearby and things like cigarettes, and Span One responded nobly and got the reputation of being the best work detail in the camp. And it wasn't only take from their side. They were awfully good at stealing certain commodities like fertilizer which were needed on the farm of Warder Hannetjie.

—1973

Similih M. Cordor

(BORN 1946) LIBERIA

Similih M. Cordor was born in Voinjama, Lofta County, in northern Liberia, in 1946. By his own account, his early education was sporadic, though he attended several schools in Voinjama and Monrovia. His interests, initially, were literature and anthropology. In the 1970s, he taught English and literature at the College of West Africa in Monrovia, while simultaneously working as a freelance journalist for the Ministry of Information, Culture and Tourism. He served as the producer of the *Writers Forum* for radio.

In 1979, Cordor attended the International Writing Program at the University of Iowa. That brief residency led to his decision to remain in the United States and pursue further studies. By the time he had completed his Ph.D., at Pennsylvania State University, political problems in Liberia curtailed his plans to return home. He has taught at a number of American colleges and universities, most recently at Florida Community College at Jacksonville.

Cordor edited several collections of Liberian literature before he came to the United States, including a volume of his own short stories, *Africa, from People to People* (1979). In the preface to that book, he states: "Various aspects of Western civilization, including Western education, Christianity, technology, modernization, urbanization, industrialization, colonialism, neocolonialism, and economic exploitation, have been brought to Africa. The African peoples have accepted some of these, but they also rejected several because they were in open conflict with the traditional cultures and values;

the African rejection was also based on the deceptive characteristics and exploitative consequences of these various concepts and institutions from the Westerners.''

Almost singlehandedly, Similih M. Cordor has worked to promote a Liberian national literature. As a writer in exile in the United States during his country's Civil War, he has continued to speak out on the need for peace and stability in the country of his birth. His most recent stories have appeared in *Share, Confrontation*, and *Short Story International*, as well as in several international fiction anthologies.

"In the Hospital" appeared in an earlier version in *More Modern African Stories* (1975). Of the revised version included here, Cordor has said: "The story is a dramatization of the humanity of a struggling African family in a big city . . . a portrayal of the plight of the semiskilled or unskilled, uneducated, and low-income masses of modern Africa who migrate to cities in search of better life for their families, but who only experience loneliness, poverty, diseases, alienation, and despair.''

IN THE HOSPITAL

1

When Kollie came home from his shop in the evening, he found his sick pregnant wife coiled on her Mandingo mat on the floor, where she had been nearly the whole day. Her face was turned very close to the wall, as if someone had nailed her head there. Marwu had wrapped herself up in her old blanket even though the room was very hot.

The forty-five-year-old carpenter stared at his wife, heaved a deep sigh, and then shrugged his broad shoulders. It wasn't until two weeks ago when he discovered that his wife was taking the wrong drugs at home from his nurse friend that he realized he should take her back to the maternity hospital in Monrovia where she had undergone an operation seven months earlier. But Kollie couldn't gather enough courage to talk Marwu into returning to the hospital. He still remembered how bitterly she had cried when she had to have her operation. So he had avoided talking about her hospitalization until Friday night.

After shaking some dust off his khaki shirt, Kollie placed his work helmet on his tiny wooden table gently, as though it were a breakable object. Then he greeted Marwu, but she took much longer than usual to answer him.

"How come you lay down on you mat like that?" Kollie asked Marwu. "You ain't feeling any better today?"

Marwu twisted her pale body on the mat, struggling to turn to her husband. "I'm too sick," she said. "My head, stomach, and all over my body's hurting me too bad."

"But my nurse friend ain't come to the house to give you some medicine today?"

"Yeah, you friend came and gave me some pills and tablets. He also gave me two shots on my buttock, but they're hurting me."

"You know we ain't able to go hospital all the time 'cause money palaver is hard on us this time."

"I know that, but . . ."

"So you've got to take some pills, tablets, and injections at home from my nurse friend."

"But my buttock all swollen from his shots. Even his pills and tablets make me sick too much now."

"But how come everything making you sickness worse this time?"

"Go ask you friend. Me, I ain't know nothing about medicine."

At first, Kollie frowned. But his anxiety faded quickly when he realized that Marwu's statements had just confirmed his belief that the nurse wasn't giving her the right drugs.

After standing quietly for a few minutes, Kollie shook his head dolefully. Then he glanced around at the dimly lit single room he and his family of six shared in the old brick house in Monrovia. His wife still lay on her mat, fanning flies and mosquitoes from her face. The children—four girls and a boy—were lying on their parents' bed, half naked and soaked in sweat. Their toys were scattered among dishes, clothes, palm-oil cans, empty gin and wine bottles, and carpentry tools. In a few minutes the children woke up, but each sat quietly on a stool near Marwu.

2

All day Kollie had been feeling uneasy at work. He was very busy at his carpentry shop, sweating heavily on that hot Friday in February, the height of the tropical dry season in Liberia, but he had kept thinking and worrying about Marwu's sickness. Since he brought his family from Voinjama to Monrovia to find a carpentry job in the national capital six years ago, Marwu had been quite sickly. But she hadn't been very ill like this. Her body was now wasting very fast; her swollen legs were bothering her; her joints were aching; and malaria was frequently troubling her.

"I too tired and hungry," Kollie said. "This carpenter work is breaking my back."

"But if you ain't work, we won't eat," Marwu said and told her oldest daughter to bring her father's food to the table. "I'm too sick to work for money in the farmers' market doing my little food business."

"You ain't supposed to worry about money in you condition. When you get well, you'll go back to the market to work."

"But things are hard on us this time. Even our food supply almost finished now. Just look in you bowls."

Kollie uncovered the rice and soup bowls his oldest daughter had placed before him on the table. There wasn't much in either one.

"Well, as for the food supply, you must go easy with the little one here," Kollie said. "My payday ain't ready to come now 'cause the moon ain't finished yet."

"But I always go easy with everything in the home," Marwu quickly protested. "It's just that we never get enough of anything and we must share every little thing with our old people upcountry."

"I know things are hard on us, but we won't forget our own people in Voinjama 'cause they're depending on us."

When Kollie had eaten his dinner, he drew his chair closer to Marwu. He had mustered enough courage to talk with Marwu about her hospitalization. He knew for sure that she wasn't going to be happy with the news.

"Try to get up," he said to her. "We've got something serious to talk about tonight."

"I ain't want any serious or big talk tonight," Marwu said. "Maybe I'm going to die, so you want to say goodbye to me now."

"Don't you bring any bad luck on me 'cause I ain't want see any dead body in the home."

Marwu laughed softly as she slowly twisted her wan body on her mat again, being very careful not to hurt her swollen legs on the hard cement floor. When she sat up, she leaned on the wall, and then covered her large breasts with her *buba* and *lappa*. Despite her pale look, Marwu still had some of the youthful beauty she had brought to Kollie at the age of nineteen, almost a dozen years ago.

"Darling wife, I think we've got to do something different about you sickness now," Kollie said.

"So what we'll do?" Marwu asked.

Kollie's face suddenly grew stern, but his voice still remained calm. "I think you must go back to the big hospital where you took you operation last time," Kollie said, reading Marwu's face carefully.

Marwu jerked violently on her Mandingo mat, as though someone had splashed boiling water on her swollen legs. Her heart began to beat very fast and she grew dizzy right away.

"No, no, I ain't want to go to any hospital," Marwu said, and burst into tears. "I scare the doctors there will operate on me again."

"Don't you worry about operation," Kollie said. "We ain't know yet if you'll take any more operation in the hospital."

"I always get sick whenever I take any operation, and maybe that the first operation making me sick like this. So I ain't know why you're pushing me to go back to the hospital. I think you want to get me out of you way."

"What do you mean by that?"

"I think you've seen my death in you sleep, so you want to dump me in the hospital and go away from me."

"Oh, Marwu, why you're talking like that?" Kollie said, almost in tears. "I ain't see you death in my dream."

Kollie stared at Marwu with his mouth wide open. The tone of her voice had somewhat scared him, but he felt a great relief.

"So when you'll take me to the hospital?" Marwu said, after she had cried for a few minutes.

"Tonight," Kollie said, rather absentmindedly. "Is that okay?"

"Go to the hospital tonight?" Marwu screamed. "Oh, no."

Kollie momentarily shifted his attention to the children. He fondled the nape of his son's neck, as his daughters stood around him. He hoped that Marwu would give birth to another boy child if she could make the journey to the hospital for a safe delivery. Kollie didn't want to admit to himself that his strong desire for another son had been the main reason for wanting Marwu to get pregnant, even though she wasn't willing because of the cesarean section she had with her last child two years ago. And he hadn't forgotten how Marwu got sick for nearly six months after the cesarean operation.

"I see you're too serious about this hospital business," Marwu said, after thinking the matter over for a few minutes. "So I guess I must agree with you. But how much money we'll pay to the hospital for all the treatment?"

"I'm talking about your sickness, and you talking about money?" Kollie said, looking hard at his wife.

Marwu threw a quick scornful look at Kollie's face.

"You ain't know we must always worry about money palaver?" Marwu said. "You know hospitals in Monrovia call for much money."

"True, but if we must sell or pawn all our belongings, you must go to the hospital," Kollie said.

"Where are the belongings we've got to sell or pawn for money?" Marwu said. "You ain't mean these old, old things in this room."

Kollie laughed sheepishly. Then he surveyed their property with his big eyes.

3

The journey to the hospital wasn't easy. Kollie, his wife, and their five children had had to walk nearly two miles to get to the main road where they would either catch a city bus or take a taxicab downtown. Then they would change to a train that would take them to the hospital on the northern outskirts of Monrovia, miles away from their home.

"Will we take the bus to town?" Marwu said, when they got on the main road. "I hope one is coming this way soon."

"Take the bus instead of the taxi; which is faster?" Kollie said. "We must go quickly 'cause it's getting dark."

"Yeah, by the bus; it's cheaper. Bus drivers kin sometimes help with children free, but with a taxi, I ain't know."

"You always get hard on money business, but that's okay."

"Yeah, you kin say that. You who work for house builders know that when one is finished it kin take you forever to find another carpenter job. In the five years we've been in Monrovia we ain't see any good luck yet."

"Well, we won't go back to Voinjama like that 'cause we came here to find work and money so we'll send our children to school."

"I know that. I myself want these little ones to learn something so they kin never suffer like us, but the hard times too much on us now."

Kollie turned around to pat his only son on the back. Then he looked at his watch. It was almost eight o'clock.

As Kollie and his family stood in the cold on the dusty road, waiting for a city bus, many people were passing them. But no one seemed to care about their trouble at all. Kollie knew that in Voinjama and other towns nobody would have passed them without talking to them. He missed this aspect of traditional rural life in the big city, where his family felt lonesome among so great a population.

When Kollie and his family finally arrived at the hospital around ten o'clock, he left Marwu and the children a few yards away from the door. Then he walked over to the entrance supervisor, who sat cross-legged, chat-

ting with three women and looking completely unconcerned about what
went on at the entrance. One of the women had to call his attention to
Kollie's greeting.

Then he rose unsteadily and looked at Kollie questioningly. "What's your
problem, sir?" the supervisor asked.

"I want to go inside the hospital with my family," Kollie said.

"No, not tonight. Visiting hours are over now."

"We aren't visiting, but . . ."

"Please don't stand in the door."

Kollie stepped back a little to give way to three persons who were going
into the maternity center. But he noticed that they all discreetly pushed
dollar bills into the supervisor's hand.

"May I go with my family now?" Kollie asked.

"No, not like that," the entrance supervisor said.

"But other people are going inside the hospital."

The entrance supervisor scratched his head. "I guess you don't know
what can be going on at night at big hospitals in Monrovia," the supervisor
said to Kollie, staring at him for a few moments. "Don't you know that
you must throw something in my hand before going inside?"

Kollie tried to convince the supervisor to let him and his family into the
hospital. When he found out that his pleading and protesting weren't getting
him anywhere, he reached into his pockets. Nothing was in any of them. So
he walked over to his wife, who was watching everything at the entrance.

"You ain't got no small money on you to throw to the door supervisor?"
he said to Marwu.

"But we ain't go inside yet, they're asking for money now?" Marwu
said. "I think I'm going to die outside here tonight."

"No, this is just to get us through the door."

"Let me see," Marwu said, carelessly fishing into her handbag. "Well, I
ain't get anything."

Kollie went back to the door supervisor. "Sir, my wife's too sick and
want to see doctor tonight," he said to the supervisor. "So please let us go
in 'cause I ain't got nothing on me tonight."

"Is your wife coming for any operation or some kind of emergency?"
the supervisor asked. "What's her problem?"

Marwu lifted her ears up when she heard about an operation.

The supervisor stared at Marwu again, and after some more questions and
answers, he let Kollie and his family into the hospital.

"What's happening here tonight?" Marwu asked Kollie as they walked into the hospital. "How come lots of people are here?"

Kollie and his family had entered the maternity center through the back door, the most dilapidated part of the building, with faded paint and worn cement and wood. Many people were rushing in and out. Marwu noticed that some of the women going out of the center had babies in baskets, and they were walking very fast with their infants.

"I think they're running away so they won't pay the hospital bills," said Kollie, " 'cause money palaver is hard on lots of people in the city."

"How kin they get away with that?" Marwu asked.

"How?" Kollie said. "You want to try it yourself?"

"Oh, not me. I won't do that. You know we come from the Lorma tribe and our people believe in being honest and trueful."

It was a long way from the entrance to the admissions office. Kollie and his family walked on steadily. But they didn't go far when Marwu slipped and fell in the hallway.

"Help me!" Marwu cried.

"What's wrong?" Kollie asked, turning around quickly to Marwu. "Is that you stomach again?"

"I think this is my end now," Marwu said to Kollie, and started to cry loudly. "This baby is too much for me."

As Kollie struggled to help his wife, a senior midwife, Miss Marcah Washington, heard Marwu's crying in the hallway and came out to see what the problem was.

"I guess this is your wife?" Miss Washington said. "What's your name?"

"Tanu Kollie, from Sinkor, Old Road area," Kollie said.

"But, Kollie, why you kept your wife until her sickness was so advanced before bringing her to the hospital?"

"We were trying by ourselves in town."

"I bet 'twas one of those rotten practical nurses giving your wife the wrong drugs at home."

"We ain't got money to be coming to hospital all the time."

"And why you brought all these children here this time of the night?" the midwife asked.

"We ain't got nobody to look after them," Kollie said.

"All right," Miss Washington said, "I'll get some nurses to take your wife to the Emergency Department."

"I want to stay with her tonight," Kollie said.

"No, take the children home and come back tomorrow."

"What will the doctors do for her tonight?"

"I don't know yet," Miss Washington said, after touching Marwu's forehead, hands, and legs. "But the way she is too sick with lots of complications, including swollen legs and hands, I think she might have to take an operation or two . . ."

Marwu shuddered.

4

All was quiet in the doctor's office as Kollie stared at the hospital documents for his wife. After giving Kollie the red emergency form and another medical questionnaire, the chief medical doctor, Joseph N. Togbah, had fallen silent. But he soon noticed that Kollie was growing pale.

Kollie had just rushed into the hospital to see his wife that Monday afternoon, a few days after she had been admitted. When he found Miss Washington, she told him that the chief doctor wanted to see him.

"Oh, right now?" Kollie nervously asked.

"Well, yes, but it's a routine call," the midwife replied.

The carpenter could feel his heart thumping as he walked into Dr. Togbah's office. He sat down quietly and folded his hands. Though the air-conditioned office was very cold, he soon began to sweat heavily. He pressed his lips tight, as if he would never talk again in his whole life.

"Can you read and write?" the doctor asked Kollie. "We've got a few papers here for you to sign."

"Yes, Dr. Togbah, I'll try," Kollie said. "I ain't go far in school, but I kin read and write a little."

Then the doctor put two sheets of paper before Kollie; one was red and the other was green. Kollie stared at them. He was afraid to touch the red hospital certificate.

"Is this my wife's death certificate?" Kollie asked in a trembling voice.

The doctor sighed deeply. "Well, yes, Kollie, the red paper is the death certificate for your wife," the doctor said. "It's our regular emergency form for major risky or critical operations, but don't worry about it. Just fill it out and sign it . . ."

"Is my wife going to have any operation soon?" Kollie asked.

"We can't tell right now, though our exams show various complications. Your wife's in a very critical condition. So we must have all the necessary papers signed for her. She might have to undergo an emergency operation."

"But why you ain't keep the death certificate?"

"Any person coming to us here for any surgery for a critical condition must sign this red emergency certificate. By signing this death certificate, you and your family are waiving all your rights to hold any doctor, nurse, midwife, or hospital administrator responsible for anything if your wife should die—or even develop any complication before, during, and after surgery."

"I think this death certificate kin bring bad luck on people."

"Don't be superstitious," the doctor said. "We have explained this one red hospital paper to many patients and their families, but nobody seems to understand what it's used for."

"There ain't no other way to help my wife 'cause she too scared of operation?"

"We'll see later what can be done for her. The main trouble with your wife is her various complications: swollen legs, frequent dizziness, elevated blood pressure, excessive vomiting, gastroenteris, and a history of cesarean section. So I don't think any medical doctor *would touch your wife on an operation table* without the death certificate being signed for her . . ."

Kollie stared at the death certificate; he knew that everybody was afraid of it. It had now become legendary enough for superstitions to grow about it. In fact, Kollie had learned from some of his friends in the neighborhood that only a few people for whom the death certificate was signed ever survived their operations.

Kollie moved his hands tremulously toward the doctor's desk. Because his hands continued to tremble while he wrote on the hospital documents, a nurse had to assist him, as if he himself were a sick person.

5

Kollie shuttled daily between the hospital and his carpentry shop to visit his wife. A week after he had signed the death certificate for Marwu, Dr. Togbah called him into his office again.

"This time we need to talk about the payment of your wife's medical bills," the doctor said. "By any chance, are you on any government health program or medical insurance?"

"No, sir," Kollie replied. "I'm working for a private house-building company, but my bossmen ain't give me any medical insurance."

"Then you must pay your wife's medical bills in full and possibly in advance."

"How much will we pay?"

"Well," the doctor said, scratching his head. "Let's say seven to nine hundred dollars, if any surgery is undertaken."

Kollie gasped. Where could such a large sum of money come from? His wages wouldn't help him out with such an amount.

"But my wife was here for an operation before, and we ain't pay much and we paid in installment," Kollie said.

"That's true," the doctor said, after reading over Marwu's hospital record. "That was a long time ago and things have changed. Anyway, if your wife doesn't need any surgery, you'll pay much less than that. But if she takes an operation, gets delivery services, stays in the hospital for a few weeks, and gets special care, you'll be looking at about a thousand dollars."

"I'll try my bossman at my working place to lend me some money 'cause money palaver is hard on me this time."

"Money palaver hard on you? But your wife's in our hospital."

Kollie felt like saying: "And so what?" But he realized that his pleading wasn't doing much for him.

Four days after his meeting with the chief medical doctor, Kollie was able to get a large advance on his wages from his employers. When he got the money, he rushed to the hospital to show it to Marwu.

Kollie waited outside the Midwives Department for Miss Washington, who had now become his best friend in the hospital. When she walked toward him, she had a big smile on her face.

"Kollie, your wife gave birth to a baby girl this morning, and the doctors didn't have to operate on her," Miss Washington said, all in one breath. "Your troubles are over now."

"Really, Miss Washington?" Kollie said excitedly.

"True. The baby and the mother aren't doing too bad yet."

"Thank God for that," Kollie said, smiling. "I want to see my wife so I kin show her the money for her hospital fees."

"I'm not sure you can see her now, but let's go and find out."

Miss Washington and Kollie walked over to the room where Marwu was resting. She was asleep, and the midwives assigned to her said the doctors had advised that Marwu shouldn't be disturbed for any reason.

"Maybe I kin see my baby and then come back tonight to visit my wife," Kollie said.

"No, no," Miss Washington said. "The baby is in the Baby Pool, and we normally don't let people in there."

The Baby Pool was a spacious room where all infants delivered in the hospital, dead or alive, were deposited until their mothers were ready to take them home.

"Why was the baby separated from the mother so soon?"

"This is a big hospital, and we must separate the babies and their mothers—especially if the mothers are sick, as in the case of your wife."

"This is the first time that I ain't see any of my babies after delivery."

"Maybe your other babies were born in a country hospital, but this is the new way of things in big city hospitals."

6

During the three weeks Marwu spent in the hospital, Kollie couldn't visit her as much as he had wanted because visiting hours were short. He couldn't even see his baby as frequently as he had wanted; visits to the Baby Pool were restricted. Marwu herself didn't get to spend much time with her baby. She was sick, and the nurses and midwives told her that "sick mothers don't play with their babies much in the hospital."

Kollie arrived early at the hospital the morning Marwu and the baby were ready to go home. He was anxious; he wanted to take a good look at his baby. He stood impatiently with Marwu before the Baby Door, the entrance to the Baby Pool. It was actually a large window through which all babies had to pass from the pool to their parents. Several other couples were also waiting.

About an hour passed, but nobody brought a baby to Marwu. Kollie's anxiety greatly increased.

"Why the nurses and midwives taking too long to bring our baby to us?" he asked Marwu.

"Be patient," Marwu said to him. "We'll soon get our baby."

Kollie tried to calm down, but when a midwife told Marwu that the nurses were looking for her baby in the pool, Kollie panicked.

"Looking for our baby in that big place?" Kollie said. "I hope they ain't give us the wrong baby."

The midwives finally brought a baby to Marwu in a wheelbasket, almost two and half hours later. Kollie looked skeptical about the features of the baby. After the midwives had laid the baby in Marwu's arms, they watched Kollie curiously as he examined the infant seriously.

And as soon as they had left, Kollie turned to his wife. "Do you think this is the baby you born in this hospital?" he asked.

"Why you asking me that kinda question?" Marwu said, laughing softly, but her face changed as soon as she remembered why Kollie was so concerned about the baby. "Well, I ain't God to make you a boy child."

"Don't you worry about that. But I think this is someone else's baby the midwives gave us."

"How do you know that?"

"Oh, you ain't see how they took too long to bring us this baby from that big-O Baby Pool?"

Kollie felt somewhat disappointed that he didn't get a boy child. But he felt that something might have gone wrong in the Baby Pool. He had heard rumors that apart from mislabeling of infants in the pool, which sometimes caused problems, an exchange of babies frequently took place. Sometimes rich men gave large amounts of money to nurses and midwives to give them the boy children if their wives had given birth to girls in the maternity hospitals. Kollie tried to believe Miss Washington, who was the first person to tell him that Marwu had delivered a girl child. But he wondered if the senior midwife wasn't part of trading in babies in the hospital.

"Let's go home now," Marwu said. "We just have take this baby since this is what God gave us."

"You had better say that this is what the nurses and midwives gave us from the Baby Pool," Kollie said.

Marwu laughed. Kollie he still looked somewhat skeptical, but his mood had changed. He had even smiled. When he looked at Marwu's *lappa* and *buba* suit, he thought she looked very much like when she graduated from the literacy class in Monrovia where she had learned to read and write simple English.

"I thank God I'm safe again," Marwu said. "I know you men always want boy children, but I ain't going to get any more big belly just to get you a boy child."

"That's all right 'cause this was the only way out for us," Kollie said. "Maybe this is our baby, but I ain't know."

—1975

René Philombe

(BORN 1930) CAMEROON

René Philombe (Philippe-Louis Ombedé) attended Catholic mission schools before he was admitted to secondary school in Yaoundé, where he first began writing poetry and prose. One of his young history teachers at the high school so radicalized him that Philombe was expelled, and thus his formal education came to an end when he was sixteen years old. But writing and political thought had already become entrenched in his personality.

While working as a secretary for his father, Philombe continued his extensive reading, which included the study of his people's indigenous traditions. By the 1950s, he was actively working for the anti-colonialist movement within Cameroon, including union organizing. While participating in the liberation struggle, he began suffering from the acute pain of a spinal tumor, the effects of which he would suffer the rest of his life. After surgery, Philombe continued his writing during periods of convalescence. In that decade, he also began an active career as a journalist.

Further encounters with the colonial authorities continued, including periods when he was incarcerated. Richard Bjornson, his translator, describes Philombe's repeated altercations with government officials as "reprisals by political authorities who resent his independence of mind." Philombe's harassment did not cease with his country's independence. Like many of his contemporaries across the continent (Chinua Achebe, Ngugi wa Thiong'o, Wole Soyinka), Philombe has always been a spokesperson for social and political injustice. Again in Bjornson's words, Philombe himself is "a man who passionately identifies with the suffering, disinherited, simple people of Africa and just as passionately cries out against oppression, injustice and cruelty. Always implicitly urging his readers to penetrate false masks and to preserve a feeling of what it is to be human. . . .''

Injustice is at the center of "The True Martyr Is Me," which Bjornson describes as a story of the colonial past, "foregrounding the corruption of a sociopolitical system and the effects of that system on human consciousness." More specifically, the story describes life within the *sixa*, "a curious institution invented by Catholic missionaries in French West Africa. Before any woman could receive the sacrament of marriage, she had to spend an indeterminate amount of time in a special compound at the mission. The compound was called a *sixa*, and the ostensible reason for its existence was moral and spiritual instruction, but because the women worked in the fields of the mission, they were sometimes kept there for unreasonably long periods and exploited for their labor."

"The True Martyr Is Me" was first published in *Tales from the Cameroon* (1984), which included the stories from both of René Philombe's collections, *Lettres de ma cambuse (Letters from My Hut)* (1965) and *Histoires queque-de-chat (Cats' Tails Tales)* (1971).

THE TRUE MARTYR IS ME

Translated by Richard Bjornson

The last shades of night had barely lifted in the village of Nsam. A fifty-year-old woman left her hut. Supporting herself on a cane, she walked over to a little neighboring house, planted herself in front of the door, and began to shout: "Edanga . . . ! Edanga . . . ! Get up. Edanga . . . ! You have more than five river crossings to make . . . ! Get up so that you can be on your way . . . !"

Not the slightest sign of life from the interior. The woman approached, and rapping her little cane on the barricaded door, she began again: "Isn't there anyone in this house, then? It seems silent as a grave. Could Edanga have left already without taking anything with him?"

She broke off, having heard the creaking of a rattan bed.

"Aha . . . ! Are you there then, Edanga, still asleep? How many legs do you have, eh? More than five river crossings and with that basket on your head . . . ! Get up, Edanga. Now is the time to be on your way. When traveling by foot, people quickly get tired in the heat of the sun!"

Inside, a voice grumbled disgustedly. Then, with a great creaking of the lock, the door opened, permitting an approximately thirty-year-old man to emerge. His pants had been patched repeatedly, and his shirt was covered with mud splotches. Without looking at the woman, he sank down upon a log: his features were drawn.

"What's wrong, Edanga?" She was worried.

"Where's the basket, Mother?" he muttered, and that was his only reply.

The woman regarded her son for a moment before wending her way back to the hut. When she returned, she was dragging an enormous basket pleated with palm leaves. She deposited it in front of him. Once more she disappeared into the hut and returned with a good-sized rooster and a hamper filled with assorted parcels.

"Go get yesterday's stalk of bananas. I can't carry it. It's too heavy. Don't forget to take the yams as well. These days your wife must be begging, if she wants to stay alive at Mbankolo. It's been many moons since you've been there."

Edanga complied, dragging his heels. He came back and placed the stalk of bananas and the yams in the bottom of the basket. Then he sat down again on the log; he was holding his head between his hands, and his gaze was lost in space. His mother could not understand why he was in such a bad mood. He had always been happy and gay, especially when it was a question of going to Mbankolo. With slow, labored motions she began to arrange the food, all the while sighing; "Here's the package of groundnuts, and here's the cucumber . . . ! Here's the packet of sesame seeds, and here's the one with the spices . . . ! There are also several bunches of onions and a little calabash of palm oil . . . ! In this package, there's some smoked fish; it could crumble into little pieces if you aren't careful how you carry the basket . . . !"

If there had been a witness to this scene, he might well have asked who the woman was talking to. Frozen into a posture of complete detachment, her son had eyes only for the surrounding vegetation, still bathed in the misty shadows of dawn, and he had ears only for the dissonant chorus of frogs, toads, crickets, and birds greeting the sunrise with their carefree songs.

"Good, that's it, Edanga! You can leave now. You can tell your wife that I'll do my best to come see her someday myself."

Edanga's mother had said it with a hint of triumph in her voice, as she finished tying up the basket with banana-tree fibers and carefully placing the good-sized rooster on top.

A moment later, like a slave who intends to obey only his own whims, the young man stood up ponderously. He stretched and ill-humoredly inspected the enormous, food-swollen basket with his eyes, before bending down . . .

"What're you doing, Edanga?" said his mother suddenly, as an idea crossed her mind. "Today is Sunday, and you want to leave for Mbankolo like that? Without washing up? Without changing clothes?"

"You're getting senile, Mother!" scolded the young man angrily. "I know old people of your age who don't talk such nonsense! To get me out of bed so early, when the basket hadn't even been loaded yet?"

Before the dumbfounded eyes of his mother, he tested the weight of the basket, lifted it, and placed it on his head. He was just preparing to get under way when an almost completely bald old fellow shot out of a nearby hut and began to take his turn at scolding: "Who are you so impudently accusing of senility, Edanga? My wife may be old, but yours who is so young and beautiful—where is she? If you were a man worthy of that name, she wouldn't still be imprisoned in the *sixa** after three years . . . ! And all that simply because you can't pass the catechism examinations . . . !"

"Aie-Kai-yai, Father!" cried Edanga with respect and fear. "I didn't insult my mother . . . ! All right, don't tease me about that. I'm going . . . !"

"Yes, go, and be quick about it!" bellowed Edanga's father as he brandished his flyswatter, "My daughter must be dying of hunger at Mbankolo . . . ! Look at his getup! It's that of a convicted criminal! Do people pay visits on their loved ones in such filthy costumes . . . ?"

Swelling in turn with threats and mockery, the paternal voice railed on as the young man disappeared around a turn. He walked along a pebble-strewn road, his head burdened with thoughts of martyrdom beneath the heavy basket of food, on top of which the good-sized rooster intermittently trumpeted a royal cockadoodledoo, as if to accentuate Edanga's torments.

It wasn't the first time that Edanga had gone to the Catholic Mission at Mbankolo. He had gone there many times during the last three years. A twenty-kilometer walk with a heavy load of food on his head eventually became an onerous burden to him. The last time was six months ago. On that day, he'd found the women of the *sixa* in a coffee plantation. Covered with sweat and under the supervision of an elderly catechist, they were clearing the land with blunt machetes dulled by long years of toil. As they worked, their tearful voices intoned this popular lament:

> *Skin and bones,*
> *I've become skin and bones,*
> *Skin and bones like a ripe fruit withering on the vine,*
> *Never having been relished by a loving tongue.*

---

* A compound in French African missions where engaged women received spiritual instruction before marriage.

I toil in the fields of Lord Fada*
I toil for whole moons and whole seasons,
And my spine grows old with it,
Yet Lord Fada *doesn't love me,*
And when I'm told that the race of Fadas
Never long to see a woman's skirt,
I know that I'm toiling in vain,
Toiling for nothing,
Toiling to harvest nothing.
When shall I toil then,
Oh, my mother,
In the fields of one who loves me?

Edanga had slipped behind a bush and made a sign. Having caught a glimpse of him, Angoni had asked permission to go shake his hand and receive her provisions. Immediately, a switch whistled through the air and flattened itself cruelly on Angoni's tender skin. Then a scolding voice: "What conduct! Who deceived you into thinking that you're out here with me to find ways of committing a sin against the sixth commandment, eh? Get back to work, and be quick about it!"

Tears in her eyes, Angoni went back to work. Edanga could not prevent himself from crying at the sight of his fiancée's tears. "Did I pay the bride price for my beautiful Angoni to watch her being mistreated by just any-body?" he asked himself, trembling with rage. Alas, what could he do but chew the cud of his bitterness in silence? No one had ever dared raise a hand against a catechist, even in the country's most unenlightened village. And all the more if he were the catechist in charge of the *sixa*. No one! That would have meant provoking the wrath of the *Fadas*. And God alone knows whether a *Fada* might not be more respected and feared than a white Commandant. People feared the white Commandant because he had brutal guards armed with long sticks that spit lightning. But a *Fada*, think about it . . . ! Not only was he of the same race as the white Commandant; he was also God's representative on earth. Not any old God, but the one who had made white men superior to black men!

Already boiling with a desire for vengeance, Edanga felt his blood turn to ice at these thoughts. Thus, completely crestfallen and defenseless, he

---

* Pidgin corruption of the English "Father."

withdrew from the coffee plantation to go, like everyone else, and wait for his fiancée in the visiting room at the Mission.

The visiting room at the Mission was a plank enclosure that witnessed countless uneasy whisperings, hastily blurted words, and half-formed tears. At four o'clock every day, it became animated with pairs of fiancés. There, separated by a cruel wall which it was forbidden to cross, engaged couples chatted, hardly able to see each other through the peepholes in the wall. And what chats they had . . . ! The old catechist marched ceaselessly back and forth, his ears pricked up like those of a sheep dog. If in all this chirping he overhead a few words he considered obscene, he would cry scandal, separate the offenders, and sometimes even threaten to delay the formal celebration of their marriage. For that reason, each couple continued to speak softly, like saints—that is, without prattling about love or exchanging amorous smiles. The women adopted a more reserved attitude. In their faces one could not see the passion which renders the world's ugliest fiancée beautiful in the presence of her beloved. Their eyes were fixed in glassy stares, like those of elderly widows who no longer expect anything from life. What sorts of pleasantries can two fiancés exchange in front of interlopers? All of a sudden, an enormous bell was tolling loud enough to split your eardrums, calling all the occupants of the *sixa* to evening prayers. And as each guest withdrew from the cursed visiting room, his heart was consumed with a throbbing grief.

On his return journey, after this mockery of a conversation, Edanga must have astonished anyone who saw him pass. Every once in a while, he'd stop abruptly in the middle of the road, brandishing an angry fist in empty space, shaking his head, clapping his hands, or simply raising three fingers into the air and shouting, "That's the last time!"

He had sworn never again to set foot at Mbankolo with a heavy basket of food on his head only to return alone, tormented by grief and far from his beautiful Angoni. Three years his heart had been bleeding in an endless wait for her whom he had chosen as his life's companion. Three years . . .! Night and day, the image of Angoni haunted him, invaded him in the form of a melancholy obsession. He had a wife, but he was vegetating in celibacy. He might have understood if Angoni had rejected his marriage proposal. He might have understood if, for one reason or another, Angoni had been held back by her parents. But that his beloved should remain imprisoned for more than three years in the *sixa*! He racked his brain to understand it and to find some justification for it. He recited his catechism like a parrot, but it was

all in vain, for never after any of the numerous examinations did his name
appear on the list of successful candidates! Yet the dowry had been paid in
full. Moreover, after the negotiations which accompany any engagement,
Angoni had in fact been handed over to him. However, she was not destined
to live with him at Nsam for more than three months.

Yes, three months; that is to say, until that day when the priest of Mbankolo,
who was on tour, arrived with a great deal of fanfare. In front of the entire
assembled population of Nsam, the missionary became red-faced with anger
as he began to rail against the old man, Edanga's father: "What a scandal
to let your child live in a state of mortal sin with his fiancée! You have but
a short time left to live on this earth, and yet you are doing everything you
can to earn a passage to hell! Do you know that all those sins your son is
committing against the sixth commandment redound upon your soul? Do
you know that?"

"Yes, *Fada*, I know it!" Edanga's elderly father muttered, trembling with
fright.

He had trembled with fright to see a vision of himself in the other world,
being fed into that immense furnace where all those who failed to toe the
line in this world would burn forever and ever, according to the decrees of
the Holy Roman Church . . .

That day had been a day of mourning for the two fiancés. His eyes swollen
with masculine tears and his body dripping with sweat, Edanga had thought
he would go mad with grief! He felt an invisible dagger bite into his heart.
But when he was somewhat cured of his mental sufferings, he had resolved
to learn the catechism by heart in order to regain his beautiful Angoni, who
had been carried off to the *sixa* by the priest of Mbankolo . . .

Turning over in his head the troubled past, Edanga asked himself as he
was walking, "What is it exactly that they teach those women in the *sixa*?
What more than a few scraps of catechism, while making them work like
beasts of burden! Besides, the worst of it is that a certain number of them
wake up one fine morning to find their stomachs bulging with the fruits of
adulteries that go unpunished . . . !" His legs no longer belonged to him.
They moved forward, stumbling more and more frequently. Each time they
knocked against a stone, he cried out, "And there you have it! Even the
stones in the highway have sometimes had enough of being stepped on by
those who pass by!" And he told himself that he, too, had enough of groan-
ing beneath the cruel regulations of those people at Mbankolo.

Without having noticed either the weight of the heavy basket or the distance traveled, the young man suddenly recognized the Catholic Mission perched on the summit of a hill, there with its church, its plantations, its *sixa*, and its mysteries . . . He plunged down a narrow path. When he arrived at the marketplace, he set down his burden in an unoccupied corner and hastened to unwrap it. Then, having arranged all the produce in front of him, he lost no time in selling it all at half price. With the profits from this discount sale in his pocket, he fled into a nearby bar, where he ordered a liter of red wine. Soon it seemed to him as if his blood was circulating with a vigor and a courage unknown to him since the day of his birth. It was in this singular state of well-being that he ascended the hill and walked toward the church, which was already buzzing with pious voices.

He sat down on a pile of adobe bricks in the main courtyard. From time to time he got up and craned his neck, keeping his eyes fixed upon the visiting room. Once in a while, in front of the horrified and shocked eyes of the faithful, whose late arrival had obliged them to follow the Mass from outside, he made a great show of urinating next to the Holy House of God. Then again he could be heard grumbling and waxing indignant over a Mass that kept dragging on. Finally, to his great satisfaction, the church doors opened, discharging a flood of people into the surrounding area. Suddenly he got up. Running at full speed, he dashed toward the visiting room, climbed the plank wall like a madman, and suddenly found himself in the forbidden enclosure. His heart was beating as if to break open his chest. He waited . . . Several minutes later, the nuns passed in front of him; they remained silent but were obviously astonished to see a person of the male sex in a cloister reserved for women. Then an endless line of fiancées flowed in. Edanga's eyes appeared to be popping out of his head as they rested first on one face and then on another . . . All of a sudden, cries of amazement echoed in the sky, and a stampede broke out among the women. Edanga had sprung forward to grab one of them by the arm. And before they could regain their composure he had dragged her toward the visiting room and smashed the plank wall to pieces with a single powerful kick, and now there he was outside the enclosure with his beautiful and charming Angoni.

"From this day, on," he barked, "you will no longer sleep here, far away from me! You will no longer sleep here in this slave camp invented by colonialist missionaries! You are my wife, and you must stay with me at Nsam!"

Edanga never stopped barking, while Angoni, who was caught fast by the

arm, advanced in self-defense. She trembled, shouted, cried, called for help
. . . It wasn't that she no longer loved her fiancé. But the abduction seemed
so strange to her, so scandalous, that she couldn't prevent herself from
trembling, shouting, crying, and calling for help.

While all this was taking place, the elderly catechist who was in charge
of the *sixa* came running. He seized the young woman by the other arm.
Then, during a quarter hour of universal merriment, there ensued a tug-of-
war in which the beautiful Angoni fell, first to one side and then to the
other, while her heartrending screams pierced the air.

For an instant, Edanga stopped pulling and shouted at the catechist,
"What do you think you're getting mixed up in, eh?"

He released his hold on Angoni and fell upon the old man, thrashing him
soundly and throwing him on the ground, to the accompaniment of peals of
laughter. All the young men regarded Edanga with admiration. To them, he
was a liberator of all the women in the *sixa*. "What cruelty to deprive men
of their wives for years! What injustice . . . !" they yelled on every side.
Only the other catechists took it into their heads to champion the cause of
their senior, who looked as if he had just been dragged from a flour sack.
But they entered the fray at their own peril. Beneath the weight of irresistible
blows of the fist, each of them suffered an identical fate.

Suddenly the peals of laughter ceased. All eyes were riveted on a white
silhouette emerging from somewhere down there and clearing its way
through the crowd. It advanced with long loping strides, as the sleeves of
its cassock were being rolled up. It was the priest of Mbankolo. This missionary was about forty years old, and he had the reputation of being a
regular Goliath. This was largely because he never hesitated to use the white
man's pugilistic arts to silence the most boisterous mouths in his parish.
That's what earned him the nickname *Fada Boxer*. He grabbed Edanga by the
collar of his shirt; then, after having shaken him violently as if he were
nothing more than a garden snake, the priest dealt him such a powerful blow
that, once released, Edanga tottered for an instant and fell flat on his face.
Edanga had just found his master! He lay there in a disconcerting immobility;
everyone believed he had fainted. But all of a sudden he was on his feet,
towering to the full height of his man's body. He raised his two hands to
his face, pressed his tear-filled eyes, and then ripped off his shirt.

"I want my wife!" he began to shout at the top of his lungs. "Nothing
more than my wife Angoni, for whom I have paid the bride price in front
of witnesses . . ."

Seated on the ground, Angoni sobbed mutely but incessantly. Edanga saw her and ran in her direction. But just as he was taking hold of her arm again, the boxer priest overpowered him and covered him with a shower of blows. Edanga released his hold on Angoni. Drawing himself up, he saw a large red face. He shouted an oath of war. He advanced toward the missionary. He circled his adversary, while patting one of his pockets from time to time. Then he suddenly plunged his right hand into it. When he raised his fist, a metallic glitter rose with it and inscribed a semicircular arc in space before disappearing into the folds of the cassock. It was in vain that the boxer priest tried to subdue the young man's arm, which moved mysteriously, frenetically in a back-and-forth motion. They watched the boxer priest weave about on his sturdy legs and, with one hand resting on his stomach, collapse onto the ground as a long-drawn-out moan issued from his lips. A thunderous chorus of exclamations resounded, almost loud enough to make the church walls come tumbling down. The panic-stricken spectators had stopped laughing. Like sheep unexpectedly overtaken by a windstorm, they ran in every direction, continually jostling against each other.

"He killed him! He killed him!"

"Tell somebody to notify the white Commandant . . . ! Arrest him! Arrest him . . . !" they were yelling in every corner of the courtyard.

But no one dared arrest Edanga. He was no longer a man, but a wild animal foaming at the mouth and spitting blood—a wild animal leaping about and running in all directions at once as he brandished a bloodstained dagger in the blinding midday sun.

"Today will be the last day for anyone who comes near me!" he shouted from the depths of his rage-congested lungs. "Where is Angoni, my beautiful Angoni, for whom I have paid the bride price in front of witnesses?"

Angoni had disappeared. Like all the women of the *sixa*, she had fled, trembling in horror, to find a secure hiding place.

Half an hour later, an automobile arrived like a whirlwind, trailing a halo of dust in its wake. As it screeched to a halt beside the motionless body that lay on the ground, it made a war-like sound. The white Commandant and his guards emerged. Before they could even ask who had committed the crime, accusing fingers were already pointing at Edanga, who alone remained at the scene: increasingly distant voices competed with each other to proclaim: "There he is! There he is!"

A swarm of hands seized hold of Edanga. Then, handcuffed and beneath a hail of punches, whiplashes, and blows from wooden clubs . . .

"I only wanted my wife, my wife Angoni, for whom I paid the bride price in front of witnesses—my wife who has been held prisoner for the past three years . . . ! And everyone saw how the *Fada* hit me first . . . ! Look at my bloody mouth! All that because I wanted my wife Angoni, my wife for whom I paid the bride price in front of witnesses."

The young man was shouting at the top of his lungs and crying; he could be heard calling out to several young people in the crowd, inviting them to testify against the boxer priest! But no one dared come forward. They all moved away and prudently ducked behind their neighbors, admonishing him: "Keep us out of your affair!"

"Don't do anything to him, Commandant!" exhorted the priest, playing out his mournful role, "I . . . am . . . dying . . . a martyr . . . !"

Several minutes later, the automobile drove away. It was carrying Edanga, who, though trussed up like a giant human sausage, continued to howl incessantly, "The true martyr is me! The true martyr is me . . . !"

—1984

Tijan M. Sallah

(BORN 1958) GAMBIA

Tijan M. Sallah's versatility as a writer has never been in question: poet, writer of fiction, editor—if these weren't enough, he has also written more than his share of official reports for the World Bank in Washington, D.C., where he currently works. The Gambian writer's books include *When Africa Was a Young Woman* (1980), *Kora Land* (1989), and *Dreams of Dusty Roads* (1993), his collections of poetry; *Before the New Earth* (1988), short stories; *Wolof* (1996), for The Heritage Library of African Peoples; *New Poets of West Africa* (1995), edited by him; as well as his work in progress, *Heart of Light*, a biography of Chinua Achebe. Oona Strathern, in *Africa: Traveller's Literary Companion*, remarks: "[Sallah] is noted in much of his work not only for his observation of the corruption of the motherland itself, but more unusually for his sensitivity to women's suffering."

Sallah was born in Sere Kunda, Gambia, in 1958. After attending local schools as a child, he came to the United States, where he earned a B.A. at Berea College and later a Ph.D. in economics at Virginia Polytechnic Institute. Before joining the World Bank as an economist, he taught in several American universities.

In one of the poems in *When Africa Was a Young Woman*, Sallah proclaims: "Tarzan never lived in my Africa"; and in "On Culture and Development," from *Dreams of Dusty Roads*, he says:

Food production is based on culture;
So is town-planning and architecture.
So is textile and other manufacture.
So is management of time and space, culture.

For without culture
Does development not despair?

Without culture,
Do we not all despair?

Somewhere in between these two quotations lies the domain of much of Sallah's short fiction.

Of "Innocent Terror," he states: "The story was inspired by a slice of Gambian reality: the government's favoritism, the preferential treatment toward the Lebanese community in the Gambia. I see the Lebanese immigrants as a source of new energy, dynamism, and enormous learning. They bring with them their mini-cultures, grafting them on foreign stems, creating hybridized beauties. In West Africa, the Lebanese have been a great source of entrepreneurial dynamism and cultural enrichment.

"But they also have had an inordinate share in public corruption, particularly in countries like Sierra Leone and, of course, the Gambia, where the Lebanese have helped disproportionally to subvert the prevailing system of law and order. In my view, Lebanese immigrants should be treated no differently from natives, and should abide by the established norms of their receiving society. They carry their accumulated memories, geographies, pride and prejudices, and we should welcome them. But we should also insist that the Lebanese immigrants be good ambassadors, not vessels of criminality.

"The Wolof saying puts it well: 'A visitor should never untie the goat of his host.' "

INNOCENT TERROR

It was one of those incidents that we saw in cowboys-and-Indians movies. Or frontiersmen of the wild American West. But it happened in our territory. It was unfortunate. Even sad. But it was one of those terrible events that arrest the long festival of innocence. Yeats would have understood it, for he wrote about it in his poetry. Out of it, a terrible beauty. A terrible beauty is born. And the ceremony of innocence is drowned.

He pulled the trigger on a cook and the rest was cold-blooded history. And it was an innocent cook. He pulled the trigger to retrieve a primitive thirst. The thirst for hunting which the city could not avail him. He had decided that in the absence of four-legged creatures, a two-legged one would suffice as game. The act, of course, was tainted with supercilious innocence. He did not load the gun. He just did the trigger-pulling. But could he be excused for pointing the mouth of even an empty gun at a cook? The reality was that the killing of the cook was monstrous. It happened in open daylight. As the fidgety finches sang in the mangoes. As the customers crowded the counter of his father's store.

His father was notoriously rich. And gold afforded the son the luxury of killing. Perhaps killing for the hell of it. Gold, that yellowish necessary devil. And how it can make inadequates into gods. Gold, King Midas died from it. Solomon did not plead for it; wise Solomon, he chose the path of sagacity. Gold, that god that can lure away reason and bribe emotions onto the path of tantrums. Gold, especially effortless gold, the genie that can elevate amateur hunters onto the stage of life so that they can treat bloody life as a pantomine. O gold, madness in the lunch basket, the sexy maiden under the periwinkle sky, beautiful in expanding the range of options but gaudy for circling the rich with myopia. And how they may not see beyond their noses, and how they may eat in the restaurant of human anguish and, at nightfall, count their coins with wine and Bach, cheering with senseless delight.

The air smelled of blood, the corpse lying in a corner of the kitchen. Flies partook of their share in the primal visit, feasting and exploring the dripping saliva from the corner of the mouth, leaping on the contours of the resigned face. Sometimes they would leap onto the kitchen table, then bounce back on the face, or just glide around the upper air of the body as if targeting some favored spot. The young man gazed at the corpse and mourned in his heart. He felt bereft. A bereavement mixing self-pity with remorse. He pondered about his family's reactions and the potential repercussions.

Two days after the incident, the newspapers ran front-page articles about it. Titles flamboyantly captured the tragedy with blinking flames. The popular *Outlook* ran a front-page feature titled "Kololian Cook Terrorized by Lebanese Youth." People who saw the title initially thought that Middle Eastern terrorism had found fresh ground, and so the title triggered immediate and enormous interest. One street commentator, a university graduate, upon seeing the feature's title hastily ran his mouth the way a child babbles verbal diarrhea. "These Arabs and Israelis," he asserted, "they have ruined their countries with violence. And now they export their anguish . . . They visit the morning of our land with their terror." A passing bank officer shrugged his head and shoulders in disapproval of the statement. But all over, the talk of the town was the dead cook and the untutored youth.

The death of a cook became one of those events that muster everyone's curiosity. If it was the shooting of a public figure, nobody would have cared. That was something to be expected. But a cook. A simple and humble cook. Unfeigning and innocent. How could ignorance have led to such cruel sport? A plain cook so draped with sweet everydayness that everyone would have wanted to pick these qualities and swallow. *Chei!** How could such innocent terror have evaded the responsibilities of a mutually human-regarding society?

A few days later, the Head of State had come over the National Radio and expressed his grief. Small indeed was beautiful. And everybody knew that.

* Wolof exclamation used in storytelling to express pity.

For where in the world would the Head of State express his sorrow publicly over the shooting of a cook? All over the world, children have died of napalm. Sometimes even from the napalm of starvation. But who gives a damn? All over, priests have been shot, their efforts frustrated and their convictions nullified. Innocent women and children kidnapped, terrorized, and thrown into the careless trash bins of the streets. So why would a Head of State express his grief over the shooting of a cook in a world accustomed to treachery, murder, and blood? *Chei!* Only in Kololi could that happen.

The Tambedou family had mourned for days. For them, the Head of State's gesture was at best one of public relations. Beyond that, it was empty. The Head of State was on the side of the merchants and therefore of the Lebanese. He had manured the ground for their success and given them the lantern light for their abuse of every norm of acceptable behavior. The catalogue of Lebanese misbehavior was lengthy—from receiving most-favored treatment from the banks and from all respectable government institutions to the rude flouting of local customs to sometimes engaging in incest and drugs. They picked the leanest meat from the markets and arrogantly displayed their wealth with unrefined alacrity. And as in Kololi, so was it all over the region.

"These Lebanese," remarked Badou, the younger Tambedou, "they think they own Africa. I heard that in Sierra Leone they run the state."

"I am not surprised," commented a friend.

"I even heard of one of them . . . a powerful one . . . in Sierra Leone, who had his private plane, private airport, and private bank."

"And I'm sure private army!"

They chuckled in a cynical laughter. Their faces locked in silent agreement.

"They run states within our states," continued the younger Tambedou. "In Sierra Leone, that rich Lebanese is so powerful that he tells the Head of State what to do. And so when the Lebanese speaks, everyone, including the boss of the government, listens."

"But how can our countries function like that?"

"You tell me, I swear to God."

A silent pause. A moment of meditative thought-gathering. A strange glow of helplessness glimmered on their faces. Helplessness like someone with a thirst to quench, in the middle of a desert: the desert of human anguish.

"How can our society allow this? For my father to vanish like the flame of a matchstick?"

"This is grab-bag independence, you know. The gold diggers receive soft strokes from the state."

"No matter for human blood spilled?"

"No matter. Human nature is like a prostitute here. It can sleep with whoever pays for the bed."

The cook had been buried. The burial, a protest ritual. It could have happened to any private Kololian, it seemed. The oscillations of arrogance supported by the pillars with pearls could not match the angelic force of a people bent to assert their essence in the ceremonial catharsis of a society of hydra-headed leaders and gold-worshipping back scratchers. All works of life came, exuded their support, washed their grief in the festival of the affirmation of life.

Weeks after the burial, the younger Tambedou filed a suit against Fouad Aziz. The storms gathered their force as Fouad's father hired one of the best lawyers in Kololi to defend his son. The younger Tambedou had no money, and therefore was up for a scorpion fight. He had decided to fight for a New Earth and did not care about the repercussions. Hurricanes may strike, he thought to himself. Even hack the branches to which soothsayers cling. But the vision of the New Earth is more noble than the fears of the moment.

The trial was held at Bul Falleh* Courthouse. Bul Falleh used to be called Borom Hallis.† But after independence, the Kololian officials changed the name, for reasons of not being too explicit about the hidden agenda of the court. The courthouse was packed like a sports stadium or a street *sabarr*.‡ The walls of the court appeared garish, combining whitewash with peeling blue paint and suspended cobwebs. The buzz word for the ill appearance of the courts was "austerity." The judge sat behind a huge and brightly polished wooden structure. On his left was a witness box, in which the plaintiff and the defendant presented their cases. The court audience listened attentively and gave a loud applause when Fouad's defense lawyer bamboozled the judge in a fit of eloquent and persuasive argument, invoking specific passages from ihe Kololian constitution.

The accused denied his guilt, contending that the killing was an accident.

---

* In Wolof, Bul Falleh means "Don't Care," a pun, in the context of the story.
† In Wolof, Borom Hallis means "A Person with Money," a pun also.
‡ Street drumming (and dancing).

"But why would you point a weapon, of all things a gun that is loaded, at an innocent human being?"

"It was an accident, your honor."

"An accident? Pointing a live weapon at a living person?"

"Yes, your honor. You know . . ."

"I know what? Answer my question!"

"You know . . . the gun is often locked in my father's safe. It was the late Koto Tambedou who unlocked it and let me have it."

"He is lying!" the young Tambedou interrupted. Then he was hushed by the judge and admonished to order.

"Continue your testimony," the judge commanded.

"Well, that's all I have to say, your honor."

In the interim, Fouad's lawyer stood up and made a case for the latter's innocence.

"Your honor, you can see from my client's testimony that there was no willful intention to kill. My client was a victim of the late cook's negligence. By deliberately opening a regularly locked safe and releasing a loaded gun to this inexperienced young man, he willfully assumed some risks. I contend that the young man be exonerated from the criminal accusations."

There was silence in the court. The younger Tambedou stared fiercely into the eyes of the Aziz family. His heart pounded faster as he waited for the judge to return with a decision. The court audience was split in their loyalties. The half that sided with the younger Tambedou waited with bated breath for the spinning coin to turn in their favor. But they had not known about the plaintiff's father unlocking a safe. This point added ambiguity to a case that his admirers reasonably thought was a foregone conclusion.

The judge returned and declared Fouad acquitted. He praised Fouad for his conduct in the court, which he labeled with such adjectives as "orderly and well-mannered" and "somebody predisposed to exercise reasonable care." Fouad's entourage of supporters stood up and hugged each other in a fit of merriment immediately as the judge finished his last word. The younger Tambedou received handshakes of encouragement from his supporters, some of whom stared bitterly at the grizzled mustache of Fouad's father. The younger Tambedou himself shifted his eyes around and flashed them on the dictatorial face of the judge. He swallowed his saliva in optimism and walked gracefully out of the courtroom.

—1988

Ken Saro-Wiwa

(1941–95) NIGERIA

Shortly before his execution by hanging on November 10, 1995, Ken Saro-Wiwa wrote: "Literature in a critical situation such as Nigeria's cannot be divorced from politics. Indeed, literature must serve society by steeping itself in politics, by intervention, and writers must not merely write to amuse or to take a bemused, critical look at society. They must play an interventionist role . . . The writer must be *l'homme engagé*: the intellectual man of action." Saro-Wiwa did not realize that these words would be his obituary.

Saro-Wiwa's execution by Nigerian authorities was swift and brutal, a travesty of human rights and a failure of international diplomacy. Writers rarely go gentle into that good night, but Saro-Wiwa's murder will certainly go down in the record as despicable. The inexperienced hangman brought in for the occasion attempted to hang the poor man five times before he succeeded. Saro-Wiwa had spent the previous two years being moved from prison to prison by Nigerian authorities because of his outspoken defense of his people, the Ogonis, and for protesting against the ecological destruction of their homelands by the international oil cartels, most notably Shell Oil.

Before his death, Saro-Wiwa was one of the most popular Nigerian literary figures of recent times. He had been a newspaper columnist for many years, and also published his own creative works, including books written for the primary-school market. Novels, poems, and plays—he excelled in all these forms, though his most famous novel, *Sozaboy* (1985), was not available in a Western edition until 1994. His enormous popularity in Nigeria, however, was largely the result of his immensely successful soap opera, *Basi & Co.*, which ran on Nigerian TV from 1985 to 1990. Saro-Wiwa wrote 150 episodes for the series.

Before he became a writer, Saro-Wiwa was a schoolteacher and a businessman in his family's grocery business. These endeavors occupied him during most of the 1970s, but the event that radicalized him and led him to take up the Ogoni cause occurred in the 1960s, when Nigeria cracked apart during the Civil War, or the Biafran War, as it is also called. At the outbreak of the fighting, Saro-Wiwa found himself in the wrong place, in Ibo secessionist territory. His sympathies, however, were with the Nigerian government, because he feared that oil-rich Ogoniland had become a political football. (By 1980, only 1.5 percent of the oil proceeds found their way back to the Ogonis. Most of the profits were siphoned off into the pockets of the country's military leaders. The Ogonis had "no representation whatsoever in all institutions of the Federal government of Nigeria," no electricity, no pipeborne water.)

Sozaboy was carved out of the author's experiences and observations during the Civil War. William Boyd has called the book "a great anti-war novel— among the very best of the twentieth century." The novel's unforgettable opening sentence fragment dangles in the air, holding the reader breathless and begging for more: "Although, everybody in Dukana was happy at first."

In his posthumously published volume, *A Month and a Day: A Detention Diary* (1996), Saro-Wiwa recorded many of the events of the last year and a half of his life, though he did not describe his final imprisonment. Of the plight of his Ogoni people he wrote: "The silence of Nigeria's social reformers, writers and legal men over this issue is deafening. Therefore, the affected peoples must immediately gird their loins and demand without equivocation their rightful patrimony. They must not be frightened by the enormity of the task, by the immorality of the present. History and world opinion are on their side."

AFRICA KILLS HER SUN

Dear Zole,

You'll be surprised, no doubt, to receive this letter. But I couldn't leave your beautiful world without saying goodbye to you who are condemned to live in it. I know that some might consider my gesture somewhat pathetic, as my colleagues, Sazan and Jimba, do, our finest moments having been achieved two or three weeks ago. However, for me, this letter is a celebration, a final act of love, a quality which, in spite of my career, in spite of tomorrow morning, I do possess in abundance, and cherish. For I've always treasured the many moments of pleasure we spent together in our youth when the world was new and fishes flew in golden ponds. In the love we then shared have I found happiness, a true resting place, a shelter from the many storms that have buffeted my brief life. Whenever I've been most alone, whenever I've been torn by conflict and pain, I've turned to that love for the resolution which has sustained and seen me through. This may surprise you, considering that this love was never consummated and that you may possibly have forgotten me, not having seen me these ten years gone. I still remember you, have always remembered you, and it's logical that on the night before tomorrow, I should write you to ask a small favor of you. But more important, the knowledge that I have unburdened myself to you will make tomorrow morning's event as pleasant and desirable to me as to the thousands of spectators who will witness it.

I know this will get to you because the prison guard's been heavily bribed to deliver it. He should rightly be with us before the firing squad tomorrow. But he's condemned, like most others, to live, to play out his assigned role in your hell of a world. I see him burning out his dull, uncomprehending life, doing his menial job for a pittance and a bribe for the next so many years. I pity his ignorance and cannot envy his complacency. Tomorrow morning, with this letter and our bribe in his pocket, he'll call us out, Sazan, Jimba and I. As usual, he'll have all our names mixed up: he always calls Sazan "Sajim" and Jimba "Samba." But that won't matter. We'll obey him, and as we walk to our death, we'll laugh at his gaucherie, his plain stupidity. As we laughed at that other thief, the High Court Judge.

You must've seen that in the papers too. We saw it, thanks to our bribe-taking friend, the prison guard, who sent us a copy of the newspaper in which it was reported. Were it not in an unfeeling nation, among a people inured to evil and taking sadistic pleasure in the loss of life, some questions might have been asked. No doubt, many will ask the questions, but they will do it in the safety and comfort of their homes, over the interminable bottles of beer, uncomprehendingly watching their boring, cheap television programs, the rejects of Europe and America, imported to fill their vacuity. They will salve their conscience with more bottles of beer, wash the answers down their gullets and pass question, conscience and answer out as waste into their open sewers choking with concentrated filth and murk. And they will forget.

I bet, though, the High Court Judge himself will never forget. He must remember it the rest of his life. Because I watched him closely that first morning. And I can't describe the shock and disbelief which I saw registered on his face. His spectacles fell to his table and it was with difficulty he regained composure. It must have been the first time in all his experience that he found persons arraigned on a charge for which the punishment upon conviction is death, entering a plea of guilty and demanding that they be sentenced and shot without further delay.

Sazan, Jimba and I had rehearsed it carefully. During the months we'd been remanded in prison custody while the prosecutors prepared their case, we'd agreed we weren't going to allow a long trial, or any possibility that they might impose differing sentences upon us: freeing one, sentencing another to life imprisonment and the third to death by firing squad.

Nor did we want to give the lawyers in their funny black funeral robes an opportunity to clown around, making arguments for pleasure, engaging in worthless casuistry. No. We voted for death. After all, we were armed robbers, bandits. We knew it. We didn't want to give the law a chance to prove itself the proverbial ass. We were being honest to ourselves, to our vocation, to our country and to mankind.

"Sentence us to death immediately and send us before the firing squad without further delay," we yelled in unison. The Judge, after he had recovered from his initial shock, asked us to be taken away that day, "for disturbing my court." I suppose he wanted to see if we'd sleep things over and change our plea. We didn't. When they brought us back the next day, we said the same thing in louder voice. We said we had robbed and killed. We were guilty. Cool. The Judge was bound hand and foot and did what he had to. We'd forced him to be honest to his vocation, to the laws of the country and to the course of justice. It was no mean achievement. The court hall was stunned; our guards were utterly amazed as we walked out of court, smiling. "Hardened criminals." "Bandits," I heard them say as we trooped out of the court. One spectator actually spat at us as we walked into the waiting Black Maria!

And now that I've confessed to banditry, you'll ask why I did it. I'll answer that question by retelling the story of the young, beautiful prostitute I met in St. Pauli in Hamburg when our ship berthed there years back. I've told my friends the story several times. I did ask her, after the event, why she was in that place. She replied that some girls chose to be secretaries in offices, others to be nurses. She had chosen prostitution as a career. Cool. I was struck by her candor. And she set me thinking. Was I in the Merchant Navy by choice or because it was the first job that presented itself to me when I left school? When we returned home, I skipped ship, thanks to the prostitute of St. Pauli, and took a situation as a clerk in the Ministry of Defense.

It was there I came face-to-face with the open looting of the national treasury, the manner of which I cannot describe without arousing in myself the deepest, basest emotions. Everyone was busy at it and there was no one to complain to. Everyone to whom I complained said to me: "If you can't beat them, join them." I was not about to join anyone; I wanted to beat them and took it upon myself to wage a war against them. In no time they had gotten rid of me. Dismissed me. I had no option but to join them then. I had to make a choice. I became an armed robber, a bandit. It was my choice, my answer. And I don't regret it.

Did I know it was dangerous? Some girls are secretaries, others choose to be prostitutes. Some men choose to be soldiers and policemen, others doctors and lawyers; I chose to be a robber. Every occupation has its hazards. A taxi driver may meet his death on the road; a businessman may die in an air crash; a robber dies before a firing squad. It's no big deal. If you ask me, the death I've chosen is possibly more dramatic, more qualitative, more eloquent than dying in bed of a ruptured liver from overindulgence in alcohol. Yes? But robbery is antisocial, you say? A proven determination to break the law. I don't want to provide an alibi. But just you think of the many men and women who are busy breaking or bending the law in all coasts and climes. Look for a copy of *The Guardian* of 19th September. That is the edition in which our plea to the Judge was reported. You'll find there the story of the Government official who stole over seven million naira. Seven million. Cool. He was antisocial, right? How many of his type do you know? And how many more go undetected? I say, if my avocation was antisocial, I'm in good company. And that company consists of Presidents of countries, transnational organizations, public servants high and low, men and women. The only difference is that while I'm prepared to pay the price for it all, the others are not. See?

I'm not asking for your understanding or sympathy. I need neither, not now nor hereafter. I'm saying it as it is. Right? Cool. I expect you'll say that armed robbery should be the special preserve of the scum of society. That no man of my education has any business being a bandit. To that I'll answer that it's about time well-endowed and well-trained people took to it. They'll bring to the profession a romantic quality, a proficiency which will ultimately conduce to the benefit of society. No, I'm not mad. Truly. Time was when the running and ruining of African nations was in the hands of half-literate politicians. Today, well-endowed and better-trained people have taken over the task. And look how well they're doing it. So that even upon that score, my conscience sleeps easy. Understand?

Talking about sleep, you should see Sazan and Jimba on the cold, hard prison floor, snoring away as if life itself depends on a good snore. It's impossible, seeing them this way, to believe that they'll be facing the firing squad tomorrow. They're men of courage. Worthy lieutenants. It's a pity their abilities will be lost to society forever, come tomorrow morning. Sazan would have made a good Army General any day, possibly a President of our country in the mold of Idi Amin or Bokassa. The Europeans and Americans would have found in him a useful ally in the progressive degradation of Africa. Jimba'd have made an excellent Inspector-General of Police, so versed is he in the ways of the Police! You know, of course, that Sazan is a dismissed Sergeant of our nation's proud army. And Jimba was once a Corporal in the Police Force. When we met, we had similar reasons for pooling our talents. And a great team we did make. Now here we all are in the death cell of a maximum security prison and they snoring away the last hours of their lives on the cold, smelly floor. It's exhilarating to find them so disdainful of life. Their style is the stuff of which history is made. In another time and in another country, they'd be Sir Francis Drake, Cortés or Sir Walter Raleigh. They'd have made empires and earned national honors. But here, our life is one big disaster, an endless tragedy. Heroism is not in our star. We are millipedes crawling on the floor of a dank, wet forest. So Sazan and Jimba will die unsung. See?

One thing, though. We swore never to kill. And we never did. Indeed, we didn't take part in the particular "operation" for which we were held, Sazan, Jimba and I. That operation would've gone quite well if the Superintendent of Police had fulfilled his part of the bargain. Because he was in it with us. The Police are involved in every single robbery that happens. They know the entire gang, the gangs. We'd not succeed if we didn't collaborate with them. Sazan, Jimba and I were the bosses. We didn't go out on "operations." The boys normally did. And they were out on that occasion. The Superintendent of Police was supposed to keep away the police escorts from the vehicle carrying workers' salaries that day. For some reason, he failed to do so. And the policeman shot at our boys. The boys responded and shot and killed him and the Security Company guards. The boys got the money all right. But the killing was contrary to our agreement with the Police. We had to pay. The Police won't stand for any of their men being killed. They took all the money from us and then they went after the boys. We said no. The boys had acted on orders. We volunteered to take their place. The Police took us in and made a lot of public noises about it. The boys, I know, will make their decisions later. I don't know what will happen to the Superintendent of Police. But he'll have to look to himself. So, if that is any comfort to you, you may rest in the knowledge that I spilt no blood. No, I wouldn't. Nor have I kept the loot. Somehow, whatever we took from people—the rich ones—always was shared by the gang, who were almost always on the bread line. Sazan, Jimba and I are not wealthy.

Many will therefore accuse us of recklessness, or of being careless with our lives. And well they might. I think I speak for my sleeping comrades when I say we went into our career because we didn't see any basic difference between what we were doing and what most others are doing throughout the land today. In every facet of our lives—in politics, in commerce and in the professions—robbery is the base line. And it's been so from time. In the early days, our forebears sold their kinsmen into slavery for minor items such as beads, mirrors, alcohol and tobacco. These days, the tune is the same, only the articles have changed into cars, transistor radios and bank accounts. Nothing else has changed, and nothing will change in the foreseeable future. But that's the problem of those of you who will live beyond tomorrow, Zole.

The cock crows now and I know dawn is about to break. I'm not speaking figuratively. In the cell here, the darkness is still all-pervasive, except for the flickering light of the candle by which I write. Sazan and Jimba remain fast asleep. So is the prison guard. He sleeps all night and is no trouble to us. We could, if we wanted, escape from here, so lax are the guards. But we consider that unnecessary, as what is going to happen later this morning is welcome relief from burdens too heavy to bear. It's the guard and you the living who are in prison, the ultimate prison from which you cannot escape because you do not know that you are incarcerated. Your happiness is the happiness of ignorance and your ignorance is it that keeps you in the prison, which is your life. As this night dissolves into day, Sazan, Jimba and I shall be free. Sazan and Jimba will have left nothing behind. I shall leave at least this letter, which, please, keep for posterity.

Zole, do I rant? Do I pour out myself to you in bitter tones? Do not lay it to the fact that I'm about to be shot by firing squad. On second thoughts, you could, you know. After all, seeing death so clearly before me might possibly have made me more perspicacious? And yet I've always seen these things clearly in my mind's eye. I never did speak about them, never discussed them. I preferred to let them weigh me down. See?

So, then, in a few hours we shall be called out. We shall clamber with others into the miserable lorry which they still call the Black Maria. Notice how everything miserable is associated with us. Black Sheep. Black Maria. Black Death. Black Leg. The Black Hole of Calcutta. The Black Maria will take us to the Beach or to the Stadium. I bet it will be the Stadium. I'd prefer the Beach. So at least to see the ocean once more. For I've still this fond regard for the sea which dates from my time in the Merchant Navy. I love its wide expanse, its anonymity, its strength, its unfathomable depth. And maybe after shooting us, they might decide to throw our bodies into the ocean. We'd then be eaten up by sharks which would in turn be caught by Japanese and Russian fishermen, be refrigerated, packaged in cartons and sold to Indian merchants and then for a handsome profit to our people. That way, I'd have helped keep people alive a bit longer. But they won't do us that favor. I'm sure they'll take us to the Stadium. To provide a true spectacle for the fun-loving unemployed. To keep them out of trouble. To keep them from thinking. To keep them laughing. And dancing.

We'll be there in the dirty clothes which we now wear. We've not had any of our things washed this past month. They will tie us to the stakes, as though that were necessary. For even if we were minded to escape, where'd we run to? I expect they'll also want to blindfold us. Sazan and Jimba have said they'll not allow themselves to be blindfolded. I agree with them. I should want to see my executors, stare the nozzles of their guns bravely in the face, see the open sky, the sun, daylight. See and hear my countrymen as they cheer us to our death. To liberation and freedom.

The Stadium will fill to capacity. And many will not find a place. They will climb trees and hang about the balconies of surrounding houses to get a clear view of us. To enjoy the free show. Cool.

And then the priest will come to us, either to pray or to ask if we have any last wishes. Sazan says he will ask for a cigarette. I'm sure they'll give it to him. I can see him puffing hard at it before the bullets cut him down. He says he's going to enjoy that cigarette more than anything he's had in life. Jimba says he'll maintain a sullen silence as a mark of his contempt. I'm going to yell at the priest. I will say, "Go to hell, you hypocrite, fornicator and adulterer." I will yell at the top of my voice in the hope that the spectators will hear me. How I wish there'd be a microphone that will reverberate through the Stadium, nay, through the country as a whole! Then the laugh would be on the priest and those who sent him!

The priest will pray for our souls. But it's not us he should be praying for. He should pray for the living, for those whose lives are a daily torment. Between his prayer and when the shots ring out, there will be dead silence. The silence of the graveyard. The transition between life and death. And it shall be seen that the distinction between them both is narrow as the neck of a calabash. The divide between us breathing like everyone else in the Stadium and us as meat for worms is, oh, so slim, it makes life a walking death! But I should be glad to be rid of the world, of a meaningless existence that grows more dreary by the day. I should miss Sazan and Jimba, though. It'll be a shame to see these elegant gentlemen cut down and destroyed.

And I'll miss you, too, my dear girl. But that will be of no consequence to the spectators.

They will troop out of the Stadium, clamber down the trees and the balconies of the houses, as though they'd just returned from another football match. They will march to their ratholes on empty stomachs, with tales enough to fill a Saturday evening. Miserable wretches!

The men who shall have eased us out of life will then untie our bodies and dump them into a lorry and thence to some open general grave. That must be a most distasteful task. I'd not do it for a million dollars. Yet some miserable fellows will do it for a miserable salary at the end of the month. A salary which will not feed them and their families till the next payday. A salary which they will have to augment with a bribe, if they are to keep body and soul together. I say, I do feel sorry for them. See?

The newspapers will faithfully record the fact of our shooting. If they have space, they'll probably carry a photograph of us to garnish your breakfasts.

I remember once long ago reading in a newspaper of a man whose one request to the priest was that he be buried along with his walking stick— his faithful companion over the years. He was pictured slumping in death, devotedly clutching his beloved walking stick. True friendship, that. Well, Zole, if ever you see such a photograph of me, make a cutting. Give it to a sculptor and ask him to make a stone sculpture of me as I appear in the photograph. He must make as faithful a representation of me as possible. I must be hard of feature and relentless in aspect. I have a small sum of money in the bank and have already instructed the bank to pay it to you for the purpose of the sculpture I have spoken about . . .

Time is running out, Zole. Sazan and Jimba are awake now. And they're surprised I haven't slept all night. Sazan says I ought at least to have done myself the favor of sound sleep on my last night on earth. I ask him if I'm not going to sleep soundly, eternally, in a few hours? This, I argue, should be our most wakeful night. Sazan doesn't appreciate that. Nor does Jimba. They stand up, yawn, stretch and rub their eyes. Then they sit down, crowding round me. They ask me to read out to them what I've written. I can't do that, I tell them. It's a love letter. And they burst out laughing. A love letter! And at the point of death! Sazan says I'm gone crazy. Jimba says he's sure I'm afraid of death and looks hard and long at me to justify his suspicion. I say I'm neither crazy nor afraid of death. I'm just telling my childhood girlfriend how I feel this special night. And sending her on an important errand. Jimba says I never told them I had a girlfriend. I reply that she was not important before this moment.

I haven't even seen her in ten years, I repeat. The really compelling need to write her is that on this very special night I have felt a need to be close to a living being, someone who can relate to others why we did what we did in and out of court.

Sazan says he agrees completely with me. He says he too would like to write his thoughts down. Do I have some paper to lend him? I say no. Besides, time is up. Day has dawned and I haven't even finished my letter. Do they mind leaving me to myself for a few minutes? I'd very much like to end the letter, envelope it and pass it on to the prison guard before he rouses himself fully from sleep and remembers to assume his official, harsh role.

They're nice chaps, are Jimba and Sazan. Sazan says to tell my girl not to bear any children because it's pointless bringing new life into the harsh life of her world. Jimba says to ask my girl to shed him a tear if she can so honor a complete stranger. They both chuckle and withdraw to a corner of the cell and I'm left alone to end my letter.

Now, I was telling you about my statue. My corpse will not be available to you. You will make a grave for me, nonetheless. And place the statue on the gravestone. And now I come to what I consider the most important part of this letter. My epitaph.

I have thought a lot about it, you know. Really. What do you say about a robber shot in a stadium before a cheering crowd? That he was a good man who strayed? That he deserved his end? That he was a scallywag? A ragamuffin? A murderer whose punishment was not heavy enough? "Here lies X, who was shot in public by firing squad for robbing a van and shooting the guards in broad daylight. He serves as an example to all thieves and would-be thieves!"

Who'd care for such an epitaph? They'd probably think it was a joke. No. That wouldn't carry. I'll settle for something different. Something plain and commonsensical. Or something truly cryptic and worthy of a man shot by choice in public by firing squad.

Not that I care. To die the way I'm going to die in the next hour or two is really nothing to worry about. I'm in excellent company. I should find myself recorded in the annals of our history. A history of violence, of murder, of disregard for life. Pleasure in inflicting pain—sadism. Is that the word for it? It's a world I should be pleased to leave. But not without an epitaph.

I recall, many years ago as a young child, reading in a newspaper of an African leader who stood on the grave of a dead lieutenant and through his tears said: "Africa kills her sons." I don't know what he meant by that, and though I've thought about it long enough, I've not been able to unravel the full mystery of those words. Now, today, this moment, they come flooding back to me. And I want to borrow from him. I'd like you to put this on my gravestone, as my epitaph: "Africa Kills Her Sun." A good epitaph, eh? Cryptic. Definite. A stroke of genius, I should say. I'm sure you'll agree with me. "Africa Kills Her Sun!" That's why she's been described as the Dark Continent? Yes?

So, now, dear girl, I'm done. My heart is light as the daylight which seeps stealthily into our dark cell. I hear the prison guard jangle his keys, put them into the keyhole. Soon he'll turn it and call us out. Our time is up. My time here expires and I must send you all my love. Goodbye.

Yours forever,

Bana

—1989

Don Mattera

(BORN 1935) SOUTH AFRICA

Don Mattera's several incarnations as a writer include poet, playwright, fabulist, and respected journalist, especially in the last capacity for Johannesburg's highly influential newspaper, the *Sowetan*. His other writing lives have further kept him occupied as a short story writer for children, as well as a recorder of his own life—in his autobiography, *Memory Is the Weapon* (1983). One of his plays, *One Time Brother*, was banned in 1984; others were widely performed in South Africa without encountering similar difficulty. All these talents have led Bernard Magubane to identify Mattera as "the bard of the people's liberation struggle."

A gentle, almost shy, and withdrawn man, Mattera startled readers with the publication of *The Storyteller* (1991). Besides his harsh "Afrika Road," included here, the stories in this collection scream out in the darkness against the horrors of life in South Africa under apartheid. "Execution" begins with a fragment of poetry:

> *I have no name.*
> *I am every man.*
> *I live everywhere.*
> *I die every day.*

—and subsequently reiterates the line: "A Man can die only once." "The Uniform" begins quietly with three sentences of stark realism: "The security key slid silently into the safety lock. It turned thrice until it clicked. One has to be extra-careful these days, especially with the escalation of violence and terrorism.'' A third story, ''Die Bushie Is Dood . . . ,'' opens with the unforgettable image: ''Johnny Jacobs lay bleeding in the road, his chesnut-brown eyes widened in disbelief.''

Mattera, who might be called a writer's writer, has been internationally praised as a humanist. In 1980, he was awarded the Kwanzaa Award Africa (USA); in 1986, the Steve Biko Prize (Sweden) and the Kurt Tuchosky Award (World PEN Association); in 1990, the NAFCOC Service to Humanity Award, the SOUTHCOC Service to the Community, and the Indicator Human Rights Award (all South Africa); in 1993, the Noma Award: Honorable Mention (Japan).

Before all this acclaim, Mattera's life was radically different. In *Sophiatown: Coming of Age in South Africa* (1987), he described his ethnic origins: ''According to the racial statistics of South Africa, I am a second-generation Coloured: the fruit of miscegenation and an in-between existence; the appendage of black and white. There are approximately four million other people like me—twilight children who live in political, social, and economic oblivion and who have been cut off from the mainstream of direct interaction with both black and white people.'' While a teenager, he became the leader of a street gang called the Vultures, which terrorized Sophiatown for seven years. Those experiences as well as his sentencing for public violence politicized him, and he joined the Youth League of the African National Congress. His literary career began shortly thereafter.

AFRIKA ROAD

There are many roads and lanes and streets and byways in South Africa but none quite like me, Afrika Road.

Each black township, no matter where it is situated, has an Afrika Road of its own. We are commonly known as the Tar Road, and those who create the townships and make the laws also conceive roads like us to facilitate the easy mobility of military and police vehicles. Usually there is a single road into and out of the townships. But the black people say they are not fools. They know the real motives of the rulers.

I am long and black and beautiful like a flat piece of licorice. Some folks say that my beauty has been spoiled by the obstinate white line because it cuts into my melanic majesty. But the line, like the Law of the land, slithers defiantly from the sun's bedroom in the west where I begin, to Masphala Hill in the east—a hot seat of conferred power which houses the Bantu Council Chambers and the police station.

I, Afrika Road, know and have endured the weight and pressure of all sorts of moving objects: human, animal, and mechanical. I groaned under the grinding repression of many military convoys and police brass bands that led the mayoral processions to the Hill of power. I also witness weddings and childbirths, and hear the noise of speeding police cars and ambulances, as well as the plaintive burial dirges of people weeping mournfully as they go. I hear the cries of the lonely of heart and I am familiar with the bustling din of jubilant folk whose merriment and laughter permeate the ghetto.

I am a mighty road.

All the dusty and soil-eroded lanes and streets converge on my body, bringing throngs of panting people. And I hold them all on my sturdy lap, year in and year out, birth in and death out.

There was a time when I was a teeming caldron of "people on the boil." The flames of mob anger and violence had razed the homes and businesses of men and women who threw in their lot and collaborated with the rulers of the land, or so the people said. Policemen and suspected informers and agents were brutally attacked. Some were even put to the torch. Yet amid the fear and frenzy of the marching and shouting masses, I, Afrika Road, caught glimpses of genuine gaiety on the people's faces. It was a welcome paradox, nonetheless. Humor and anger marching side by side.

That day the marchers varied in shade between chocolate-brown and shining ebony and fair apricot-skinned activists—rich characteristics for the human centipede that took to the streets.

It was one of many dates anywhere on the calendar of black resistance. The masses had heaved and swayed and breathed in the wild wind of their own passions. Occasionally the main body of the crowd opened up its floodgates and swallowed several hundreds of new protesters and their assortment of crude weaponry: sticks, stones, axes, homemade swords, knives, and dustbin lids. Four hundred people poured out of Mpanza Street; five hundred from Matambo and a half-drunk dozen from Sis Sonti's *shebeen*. The call to arms had a magnetic pull even for the imbibers. A soldier was a soldier drunk or sober, or so the leaders said. What mattered most were numbers.

Between Goba and Zamani streets, where the elite owner-built homes stand proud and indifferent, only three youngsters joined the swelling ranks. The Mkhuku Shanty Town dwellers mingled eagerly in their hundreds. The march gained momentum. Men, women, children, and the fire-eating T-shirted comrades—soldiers without uniforms or conventional armory—were carried along the hard journey of insurrection, aware that death waited for them on Masphala Hill.

And they sang defiantly.

Songs that challenged and mocked the armed keepers of the Hill, that hated Hill which many blacks see as one of countless links in the chain of bondage and humiliation, or so the people said. Those who served in state-created institutions and sought and found sanctuary inside the high barbed-wire walls of the Hill were branded puppets, sellouts, and *mpimpi*—the word used to describe informers and fifth-columnists.

I, Afrika Road, bore that maddened crowd as it rambled and swayed in the fervor of revolt toward the Hill of confrontation where hundreds of heavily armed battalions of soldiers, policemen, and the local greenbean law enforcers kept vigil. Their automatic weapons caught flashes of the shimmering gold and orange sunrays that blistered from a cloudless sky. The singing reached fever pitch when a group of chanting, flag-carrying militant youth took the lead toward the waiting death machine.

The songs spoke of imminent battle and vengeance, and of the people's hunger for liberation. Songs which exhorted the Bothas to release Nelson Mandela and all the other political prisoners. There were martial strophes which alluded to the impending acquisition of AK-47s, Scorpion automatic pistols, and bazooka rocket launchers. Then came the electrifying *toi-toi* war dance, which appeared to penetrate and possess the very souls of the marchers. It seemed to me that the masses yearned to touch the faces of death or victory—whichever came first.

The *toi-toi* is a ritual dance which people have come to fear and hate or love and revere depending on which side of the political trenches a person stood—with the masses or the "masters."

A truly awe-inspiring sight, thousands of angry and anxious feet in an exuberant display of bravado and daring. Up and down, back and forth; then forward and ever onward—spilling the froth and sweat of excitement on my black brow.

And I, Afrika Road, saw schoolchildren in khaki uniforms raise their wooden guns at the law enforcers on the Hill. Bullets made of hot breath and noise and spit reverberated in the air. "We are going to kill them in the company of their children," the khaki-clad warriors chanted. Death waited for them on the Hill as the crowd drew closer and closer. It would be the final confrontation: more than sixty thousand marchers heading for the showdown. Heading for freedom, or so they said.

You see it in their youthful eyes: a readiness to feel the familiar thud on the chest, and to hear the cracking of bone and the ripping of lung as the firepower of the law enforcers makes its forced entry and exit through the dark dissident flesh.

You see it in the flailing young arms of the children—always the children in the firing line—in tattered clothes or in school uniforms; T-shirted or naked chests; you see their hands fisted in the ardor of transient emotions; lives destined never to fully experience the essence of a natural childhood. You see them.

And I, Afrika Road, have seen them rise and then run undaunted against the ill wind; falling but emerging anew through sheaves of resisting corn—giving the earth life that genuine life might be reborn—or so I have heard the people's poets say during the many long marches.

A late-model car zoomed out of a small, nondescript lane between Zwide and Zwane streets. The well-dressed, well-fed driver, a wealthy local businessman and Bantu councilor, was en route to his sanctuary on Masphala Hill. He swerved noisily onto me. People dived to safety as the expensive imported vehicle screeched, skidded, and smoked at the wheels, and burned me.

Someone shouted, *"Mpimpi!"*

The human telegraph wire relayed the hated word and echoed it against the blue sky. The leaders in front got the message, stopped, and gave their backs to the waiting militia, who instinctively raised their guns at the ready in anticipation of attack.

The laminated windows of the car sagged under the weight of flying rock. Some of the youngsters jumped on it and smashed the front windshield. The terror-stricken man sat openmouthed, immobilized by his fear of death.

And I, Afrika Road, watched, knowing the fateful outcome. I have witnessed it too many times.

"Mpimpi!"

The chilling indictment rang out one final time.

A huge stone crushed the driver's skull. His eyes blinked and then went blank. Blood poured from his ears, nose, and mouth. They dragged him out. The back of his head cracked against me. I drank his blood just like I tasted the blood of many before him, and many more to come.

It is the law and the legacy.

Someone rolled a tire. Someone lifted a petrol can. Someone struck a match on Afrika Road . . .

—1991

Yvonne Vera

(BORN 1964) ZIMBABWE

Since the early 1990s, Yvonne Vera has been widely identified as one of southern Africa's major women writers. She began her writing career with the publication of a novel, *Without a Name* (1991), short-listed for the Commonwealth Writers Award (Africa Region). That work was followed by a collection of short stories, *Why Don't You Carve Other Animals* (1992), and two novels, *Nehanda* (1993) and *Milk and Moon* (1996). Her fiction has been praised for its haunting portraits of women who must come to grips with the disturbing realities of their pasts.

Vera was born in Bulawayo, Zimbabwe. After attending local schools, she continued her work at the University of York, in Toronto, Canada. In her short story "Crossing Boundaries," she passionately describes the inner conflict of many internationals today, though the following statement also applies to the peripatetic contemporary writer: "The exiled soul insists on finding a connection between moments and histories, on securing a promise from the future that there shall be compensation. The banished wanderer insists on narrating, and on situating solutions that have been evaded by the past. Caught between memory and dreaming, the hopeful exile weaves a comforting performance out of a tale of agony."

Yvonne Vera has completed a doctorate at York University.

WHY DON'T YOU CARVE
OTHER ANIMALS

He sits outside the gates of the Africans-Only hospital, making models out of wood. The finished products are on old newspapers on the ground around him. A painter sits to his right, his finished work leaning against the hospital fence behind them. In the dense township, cars screech, crowds flow by, voices rise, and ambulances speed into the emergency unit of the hospital, their flashing orange light giving fair warning to oncoming traffic. Through the elephants he carves, and also the giraffes, with oddly slanting necks, the sculptor brings the jungle to the city. His animals walk on the printed newspaper sheets, but he mourns that they have no life in them. Sometimes in a fit of anger he collects his animals and throws them frenziedly into his cardboard box, desiring not to see their lifeless forms against the chaotic movement of traffic which flows through the hospital gates.

"Do you want that crocodile? It's a good crocodile. Do you want it?" A mother coaxes a little boy who has been crying after his hospital visit. A white bandage is wrapped tight around his right arm. The boy holds his arm with his other hand, aware of the mother's attention, which makes him draw attention to his temporary deformity. She kneels beside him and looks into his eyes, pleading.

"He had an injection. You know how the children fear the needle," the mother informs the man. She buys the crocodile, and hands it to the boy. The man watches one of his animals go, carried between the little boy's tiny fingers. His animals have no life in them, and the man is tempted to put them back in the box. He wonders if the child will ever see a moving crocodile, surrounded as he is by the barren city, where the only rivers are the tarred roads.

A man in a white coat stands looking at the elephants, and at the man who continues carving. He picks a red elephant, whose tusk is carved along its body, so that it cannot raise it. A red elephant? The stranger is perplexed, and amused, and decides to buy the elephant, though it is poorly carved and cannot lift its tusk. He will place it beside the window in his office, where it can look out at the patients in line. Why are there no eyes carved on the elephant? Perhaps the paint has covered them up.

The carver suddenly curses.

"What is wrong?" the painter asks.

"Look at the neck of this giraffe."

The painter looks at the giraffe, and the two men explode into uneasy laughter. It is not easy to laugh when one sits so close to the sick.

The carver wonders if he has not carved some image of himself, or of some afflicted person who stopped and looked at his breathless animals. He looks at the cardboard box beside him and decides to place it in the shade, away from view.

"Why don't you carve other animals? Like lions and chimpanzees?" the painter asks. "You are always carving giraffes and your only crocodile has been bought!" The painter has had some influence on the work of the carver, lending him the paints to color his animals. The red elephant was his idea.

"The elephant has ruled the forest for a long time, he is older than the forest, but the giraffe extends his neck and struts above the trees, as though the forest belonged to him. He eats the topmost leaves, while the elephant spends the day rolling in the mud. Do you not find it interesting? This struggle between the elephant and the giraffe, to eat the topmost leaves in the forest?" The ambulances whiz past, into the emergency unit of the Africans-Only hospital.

The painter thinks briefly, while he puts the final touches on an image of the Victoria Falls which he paints from a memory gathered from newspapers and magazines. He has never seen the Falls. The water must be blue, to give emotion to the picture, he thinks. He has been told that when the water is shown on a map, it has to be blue, and that indeed when there is a lot of it, as in the sea, the water looks like the sky. So he is generous in his depiction, and shocking blue waves cascade unnaturally over the rocky precipice.

"The giraffe walks proudly, majestically, because of the beautiful tapestry that he carries on his back. That is what the struggle is about. Otherwise, they are equals. The elephant has his long tusk to reach the leaves and the giraffe has his long neck."

He inserts two lovers at the corner of the picture, their arms around each other as they stare their love into the blue water. He wants to make the water sing to them. So he paints a bird at the top of the painting, hovering over the falls, its beak open in song. He wishes he had painted a dove, instead of this black bird which looks like a crow.

The carver borrows some paint and puts yellow and black spots on the giraffe with the short neck. He has long accepted that he cannot carve perfect animals, but will not throw them away. Maybe someone, walking out of the Africans-Only hospital, will seek some cheer in his piece. But when he has finished applying the dots, the paint runs down the sides of the animal, and it looks a little like a zebra.

"Why do you never carve a dog or a cat? Something that city people have seen. Even a rat would be good, there are lots of rats in the township!" There is much laughter. The painter realizes that a lot of spray from the falls must be reaching the lovers, so he paints off their heads with a red umbrella. He notices suddenly that something is missing in the picture, so he extends the lovers' free hands, and gives them some yellow ice cream. The picture is now full of life.

"What is the point of carving a dog? Why do you not paint dogs and cats and mice?" The carver has never seen the elephant or the giraffe that he carves so ardently. He picks up a piece of unformed wood.

Will it be a giraffe or an elephant? His carving is also his dreaming.

—1992

Véronique Tadjo

(BORN 1955) IVORY COAST

In her critical study, *Francophone African Women Writers: Destroying the Emptiness of Silence* (1994), Irène Assiba d'Almeida claims that Véronique Tadjo's groundbreaking first novel, *Au Vol d'oiseau* (*As the Crow Flies*), is "one of the most original pieces of Francophone writing, and one that defies easy classification. It is surely a 'text' in the primary meaning of the word, that is, 'something woven.' Tadjo's cloth is patterned from ninety-two independent yet related pieces, most accurately described as vignettes, that can stand on their own or be put together to form an immense appliqué representing an African social reality. The vignettes are written mainly in prose, but Tadjo's language is never far from poetry, and here it shows her ability to use very simple words to create a superb poetic prose."

Véronique Tadjo was born in Paris in 1955, and she grew up in Abidjan, in the Ivory Coast, where she attended local schools. She earned a B.A. in English from the University of Abidjan, followed by a doctorate from the Sorbonne in Paris, also in English. In 1983, she attended Howard University, in Washington, D.C., on a Fulbright research scholarship. She taught at the University of Abidjan during the early 1980s, and in 1994 moved to Nairobi with her husband, a journalist.

Tadjo's initial publications were poems, collected in the volume *Latérite* in 1984. In addition to several children's books, she has had two collections of short fiction published: *La Chanson de la Vie* (1989) and *Le Royaume Aveugle*

(1990). "The Magician and the Girl"—translated by the author—is from *Au Vol d'oiseau*, published in Paris in 1992.

Asked to comment on her writing, Tadjo responded: "I write because I want to understand the world I am living in, and because I want to communicate with others my experience of what it is to be living in Africa today. I use my eyes like a camera, trying to record everything, from the most personal emotions to the major crises like wars, death, and AIDS. When asked what my novels are about, I usually sigh heavily and say, 'About life,' because I cannot explain it in any other way. I am interested in life in its entirety, and this is why I have an aversion to giving names to my characters. I want the readers to see them as human beings first of all. And these human beings are faced with challenges and struggles they must overcome if they want to retain their humanity in the unfavourable context of an African society in crisis."

THE MAGICIAN AND THE GIRL

Translated from the French by the author

He was a magician of great power and of renowned beauty. His knowledge of secrets knew no boundaries.

People came from all over the world to meet him. It was said he could do anything he wanted. People believed he had the formula for eternal happiness, and he himself claimed to possess it. "Happiness," he would explain, "is the absence of happiness. Do you know how to walk with your eyes shut? Can you sleep forever? Do you master silence?"

People were amazed. They could not comprehend the meaning of his words. "Happiness is love, money, or power," they declared. By coming to him, they expected to acquire one or the other. Unfortunately, they didn't get anything from him.

As a result, a lot of people were disappointed. They went back to their countries and told their friends that the man was a fraud. "Can you imagine?" they said. "We waited for days on end to have the chance to talk to him, and all for absolutely nothing."

Others, however, decided to stay close to him in the hope of discovering his secrets. They were probably very unhappy because they had nowhere else to go. They depended entirely on him. If he raised his arm, they immediately tried to analyze the meaning of his gesture. They organized conferences and round tables. They worked hard to grasp the deep significance behind all his movements. Whether he scratched his head, coughed, yawned, or cracked his fingers, the disciples took note of it at once. Some even made drawings of him.

They did so because the man never answered questions.

The girl arrived right in the middle of an evening of debate. The magician had just gone to bed and the disciples were sitting in a circle, discussing the significance of his many yawns:

"The master yawned twenty times."

"No! Twenty-one, I counted!"

A brouhaha ensued and a new debate exploded.

The girl came from a family of magicians. Her father was a magician and her mother had extraordinary powers. She stayed at the back of the room and listened to each one of them. Then she decided to take a chance.

The following morning, she sat in the middle of the floor, crossed her legs, and summoned all the vital energies into herself. She closed her eyes. When she felt that she was ready, she suddenly opened her eyes and looked. The magician was standing right in front of her, watching. She waited.

He held out his hand. "What do you want?" he asked her. "Why are you here?"

"I don't know. I am very confused."

"You look happy, though. Your face is radiant and your energy attracts people. If you fail, you will lose what you already have."

"I want to try. I do not know the nature of my joy. It comes and goes. Nothing seems to stay. Everything changes and I am caught in a whirl. I have lost the difference between dream and reality."

There was a moment of silence. Then the magician smiled at her and said: "I understand. Follow me, but do not ask any questions."

They entered a maze. The girl remained at his side. She did not know where they were going, and it was obvious she would never be able to find her way back alone. It frightened her a little.

They arrived in a room lined with thick curtains. She wondered if there were windows behind them. The atmosphere was peaceful. She noticed the bareness of the place. There was no decoration.

The man came close to her, put his arms over her shoulders, and kissed her.

Later on, she ran her fingers over the naked skin of the man who had made love to her as only a wizard could do. She stroked the nape of his neck, the deep curve of his back, and his thighs. She could feel each cell, each atom pulsating. He was sleeping in silence.

She parted from him, laid her hands on his forehead, and opened his skull. What she saw inside frightened her. It was a desert of sadness and solitude. It looked like a battlefield. There were trenches and shell craters. Corpses covered the ground. She regretted having come and with a heavy heart she started going away, when, in the distance, she spotted a lake and, beyond that, a plain on which the grass seemed green and smiling. The earth there was rich.

She closed his skull and fell asleep.

From that time on, she spent her days devising a means of reaching the valley which spread in the horizon of his mind. She wanted to roll in the grass, smell the strong scent of the wet soil, the warm and reassuring soil. It had become her obsession.

She was with the magician day and night. To avoid his constant yawning, she told him stories that, very often, she invented on the spot. She enjoyed making him burst into long laughter, his head thrown back, his neck bare and vulnerable. But what she feared most were his thick and unfathomable silences which echoed in her head like the stampeding of wild horses.

She decided to get into his skull again. However, before starting the final journey, she had to prepare herself carefully. She had to be cautious. She would have to use all her powers.

So she cracked an egg, washed her face three times, and drew close to the man who was sleeping. She laid her hands on his forehead and opened his skull.

She walked with great care but ripped her dress on thorns and hurt herself when she fell into a trap. Nevertheless, she successfully avoided the shells buried in the ground and managed to hold her breath against the smell of putrefied bodies. In the end, she reached the lake. By then, she was terribly hot and thirsty. She sat on the bank and drank some of the clear water. A light breeze was blowing. On the other side, the valley extended as far as the eye could see.

When she had regained her strength, she took a deep breath and dived.

In the bed, the magician stirred. He tossed about in his sleep and then abruptly opened his eyes. He looked around the room and after a while jumped out of the sheets. The girl had disappeared. He called her name at the entrance to the maze.

The girl was being pulled down to the bottom of the lake by a superior force. She was aware of sinking deeper and deeper. Water was getting into her mouth, her ears, her nose. She could see the algae dancing. She couldn't call out.

She could only think of the shore.

—1992

Ben Okri

(BORN 1959) NIGERIA

Ben Okri's star-studded literary career began in 1980, when *Flowers and Shadows* was published. Okri was nineteen. Rooted in the fast-paced lives of many urban Nigerians at the end of the 1970s, the novel is set in the growth years of the country's economy: after the Civil War, when the oil boom brought about rapid social change and many people were out to make a quick fortune. The novel's realism provides a glimpse of the future direction of Okri's writing. The flowers of the title are real, though in time they will wither and grow old; the shadows are constantly changing and elusive— perhaps untouchable.

In the fiction that was published after his first novel—a second novel, *The Landscapes Within* (1982), and two collections of short stories, *Incidents at the Shrine* (1987) and *Stars of the New Curfew* (1988)—Okri shifted from realism to fabulism. Many of the short stories move effortlessly between the two realms, recording incidents that are often difficult to identify as real. In the title story of *Stars of the New Curfew*, a young man named Arthur resists the criminal opportunities of his immediate world, yet eventually peddles quack medicine to innocent people who are looking for a quick fix for their miseries. Though Arthur himself is concerned about the gullibility of his customers, the fraudulent drug manufacturers are happy enough to take further advantage of their victims.

With *The Famished Road* (1991) and its sequel, *Songs of Enchantment* (1993), Okri's fictive domain shifted more directly into the unseen world. Azaro, the main character of both novels, is an *abiku*, a spirit-child, fated to a cycle of deaths and rebirths into the same world. *The Famished Road* describes his mother's almost pathological anguish that Azaro will never be of this world, though Azaro himself describes his condition in much more benevolent terms:

"There was not one among us who looked forward to being born. We disliked the rigors of existence, the unfulfilled longing, the enshrined injustices of the world, the labyrinths of love, the ignorance of parents, the fact of dying, and the amazing indifference of the living in the midst of simple beauties of the universe. We feared the heartlessness of human beings, of all who are born blind, few of whom ever learn to see."

The Famished Road was the winner of the 1991 Booker Prize. Earlier, Okri had won the Commonwealth Writers' Award for Africa and the *Paris Review* Aga Khan prize for fiction. He received the Chianti Rufino—Antico Fattore International Literary Prize and the Premio Grinzane Cavour Prize in 1994.

In 1995, Okri's most daring novel to date, *Astonishing the Gods*, was published—simultaneously a spiritual autobiography for the author and a visionary fable for mankind in general. Okri has also served as the poetry editor for *West Africa* and published a volume of his own poems, *An African Elegy*, as well as a sixth novel, *Dangerous Love*, in 1996.

"A Prayer from the Living" appeared in 1993 on the op-ed page of *The New York Times*. In this powerful response to the famine in Somalia (and, more specifically, to the arrival of American troops in the country), Okri defines a central moral issue of our time: the justification of intervention in cultures other than our own, which too often for the West has meant misunderstanding and ignorance of other people's ways.

A PRAYER FROM THE LIVING

We entered the town of the dying at sunset. We went from house to house. Everything was as expected, run-down, a desert, luminous with death and hidden life.

The gunrunners were everywhere. The world was now at the perfection of chaos. The little godfathers who controlled everything raided the food brought for us. They raided the airlifts and the relief aid and distributed most of the food among themselves and members of their clan.

We no longer cared. Food no longer mattered. I had done without for three weeks. Now I feed on the air and on the quest.

Every day, as I grow leaner, I see more things around us. I see the dead— all who had died of starvation. They are more joyful now; they are happier than we are; and they are everywhere, living their luminous lives as if nothing had happened, or as if they were more alive than we are.

The hungrier I became, the more I saw them—my old friends who had died before me, clutching onto flies. Now they feed on the light of the air. And they look at us—the living—with so much pity and compassion.

I suppose this is what the white ones cannot understand when they come with their TV cameras and their aid. They expect to see us weeping. Instead, they see us staring at them, without begging, and with a bulging placidity in our eyes. Maybe they are secretly horrified that we are not afraid of dying this way.

But after three weeks of hunger the mind no longer notices; you're more dead than alive; and it's the soul wanting to leave that suffers. It suffers because of the body's tenacity.

We should have come into the town at dawn. In the town everyone had died. The horses and cows were dying, too. I could say that the air stank of death, but that wouldn't be true. It smelled of rancid butter and poisoned heat and bad sewage. There was even the faint irony of flowers.

The only people who weren't dead were the dead. Singing golden songs in chorus, jubilant everywhere, they carried on their familiar lives. The only others who weren't dead were the soldiers. And they fought among themselves eternally. It didn't seem to matter to them how many died. All that mattered was how well they handled the grim mathematics of the wars, so that they could win the most important battle of all, which was for the leadership of the fabulous graveyard of this once beautiful and civilized land.

I was searching for my family and my lover. I wanted to know if they had died or not. If I didn't find out, I intended to hang on to life by its last tattered thread. If I knew that they, too, were dead and no longer needed me, I would die at peace.

All my information led me to this town. If my lover, my brothers, my family are anywhere, they are here. This is the last town in the world. Beyond its rusted gate lies the desert. The desert stretches all the way into the past; into history, to the Western world, and to the source of drought and famine—the mighty mountain of lovelessness. From its peaks, at night, the grim spirits of negation chant their awesome soul-shrinking songs. Their songs steal hope from us and make us yield to the air our energies. Their songs are cool and make us submit to the clarity of dying.

Behind us, in the past, before all this came to be, there were all the possibilities in the world. There were all the opportunities for starting from small things to create a sweet new history and future, if only we had seen them. But now, ahead, there lie only the songs of the mountain of death.

We search for our loved ones mechanically and with a dryness in our eyes. Our stomachs no longer exist. Nothing exists except the search. We turn the bodies over, looking for familiar faces. All the faces are familiar; death made them all my kin.

I search on, I come across an unfamiliar face; it is my brother. I nod. I pour dust on his flesh. Hours later, near a dry well, I come across the other members of my family. My mother holds on tightly to a bone so dry it wouldn't even nourish the flies. I nod twice. I pour dust on their bodies. I search on. There is one more face whose beautiful unfamiliarity will console me. When I have found the face, then I will submit myself to the mountain songs.

Sunset was approaching when, from an unfinished school building, I heard singing. It was the most magical sound I had ever heard and I thought only those who know how sweet life is can sing like that, can sing as if breathing were a prayer.

The singing was like the joyous beginning of all creation, the holy yes to the breath and light infusing all things, which makes the water shimmer, the plants sprout, the animals jump and play in the fields, and which makes the men and women look out into the first radiance of colors, the green of plants, the blue of sea, the gold of the air, the silver of the stars. It was the true end of my quest, the music to crown this treacherous life of mine, the end I couldn't have hoped for, or imagined.

It seemed to take an infinity of time to get to the school building. I had no strength left, and it was only the song's last echo, resounding through the vast spaces of my hunger, that sustained me. After maybe a century, when history had repeated itself and brought about exactly the same circumstances, because none of us ever learned our lesson, or loved enough to learn from our pain, I finally made it to the schoolroom door. But a cow, the only living thing left in the town, went in through the door before I did. It, too, must have been drawn by the singing. The cow went into the room, and I followed.

Inside, all the space was taken up with the dead. But here the air didn't have death in it. The air had prayer in it. The prayers stank more than the deaths. But all the dead here were differently dead from the corpses outside. The dead in the school were—forgive the paradox—*alive*. I have no other word to explain the serenity. I felt they had made the room holy because they had, in their last moments, thought not of themselves but of all people who suffer. I felt that to be the case because I felt myself doing the same thing. I crawled to a corner, sat against a wall, and felt myself praying for the whole human race.

I prayed—knowing full well that prayers are possibly an utter waste of time—but I prayed for everything that lived, for mountains and trees, for animals and streams, and for human beings, wherever they might be. I heard the great anguished cry of all mankind, its great haunting music as well. And I, too, without moving my mouth, for I had no energy, began to sing in silence. I sang all through the evening. And when I looked at the body next to me and found the luminous unfamiliarity of its face to be that of my lover's—I sang all through the recognition. I sang silently even when a good-hearted white man came into the school building with a television camera and, weeping, recorded the roomful of the dead for the world—and I hoped he recorded my singing, too.

And the dead were all about me, smiling, serene. They didn't urge me on; they were just quietly and intensely joyful. They did not ask me to hurry to them, but left it to me. What could I choose? Human life—full of greed and bitterness, dim, low-oxygenated, judgmental and callous, gentle, too, and wonderful as well, but . . . human life had betrayed me. And besides, there was nothing left to save in me. Even my soul was dying of starvation.

I opened my eyes for the last time. I saw the cameras on us all. To them, we were the dead. As I passed through the agony of the light, I saw them as the dead, marooned in a world without pity or love.

As the cow wandered about in the apparent desolation of the room, it must have seemed odd to the people recording it all that I should have made myself so comfortable among the dead. I did. I stretched myself out and held the hand of my lover. With a painful breath and a gasp and a smile, I let myself go.

The smile must have puzzled the reporters. If they had understood my language, they would have known that it was my way of saying goodbye.

—1993

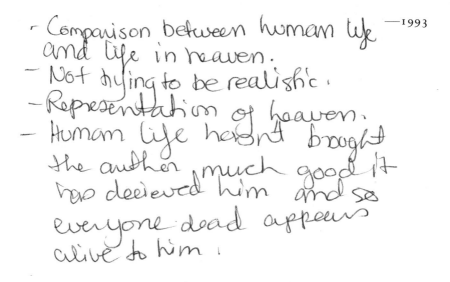

- Comparison between human life and life in heaven.
- Not trying to be realistic.
- Representation of heaven.
- Human life hasn't brought the author much good, it has deceived him and so everyone dead appears alive to him.

Alexander Kanengoni

(BORN 1951) ZIMBABWE

The past—particularly the recent struggle for freedom—looms ominously in many of Alexander Kanengoni's short stories. The title of one of them ("Things We'd Rather Not Talk About") itself suggests the tortured lives of men caught up in the resistance activities that led to Zimbabwe's independence. In another powerful story, "The Black Christ of Musami," the narrator seeks comfort in his own ancestry, also against the backdrop of guerrilla activities. The story concludes: "There was a huge old *mukamba* tree watching silently over our home from a small hill in the east which never seemed to shed any of its brittle, evergreen leaves. It was a towering giant that marked our home from miles around. Each time I came home from the city, I went up the hill and crouched under the tree, talking to it, talking to my deceased grandfather. . . ."

Alexander Kanengoni was born in 1951, in Chivu, Rhodesia. He attended Marymount Mission in Mt. Darwin and had his secondary education at Kutama College, St. Paul's Teacher Training College, as well as the University of Zimbabwe, where his major was English. He taught briefly before leaving the country to join the liberation war in 1974. At the time of independence in 1980, he was appointed to a position in the Ministry of Education and Culture. Currently, he heads the Television Services of the Zimbabwe Broadcasting Corporation.

Kanengoni has published three books, the novels *Vicious Circle* (1983) and *Echoing Silence* (1996), as well as a collection of short stories, *Effortless Tears* (1993). He writes, he says, "to reconcile raging turmoils" inside him.

EFFORTLESS TEARS

We buried my cousin, George Pasi, one bleak windswept afternoon: one of those afternoons that seem fit for nothing but funerals. Almost everyone there knew that George had died of an AIDS-related illness but no one mentioned it. What showed was only the fear and uncertainty in people's eyes; beyond that, silence.

Even as we traveled from Harare on that hired bus that morning, every one of us feared that at last AIDS had caught up with us. In the beginning, it was a distant, blurred phenomenon which we only came across in the newspapers and on radio and television, something peculiar to homosexuals. Then we began hearing isolated stories of people dying of AIDS in far-flung districts. After that came the rumors of sealed wards at Harare and Parirenyatwa, and of other hospitals teeming with people suffering from AIDS. But the truth is that it still seemed rather remote and did not seem to have any direct bearing on most of us.

When AIDS finally reached Highfield and Zengeza, and started claiming lives in the streets where we lived, that triggered the alarm bells inside our heads. AIDS had finally knocked on our doors.

For two months, we had watched George waste away at Harare Hospital. In desperation, his father—just like the rest of us—skeptical of the healing properties of modern medicine, had turned to traditional healers. Somehow, we just could not watch him die. We made futile journeys to all corners of

the country while George wasted away. He finally died on our way home
from some traditional healer in Mutare.

All the way from Harare to Wedza, the atmosphere was limp. January's
scorching sun in the naked sky and the suffocating air intensified into a sense
of looming crisis that could not be expressed in words. The rains were
already very late and the frequent sight of untilled fields, helplessly confronting an unfulfilling sky, created images of seasons that could no longer be
understood. The crops that had been planted with the first and only rains
of the season had emerged only to fight a relentless war with the sun. Most
had wilted and died. The few plants that still survived were struggling in
the stifling heat. *Plants personified as humans w/ Aids.*

Now, as we stood forlornly round the grave, the choir sang an ominous
song about death: we named the prophets yielded up to heaven while the
refrain repeated: "Can you see your name? Where is your name?"

This eerie question rang again and again in our minds until it became part
of one's soul, exposing it to the nakedness of the Mutekedza communal land:
land that was overcrowded, old, and tired. Interminable rows of huts
stretched into the horizon, along winding roads that only seemed to lead to
other funerals.

Not far away, a tattered scarecrow from some forgotten season flapped a
silent dirge beneath the burning sun.

Lean cattle, their bones sticking out, their ribs moving painfully under
their taut skin, nibbled at something on the dry ground: what it was, no
one could make out. And around the grave the atmosphere was subdued
and silent. Even the once phenomenal Save River, only a stone's throw away
to the east, lay silent. This gigantic river, reduced to puddles between heaps
of sand, seemed to be brooding on its sad predicament. And behind the
dying river, Wedza Mountain stared at us with resignation, as if it, too, had
given up trying to understand some of the strange things that were happening.

The preacher told the parable of the Ten Virgins. He warned that when
the Lord unexpectedly came and knocked on our door, like the clever five
virgins, we should be found ready and waiting to receive Him.

Everyone nodded silently.

George's grandfather mourned the strange doings of this earth. He wished
it was he who had been taken away. But then such were the weird ways of
witches and wizards that they preferred to pluck the youngest and plump-
est—although George had grown thinner than the cattle we could see around

The aspect of the dead as the living.

us. We listened helplessly as the old man talked and talked until at last he broke down and cried like a small child.

George's father talked of an invisible enemy that had sneaked into our midst and threatened the very core of our existence. He warned us that we should change our ways immediately or die.

He never mentioned the word "Aids," the acronym AIDS.

George's wife was beyond all weeping. She talked of a need for moral strength during such critical times. She readily admitted that she did not know where such strength could come from: it could be from the people; it could be from those gone beyond; it could be from God. But wherever it was from, she needed it. As if acting upon some invisible signal, people began to cry. We were not weeping for the dead. We were weeping for the living. And behind us, while Wedza Mountain gazed at us dejectedly, the Save River was silently dying.

The coffin was slowly lowered into the grave and we filed past, throwing in clods of soil. In the casket lay George, reduced to skin and bone. (Most people had refused a last glimpse of him.) during his heyday we had called him Mr. Bigstuff because of his fast and flashy style—that was long ago.

As we trudged back to the village, away from the wretched burial area, most of us were trying to decide which memory of George to take back with us: Mr. Bigstuff or that thread, that bundle of skin and bones which had died on our way back from some traditional healer in Mutare.

Out there, around the fire, late that Monday evening, all discussion was imbued with an a painful sense of futility, a menacing uncertainty, and an overwhelming feeling that we were going nowhere.

Drought.

"Compared to the ravaging drought of 1947, this is child's play," said George's grandfather. "At that time, people survived on grass like cattle," he concluded, looking skeptically up into the deep night sky.

No one helped him take the discussion further.

Politics.

The village chairman of the party attempted a spirited explanation of the advantages of the government's economic reform program: "It means a general availability of goods and services and it means higher prices for the people's agricultural produce," he went on, looking up at the dark, cloudless sky. Then, with an inexplicable renewal of optimism peculiar to politicians, he went on to talk of programs and projects until, somehow, he, too, was overcome by the general weariness and took refuge in the silence around the dying fire.

"Aren't these religious denominations that are daily sprouting up a sign that the end of the world is coming?" asked George's grandfather.

"No, it's just people out to make a quick buck, nothing else," said George's younger brother.

"Don't you know that the end of the world is foretold in the Scriptures," said the Methodist lay preacher with sharp urgency. He continued: "All these things"—he waved his arms in a large general movement—"are undoubtedly signs of the Second Coming." Everyone looked down and sighed.

And then, inevitably, AIDS came up. It was a topic that everyone had been making a conscious effort to avoid, but then, like everything else, its turn came. Everyone referred to it in indirect terms: that animal, that phantom, that creature, that beast. It was not out of any respect for George. It was out of fear and despair.

"Whatever this scourge is"—George's father chuckled—"it has claimed more lives than all my three years in the Imperial Army against Hitler." He chuckled again helplessly.

"It seems as if these endless funerals have taken the place of farming."

"They are lucky, the ones who are still getting decent burials," chipped in someone from out of the dark. "Very soon, there will be no one to bury anybody."

The last glowing ember in the collected heap of ashes grew dimmer and finally died away. George's grandfather asked for an ox-hide drum and began playing it slowly at first and then with gathering ferocity. Something in me snapped.

Then he began to sing. The song told of an unfortunate woman's repeated pregnancies which always ended in miscarriages. I felt trapped.

When at last the old man, my father, stood up and began to dance, stamping the dry earth with his worn-out car-tire sandals, I knew there was no escape. I edged George's grandfather away from the drum and began a futile prayer on that moonless night. The throbbing resonance of the drum rose above our voices as we all became part of one great nothingness. Suddenly I was crying for the first time since George's death. Tears ran from my eyes like rivers in a good season. During those years, most of us firmly believed that the mighty Save River would roll on forever, perhaps until the end of time.

But not now, not any longer.

—1993

Mzamane Nhlapo

(BORN 1960) LESOTHO

Upon completing his secondary schooling in 1981, Mzamane Nhlapo left Lesotho and worked in the South African mines for two years. He continued his education, earning a Secondary Teaching Certificate in 1988, but instead of teaching he went to work for the Highlands Water Project in the mountains of Lesotho as a site administrator. A year later, he went back to school, matriculating at the National University of Lesotho. Nhlapo completed his B.A. in education in 1993. Since that time, he has served as the headmaster of a secondary school in the Mafeteng District, while working on his writing in his free time.

According to the editors of *The Kalahari Review*, where "Give Me a Chance" was originally published, Nhlapo "wishes to engage in 'the emancipation of women in the world' " in his writing. Based on an actual incident in his mother's life, the story begs the question of what is true storytelling: fact or fiction?

About "Give Me a Chance," Nhlapo says: "First, I wrote the story to show how bold my mother was in trying to break away from the cultural bondage in which a woman is a helpless minor who should seek permission from her husband to get—among other things—employment, even when her husband was failing to provide for the family. My mother refused to be passive and let herself and her children die of hunger. She is the voice of many women who should boldly stand up and demand their chance to determine their destiny.

"Second, in our culture boys must look after animals and do other 'manly' chores at a young age. This denies them a chance to be closer to their mothers. Writing the story brought me closer to my mother for the first time, since I had to talk to her to ask for details and reasons for her actions. For the first time, I felt the warmth of motherhood. I could laugh and cry with her. Like their mothers, young boys in our culture should stand up and demand their chance for a balanced and healthy growth to adulthood."

In addition to *The Kalahari Review*, the author's stories have appeared in *Basali! Stories by and about Women in Lesotho* (1995) and in *'Na Le Uena— Anthology of Creative Writing in Lesotho* (1995).

GIVE ME A CHANCE

Mama KaZili woke up early with her eyes red and watery as though she had been crying the whole night. I suspected that something was going to happen. At the age of nine I could see and observe well. Life at home demanded as much.

That was the day when she decided never to let us die of hunger. My father had not been sending her money from the South African mines for more than a year. It was said that he had another wife in the mines. His parents refused to listen to Mama KaZili's complaints about that. They wanted her to accept that for a husband to have numerous wives was the norm, something a "good" wife did not have to complain about. They did not seem to understand the economic realities facing her and her children.

But in a way it was understandable why my grandparents didn't care. Now of late, if my father had to send money at all, he sent it to his mother, who was to decide whether to pass it on to Mama KaZili. And in most cases Mama KaZili never received a cent. My father knew this, but he, too, could not afford a complaining wife.

"Today we are going to Makhoakhoeng, to some relatives of your father," my mother announced that morning after we had eaten *pap mpothe* (mealie pap alone, a mixture of cornmeal and water).

"Why, Mother?" I asked. She took time to answer my question. I saw her swallow something hard first.

"Because if we stay here you won't have something to eat," she said eventually.

Makhoakhoeng is forty kilometers from Habelo, my home village. To go there we took an old bus from Botha-Bothe, my hometown. After traveling for thirty kilometers, there was no road for the bus to go farther. The Maluti Mountains began to get rugged—steep, rocky, rough. Worse still, it was snowing that day. The air was chilly and freezing to the bone marrow, more so when we were wrapped in tattered blankets and had no shoes on our feet. A sympathetic woman must have lent my mother some money at home so that we could take the bus to those mountains. They were so white and so huge!

Slowly we began to climb those cold, slippery, and uncompromising mountains. My younger sister, Nopaseka, fell down time and again, getting more damp from the snow each time. Once I decided to carry her on my back because my mother had the youngest baby, Mkhathini, on hers. Nopaseka was too heavy for me, and we fell down together. My mother fell also, only twice or thrice. Mothers are tough; they don't fall easily. But the last time she fell, it was heavily, and I heard her mention my father's name in disgust: "Moshe!" She also mentioned the names of my older brother and sister, who left at home, as if to say, "What will they do tonight?" When I walked close enough to her, her eyes were still a little red and looked like they had water in them.

We struggled up the mountains in a numbing temperature. I could not feel my toes. Our cheeks were stung by the chilling winter winds. A vicious icy snow pelted us in the face. Our bodies were bruised, hungry, and exhausted. But we were determined to reach the place of our father's relatives, where we would eat *papa* before we went to sleep. The determination of Mama KaZili rekindled ours.

We wrestled endlessly with the treacherous mountains to cover the ten kilometers. I could not calculate the passage of time. My mother kept swallowing something hard. She also spoke alone, uttering words like, "I'll go back to work hard for them . . . Tonight you will eat . . ."

When we were close to the village we were going to, we stopped. Mama KaZili wanted to breast-feed the baby. The baby did not suck her breasts as usual. He was very stiff and looked very pale. And he was not breathing. For the first time in my life, I heard my mother cry.

The death of Mkhathini reduced our number to six in the home.

It is difficult to tell in detail exactly what went on in that snowy weather.

But I do remember that we were taken to the village on horseback. Observant villagers had seen that we had stopped at one spot for a long time in the snow, and they must have wondered why. Then horsemen came to fetch us. People in the mountains are more concerned about others than people in the lowlands or towns.

When we arrived at my father's relatives', there was a mixture of happiness and grief. They were happy to see us, children of their brother. But the sight of Mama KaZili carrying the dead child was a great shock.

They might have been struck by the sight of death, but by this time Mama KaZili was sober, clear, and determined. She was in her best poised manner. She was no longer a cold, crying woman trapped in the snow with small kids falling down numerous times behind her. I saw a mixture of anger, grit, and willpower in her. That was my mother at her best.

She was expecting the accusation: "If you respected your husband and his parents, the child wouldn't have died."

She knew that they, too, would be more concerned about the cultural norms and respect for the Nhlapo family than the circumstances that compelled her to come to them. One step wrong, she knew, and she would be told she was not married from Swaziland to kill children but to "make" them for the family to grow.

After the initial shock of Mkhathini's death was absorbed and discussion about burying him had finished, Mama KaZili had to answer a few questions, just as she had expected. The house was full of curious relatives, each one of them listening very attentively. The atmosphere was that of a serious village court case.

"You mean you didn't ask permission to come here from your husband or from your parents?" Matweba, my father's oldest brother, asked with serenity.

"Yes, after all, I know they would have refused," answered Mama KaZili coolly.

"And what lesson do you think you are teaching other wives in this big Nhlapo family?"

Mama KaZili kept silent.

"Talk!" scolded Matweba, with muttered support from the group of men.

"Talk!" repeated Matweba, shouting at the top of his voice.

Mama KaZili looked at him straight in the eye and said, "I'm teaching them that when husbands don't fulfill their duties as heads and breadwinners of families, to an extent that children die of hunger, they should not sit there and do nothing, waiting for manna from heaven. I have brought my children to you for a month or two to have something to eat while I look for employment.''

"And again without permission?"

"Yes," Mama KaZili answered with firmness.

Once again, there were rumbling voices from the men, this time louder and more threatening. I remembered one case two years ago in Habelo when one woman had told her husband outright that he was lazy. Every corner of the village had groups of men cursing,

"What an insult! A woman tell her husband he is lazy!" By the end of the week, the woman had disappeared. Her husband had beaten her severely. Nobody knew whether she had been admitted to the hospital or had run back to her parents, *a ngalile* (a wife who runs away from her husband back to her parents), or had joined other runaway wives, who were eventually called prostitutes. (Because separation and divorce are more common nowadays, that has changed.) There were rumors and speculations, until a few days later, when dogs dug up the decaying body of the woman in her garden.

"Order!" Matweba demanded silence.

In addition to the rumblings, there was an uncomfortable chaotic movement in the house. Men felt insulted by Mama KaZili, and obviously some of them wanted to "touch" or "lay hands" on her. Others gaped at her with utter scorn.

"She must go back to Swaziland!" a voice shot to the roof.

"O-o-o-o-order!" Matweba shouted vehemently in a roar that could have frightened a lion. There was a smell of onion from the other room. My stomach groaned. My mouth watered. If only we would eat in a few minutes! At least by now we were warmed by the yellowish-blue flames of burning dung. But we were still starving. Would we ever eat, amid these heated quarrels of grownups? I wondered.

A band of birds passed next to the window, singing their old melodious song happily, as though it was not snowing outside. In the house, a deafening silence fell once more for Mama KaZili to speak.

"May I remind you that I'm a legal citizen of Lesotho through marriage? I don't intend to go back to Swaziland. And no one can force me to go, not even my husband."

"Does this woman ever read the Bible? Will she ever learn to respect us?" one man asked loudly near the door. Other voices joined in.

"Yes, the Bible. And respect to us?" The question was directed to Mama KaZili via Matweba.

"Yes, I know the Bible," she answered. "It says women should keep silent. 'They are commanded to be under obedience, as also saith the law.' Customary laws also treat women as children who are expected to be under the man's guidance and protection. Women are considered weak and naïve. They have to seek permission even for little things like visiting friends and parents, looking for employment, seeking to attend school, or asking for a scholarship or loan or applying for a site. . . . Name them all," Mama KaZili told them in a clear, firm tone. Her voice had a ring to it, like a medium-sized school bell. It reflected self-confidence, industriousness, fairness, and humbleness, just a touch of hunger, loneliness, and tiredness. The way everybody listened quietly in the house, you would have thought they were hypnotized.

Mama KaZili continued undisturbed. "All these forms of injustice take place in a government [Basutoland National Party] that repeatedly points out with pride that it has been elected by women because men, who are predominantly away in the South African mines, are mostly pro-BCP [Basutoland Congress Party]. Society and government don't want to give women a chance. Women have to seek permission for everything that can improve their lives. Before I pass away in this world, I want to have had a chance to improve my life and the lives of my children."

Everybody in the house was looking at her in disbelief, openmouthed, eyebrows raised. Mama KaZili must have given them more than enough to chew at a go. Men sighed without a word. One after the other they started going out of the house silently.

The last to go was Matweba, who said in a declarative tone: "Men solve family problems best at the kraal. We shall be back soon to give our final word on the matter." He closed the door behind him with what I thought was a bang.

Fortunately for them, it had stopped snowing, although it was still freezing outside. I heard a cow moo at the kraal, obviously mistaking the men for herdboys.

As soon as the men had gone, plates of food were brought in for us to eat. That was what Mama KaZili had brought us to Makhoakhoeng for: to have something to eat before we went to sleep. The food was delicious: *papa, papasane* (a wild vegetable which is resistant to winter cold), and mutton. It was two years since I had eaten meat. The smell of onion was there.

I had always been told that my nickname, Richman, was derived from one old Nhlapo whom I was named after who lived at Makhoakhoeng some-time in the late 1890s and owned a lot of sheep. That day, with mutton on my plate, the nickname made a lot of sense.

There were mixed feelings about what Mama KaZili had said to the men. Elderly wives thought she shouldn't have spoken like that to the heads of families, and that she should offer an apology when they came back from the kraal. Younger wives thought the truth had finally been told. It was high time they stood up on their feet to do something about their lives, they said. Even if men did not admit it, economic pressures in the families appeared too heavy for them to lift alone. It was time they swallowed their pride and accepted reality. Mama KaZili nodded her head with satisfaction, agreeing with the younger women. Her preaching was developing roots.

One by one, in single file, the men came in. They were silent and frightening. Dusk made them look like tall black shades moving in silhouette. One by one, they sat down in their chairs, while the women remained seated on the floor. Once again, Matweba took the chairmanship.

Soon there was a frightening silence in the house. Those who hadn't finished eating had to stop abruptly. The atmosphere became electric. Everybody knew that decisions made from the kraal could not be questioned. In a way, the decisions were regarded as holy because men were made heads of families by the Almighty God.

The last man came in from the other house, carrying a bundle in his hands, wrapped in a white sheet. He put the bundle next to my mother. It was the corpse of Mkhathini, the deceased child. The audience remained breathless.

With a thundering note of finality in his voice, Matweba broke the silence: "I, Matweba, the brother of your husband, together with his other close relatives, have decided that you, Mama KaZili, are bringing disrespectful and misleading lessons to our wives here at Makhoakhoeng. If they allow you to do that at Habelo, we cannot allow it here. We have therefore decided that, because of snow, the children will remain here for a week or so. As soon as the snow is over, they will be sent back to Habelo, back to you. We cannot allow you to humiliate Moshe, your husband, our brother, by scattering his children all around in the name of looking for employment without anybody's permission. If we can allow you to humiliate him, our wives can also go out of hand and humiliate us. We cannot allow the breakup of the Nhlapo family. Those of us who have not been fortunate enough to get employment in the mines have the duty of keeping the Nhlapo family intact.

"Tomorrow morning some of us will accompany you back to Habelo to help with the burial service for the deceased. You will have to carry the corpse back home on your back, just like you brought it here today. I have spoken."

As soon as he had finished, everyone stood up to disperse to their families in silence.

Matweba and his men might have been keeping culture, customs, and the Nhlapo family intact, but they were still in for another surprise, another challenge. The decision from the kraal was not definite and final enough for Mama KaZili. She stood up to speak. Members of the family who were already going had to stop to listen.

"You may have spoken. But I also have meant every word I spoke to you and to everybody. It is up to us women to stand up for our lives and the lives of our children . . . I'll go back to work hard, hard for them and for myself . . ." She spoke aloud in a tone that changed to a familiar one I had heard several hours ago when we were struggling to climb the slippery, snowy mountain.

She did not finish all she wanted to say because she fell down heavily, just like the last time she did on the mountain with a baby on her back. But this time she did not utter the name of my father in disgust when she fell. It was just a heavy and very silent fall. Her body lay painfully crooked next to the body of Mkhathini.

My sister and I were the first to cry hysterically. We did not like the thought that our mother might have died too, leaving us alone in the brutal, uncaring world.

Very quickly we were taken to the other house, because we were making unbearable noise and disturbing the adults. They were pouring cold water on Mama KaZili's head to wake her up.

I recalled all the events of the day and all that Mama KaZili had said. In one instance, she had said: "Before I pass away in this world I want to have had a chance to improve my life and the lives of my children." I wondered if this would ever happen.

By the end of the year she would be working as a primary teacher without my father's or his parents' permission. From her meager salary she sent us to school, again without anybody's permission. From then on, there was always something to eat before we went to sleep.

—1994

Steve Chimombo

(BORN 1945) MALAWI

Steve Chimombo has been an active force in Malawi's literary resurgence for the past twenty years. A professor of English at Chancellor College, University of Malawi, he has edited and encouraged student work in addition to founding Writers and Artists Services International. His education has been international: a B.A. from the University of Malawi, an M.A. from Leeds, an Ed.D. from Columbia, and stints as a creative writer at the Iowa International Writers Workshop and the Macdowell Colony. He has also taught briefly in the United States, in addition to his more lengthy career as an academic in Malawi.

The scope of Chimombo's writing is equally broad. His six volumes of poetry include *Napolo and the Python* (1994). He has had one novel, *The Basket Girl* (1990), published and has had several plays presented in Malawi, including *The Rainmaker* (1975). A collection of short stories, *Tell Me a Story* (1992), several children's books, and a volume of folklore (*Malawian Oral Literature*, 1988) are part of his extensive output, in addition to several academic guides to Malawian literature.

In an interview with Lee Nichols, commentator for the Voice of America, Chimombo stated that the main goal of all his writing has been to show "the cyclical nature of things, the rhythms of life, night and day, birth, death, and so on." As the story "Taken" implies, until recently conditions for the writer in Malawi have not been particularly supportive of creative work. Chimombo has said: "The story recaptures the processes of eliminating writers under Dr. Hastings Kamuzu Banda's regime between 1964 and 1994. Writers, artists, and dissenters were systematically arrested, detained, killed, or forced into exile. Although the story was written under such conditions, it could not be published until democracy and multi-partyism were ushered in during the second republic. In fact, an editor of a U.K. journal of letters refused to publish it before this period for fear it might jeopardize the writer. The characters involved in the story are well known in Malawi's academic circles and have granted the author permission to publish the story as it is. The names and places, however, are pure fiction.''

Of his own attempts to survive as a writer during the Banda years, the author remarks: "My writings—poetry, fiction, and even faction—over the past thirty years have been forced to be expressed in mythological terms. Writing openly or plainly during Banda's reign of terror was an invitation to be 'meat for the crocodiles'; hence my taking refuge in symbol and myth. Those who know the system of metaphors I use understand what I am talking about. The system is still accessible to those who are foreign to it. In the story, however, I am dealing with actualities. I was involved in some of the events and there was no room for mythologizing anymore. Even myth offered no route for escape.''

TAKEN

1

It was a few minutes before noon, and I was packing my briefcase slowly, when Zinenani, an old friend now working in the capital city, burst in.

"Alekeni!" he shouted unceremoniously.

"Hi!"

"When did you get back?"

"Get back?"

"I thought you'd gone abroad."

"It won't be for a month or so."

"But the whole capital is full of rumors of your having gone already, and decided to stay on."

"Stay on?"

"Defected is the word."

"Defected? Why?"

"Because of what happened to Ndasauka."

"But I wasn't involved in that."

"Rumor has it that since your fellow writer was detained you decided to skip the country."

"But why should I do that? I haven't done anything that would make me go into exile."

"Believe me, when I saw you walk up to your office a few minutes ago,

I thought I was seeing a ghost. The rumors were that strong. I came up just to make sure I was seeing right.''

"But I was on the radio two days ago.''

"That could have been prerecorded.''

"That's true. Anyway, you can tell my well-wishers in the capital that I'm still around.''

"But you'll still be going abroad?''

"I can't miss that opportunity.''

"The rumors aren't anticipating your exile?''

"Believe me, if I had wanted to go into exile, I would have done so years ago when I was away studying in the U.K. and U.S.A. The thought seriously occurred to me then, but after toying with it, I realized I'm, deep down, an ancestor worshiper. I also discovered that I cannot write the genuine stuff when I'm on foreign soil. I decided to brave my own country.''

"It's good the rumors were just that. We need fellows like you around.''

"What are you doing here?''

"Consultations.''

The phone rang. I let it ring.

"It's nice to see you, all the same.''

"I've got to be going.'' Zinenani turned to the door.

I waved him off and lifted the receiver. "Hello?''

"This is Chodziwa-dziwa.''

It was my kid brother. He had not been in touch for a long time. He, too, worked in the capital.

"How are you?''

"Fine. I'm actually speaking from your house.''

"When did you come down?''

"I just arrived. I wanted to talk to you.''

"I'll be right over. It's lunchtime, anyhow.''

As I finished packing my briefcase, I puzzled over what Zinenani had said. The rumor was getting slightly stale. Just yesterday, I had been waylaid by a colleague's wife in the supermarket.

"Alekeni, come here!''

She took me by the hand and literally dragged me between two food counters. She was so enthusiastic I worried someone might suspect we were going to embrace or something, the way she furtively looked around and then drew near me as if she wanted to touch me.

"So"—she heaved a sigh of relief—"you're not gone!"

"Gone where?"

"Taken by the police."

"Why should the police take me?"

"Because of Ndasauka."

"But I don't even know what he's inside for."

"You don't need to know to be implicated. You're a friend of his, and a writer, too."

"Even then."

It had ended like that, leaving me thoroughly peeved at the source of the rumor. In Mtalika, rumor diffused at the speed of sound: word of mouth, telephone, letter, even telepathy. It was said that before you decided to seduce your friend's wife, people would already know about it and actively make sure it came about. Before long, I would end up believing in the rumor myself, even when right now I was still in Mtalika, getting into my own car to drive from my office home to have lunch with my family and kid brother. A free man.

"Daddy! Daddy!"

My five-year-old always ran up to the garage doors to meet me as soon as he heard the car in the driveway. Between our dog and him, I could not tell who gave me the warmer welcome. Sometimes they almost tripped over each other in the rush to meet me with cries and barks. It was overwhelming.

"Your brother is in the sitting room" were my wife's welcoming words.

I walked through the dining room to the lounge to find Chodziwa-dziwa flipping through a popular magazine. He looked up and grinned sheepishly. Something was bothering him.

"So it's not true" was his greeting.

"What?"

"That you are missing."

"Missing?" This was getting to be too enormous to be funny.

"A man came round to my place two days ago to say that something had happened involving a friend of yours, that your friend had been taken, and that you had disappeared without a trace."

"This is ridiculous. Who was the man?"

"I don't know, and he refused to identify himself. He said he just wanted your relatives to know that you could not be found."

It was wearisome, if not monstrous. I reviewed my involvement with Ndasauka again.

2

I was going too fast but could do nothing about it. I was too agitated to be driving at that speed, yet I still maintained it, even when I kept going off the road at each minor bend. I had had one too many, but it was too late to start regretting that. I could not talk about Ndasauka rationally with his best friend by my side.

"Surely"—I detected the hoarseness in my voice—"you must know something he was involved in?"

"I'm telling you I don't."

"You don't know, or you don't want to discuss it?"

"I don't know anything that he was doing for the police to be interested in him."

"You're his closest friend."

"That doesn't mean he told me his entire life history."

"You were there when the police came to get him."

"It's very simple. I had invited him out to lunch at the club for a change. We had just finished the meal and were having a drink before going back to work when they found us at the bar."

"They knew you were there?"

"That's where they found us. I didn't know what was happening at first. One of them came over and called Ndasauka out. After a few minutes, another one came in, looking for nothing in particular. When Ndasauka didn't come back after fifteen minutes, I went out to investigate. I found him in handcuffs."

"You mean they handcuffed him right outside the club?"

"It created quite a sensation. There was a small crowd when I went out. I followed the police van to the office. There was another crowd as they took him up to his office."

"Still in handcuffs?"

"Yes. Another contingent was already in the office going through his papers. I learned this from the secretary."

"How did she take it?"

"Scared. So gray she looked almost white. She couldn't type, read, crochet, or phone. I understand they threatened to arrest her, too, if she so much as moved from her chair."

"What were they looking for?"

"Search me."

"It comes back to what you know about all this. If you don't know, and his colleagues don't either, who is there to tell us what is happening?''

"The police."

I nearly exploded, the car swerved, and I hastily righted it again.

I felt cheated out of something in life and frustrated by the tantalizing thought that perhaps beneath it all there was really nothing at all to discover. Perhaps the police did not even know what they were looking for. Maybe they only had Ndasauka on suspicion, pending further investigations. If that was the case, Ndasauka would be in for a long, long time. He might not ever come out.

The normal detention orders operated for twenty-eight days without formal charges. After that period, formal charges had to be filed, a statement issued, or the detainee released. The Republic of Mandania, however, operated neither with normal detention procedures nor with formal charges. A decade or so before, the country had gone through a spate of detentions of several highly placed persons in the civil service, the armed forces, and the university. All were supposedly suspected of planning a coup. Although five years later most of the detainees had been released, some members of that group were still rotting in the numerous camps dotted around the country.

"Are we going back to the seventies?" was the question everyone asked as soon as Ndasauka was taken, and it was rumored—but never verified— that other members of the citizenry had also been or were about to be detained.

"When the police behave like that, it means they have reached the final act," someone who had lived through the terrors of the seventies said, meaning that the swoop was too dramatic and public to be followed by others of a similar nature.

In the seventies, enough terror had been generated for you to distrust even your closest relative and neighbor, for fear they might turn out to be one of the numerous informers in the pay of the police. People had disappeared into detention, demise, or exile. The whole period was shrouded in such a terrifying cloak of mystery the media never covered it, no one talked about it in public, social places were emptied because it was safer to retire to your home after work. However, even within the safety of your home, you feared your servant, even your wife and children, and dreaded a knock at the door, lest it should be your turn to be taken.

3

"Don't get involved in this."

It was the parish priest. He had gone to visit Ndasauka's family and then dropped in to see me.

"How can I get involved in something I don't know anything about?"

I was exasperated. Why was everyone implicating me in the whole thing? The first hint that people thought I would be the next one to go was the surprised faces I met at work the day after Ndasauka was taken.

"When did they let you out?" the secretary had asked me.

"Who? What?"

"People said you were also taken yesterday. Someone saw the flashing lights of a police van in your drive at seven o'clock last night."

"It's a long drive and the driver might have been reversing."

"But what was it doing there, of all places, and at that hour?"

I could never figure out the answer to that one. Nor to the next, which I got from a colleague at coffee time the same day. "Someone told me you were taken for at least a few hours, if not the whole of last night."

"Who's spreading all these rumors?" I exploded. "I was at home and in bed the whole of last night. Why don't people ask me or my wife or my children before jumping to conclusions based on non-evidence? I know I went to Ndasauka's office after I'd heard what had happened to him. I saw the police there. I know I went to his house when I didn't find him at the office. I found the police and Ndasauka there. I was there to see him finally bundled into the police Land Rover to be heard of no more. But that was all I did."

It had not been all I did, though. I'd arrived at Ndasauka's home just as he was writing postdated checks to give to his children—his wife was away in the capital on a six-month course. I paced up and down outside, not knowing whether or not I could go in to speak to him, or, in fact, what I would say to him if I could.

The police crowded him out of the house.

"You must take me, too!" Ndasauka's seventy-year-old mother cried as she tottered on crutches, following the group outside. It was the only clear sign of emotion that was expressed by any member of the family. I do not think the children fully understood what was happening, the oldest being only thirteen.

"Don't worry, Mother, he'll come back soon," one of the plainclothesmen said unconvincingly as they went over to the Land Rover parked just beyond the garage. Another police wagon was next to it. So many cars and officers for just one man.

"Excuse me," I introduced myself. "I'm a friend of Ndasauka's and I would like to know what's happening."

"Orders from the government: We are to take him to the capital."

"Where in the capital?" It was an automatic question.

"We can't say."

"But I have to tell his wife where he's being taken."

"You can't do that. You must not discuss with anyone what has happened today, until you hear from us."

"When will that be?"

"Tomorrow morning."

"But these kids will be alone all night with their old grandmother if his wife is not informed immediately. Who's going to look after them tonight?"

"I'm sorry, those are our instructions."

"Can I talk to Ndasauka?"

"Of course."

I went over to him.

"Look," I whispered, although the police could hear me, "do you know what this is all about?"

"All I know," he said loudly, "is that I'm being taken to the capital on government orders."

"What would you like me to do?"

He looked at his mute children. I thought someone would burst into tears.

He cleared his throat. "Look after the kids." He straightened up.

I watched him walk to the police car, flanked by the Special Branch men. They climbed in the back door of the Land Rover, putting him in the middle. The wagon followed. No sirens. No tears. That was the last we saw of him.

"Pirira is arriving by the trailer tonight." The parish priest brought me back to the present.

"She knows?"

"Of course. Could you pick her up? I have a meeting with the bishop, and it threatens to be a long one."

"That's all right. I'll meet her."

And so began the longest night in my life. The "trailer," as the late-night bus was called, was aptly nicknamed. It took the whole night to reach Mtalika from the capital, when other buses took no more than three hours. I had not known these details before and had gone to the bus station at nine o'clock to check on Ndasauka's wife. They told me the bus would arrive at eleven. At eleven, it still did not appear. Nor at one.

I parked by one of the shops with lighted fronts near the bus station and tried to sleep in the car. At three, another car came and parked behind mine. I raised a sleepy head.

The other man recognized me. "You're not waiting for the trailer, are you?"

"Yes."

"You're too early. It won't be here till four-thirty or later."

"But why didn't they tell me that before, so I could sleep at home?"

"They didn't know, either. It's quite erratic."

"Surely they could have phoned?"

"Once it has left the capital, it stops to drop or pick up any mail or passengers at every single trading center. It's useless to try to keep track of it. Those who know about its unpredictability wait until dawn before venturing to meet it."

I looked at my watch: three-fifteen. If I went home, I would probably sleep until midday. I decided to stay where I was.

The trailer groaned to a halt at four-thirty, dragging the mail van, from whence its nickname. I walked across the lot.

"Pirira," I greeted Ndasauka's wife. It was painful to try to smile.

"What happened?" She sobbed. She looked as if she had been crying all the way and was on the verge of collapse.

"The car is over there."

I got her bag and walked briskly. She had to trot after me.

"It's like this," I said as I drove off. "We really don't know what's happening."

It was no consolation. I let her get what was left out of her system and drove in silence all the way to her house.

"Mommy!" was the delighted cry of the youngest boy as he rushed out to my car. The joy of seeing his mother and the reason for her being there were irreconcilable.

"I'll be in touch." I hastily drove off.

"I'm sorry to get you involved like this," the parish priest had continued. "You're a fellow writer and a friend of his. You should check your travel documents."

4

I turned into the side road leading up to the police camp and stopped at the barrier just inside the iron gates. There was a flurry of activity in the little hut on the side of the road. Two armed men emerged.

One marched purposefully toward the car. "Name and address?"

He leaned through the open window, surveyed me and the interior of the car. He paused by my left hand, which was still holding the gearshift. I ignored the bayonet waving half a foot away from my throat and supplied the information.

"Can we help you?"

I mentioned my desire to visit one of the top-ranking officers.

"Just a moment, sir." He marched back to the hut. I could see him phoning.

I wondered why there were roadblocks manned by heavily armed police at several points on either side of Mtalika town. It seemed as if Mandania was in a perpetual state of siege or under curfew. As far as I knew, the nearest war was across the border, and it had nothing to do with us.

"Just obeying orders, sir." The man came back. "I have to ask his permission to let you through."

I shrugged and asked for directions. The barrier was lifted, I drove past slowly, and waved back at the mock salute I was given by the other man.

"Alekeni! Long time no see!"

The officer, in civilian clothes, pumped my hand with exaggerated enthusiasm, as I got out of the car. "Come in."

I didn't know if my mission could be discussed in the house with so many children milling around. "Thank you!" I said all the same.

The sitting room was filled with enough furniture for two houses. He waved me to a sumptuous chair, into which I sank up to my waist. I bobbed up again and sat forward on the edge of the seat.

"This is Alekeni, my old schoolmate." He introduced me to a parade of sons and daughters, who detached themselves from various corners and rooms and advanced an arm and a shy smile. They filed back to their occupations afterwards like a small regiment.

Brief pause.

I decided to plunge straight into the purpose of my visit.

He jerked forward. "Yes." He spoke rapidly. "Ndasauka. I heard about it. Routine, of course. I'm kept informed of what is happening."

"The problem is," I continued, "that we don't know what is happening and we are really worried about it. It's a week now, and there's no news of his whereabouts or even the reasons for his being taken in."

"But why come to me?" He was very agitated. "It's not really my department."

"For the simple reason that we were at school together, we were friends. His wife also said you go to the same church. She, in fact, is the one who suggested I should come to see you."

"You realize this is a delicate matter?"

"But we don't know anything."

"I'm telling you it's a delicate matter. If anyone knew you came to see me about it, I would be in trouble."

"Surely you can mention at least to his wife the nature of the suspicions or the speculations as to why he was taken?"

"It's too sensitive."

"I take it it's not a criminal charge, then."

"In his case, it wouldn't be that."

"It's political, then?"

"Look, I only got to know about it as a matter of routine. I didn't inquire further into the details, although I saw his name on the list."

"There are others involved, too?"

"Yes, and I trust you appreciate the fact that I can't just lift the phone and call the Special Branch?"

"I do, but surely on the list there was some explanation why the people had to be taken?"

"That's why I'm saying it's too delicate to discuss with you at the moment. Give me a few days and perhaps I can let you know what can be safely told."

"When can I get in touch with you again?"

"I'll get in touch with you."

When we parted, I had a strong suspicion he would not contact me again and that I had lost an old school friend forever. As I drove out past the armed guards, I wondered if the country hadn't been in a state of emergency all along and I hadn't known. It was too delicate to announce publicly, and so, too, would it be when the next one was taken.

—1996

Sindiwe Magona

(BORN 1943) SOUTH AFRICA

Born in the Transkei (a former South African homeland), Sindiwe Magona grew up in Cape Town's black townships. She attended the University of London from 1971 to 1973, eventually earning her B.A. in psychology and history from the University of South Africa in Pretoria. Graduate work took her to Columbia University from 1981 to 1983, where she earned a Master of Science in Organizational Social Work, with a minor in Business Administration. In 1992, she was awarded an Honorary Doctorate in Humane Letters from Hartwick College in Oneonta, New York.

Magona began her writing career with a two-part biography: *To My Children's Children* (1990) and *Forced to Grow* (1992). During 1993 and 1994, she translated the former into Xhosa and wrote *Imida* (1995), a book of essays, also in Xhosa. Her two collections of short stories—*Living, Loving and Lying Awake at Night* (1991) and *Push-Push! and Other Stories* (1996)—have been widely praised and reprinted. Her current writing includes a one-woman play, *I Promised Myself a Fabulous Middle Age*, and a forthcoming novel, *Perhaps I Do Not Die in Vain*.

Magona is active in the South African literary scene, giving frequent lectures and readings as well as participating in the *Weekly Mail* and the *Guardian Book Week* annual literary events. She lives in New York City, where she works for the United Nations.

The author says about "I'm Not Talking About That, Now": "In this story, an ordinary family living in one of South African townships takes center stage during the post-1976 political upheavals in that country. . . . My aim was to show how the political impinged on the personal; people's lives were affected in ways they had perhaps never imagined; the heroism of the day, which we hear a lot about, had another face—beastly behavior from men, women, and people so young we still referred to them as 'children'—all people who, in another time, would not have known they could be capable of such. Someone refusing to take a wounded neighbor to the doctor? A father refusing to take action so that he could go and bury his own child? Singing and dancing over the writhing, flaming body of a victim of an attack who'd been deliberately set alight?

"Yet most, if not all, of the actors in the South African drama were ordinary people, not know for thuggery before they did what they did. I suppose you could say I'm grappling with the transmogrifying power of a certain type of event. Understanding that, perhaps, might we come to judge less harshly? Or not judge at all? I really don't know. Like a lot of other people, I'm just trying to understand what really happened to the gentle, humane, kindly people of my childhood. Could they be the same as these that people the stories that come out of the South Africa of the last thirty years? I am mourning the lost innocence of families where the husband's snoring was a major disturbing event, the wife's industriousness, or lack thereof, a calamity."

I'M NOT TALKING ABOUT THAT, NOW

Mamvulane lay very still, her eyes wide open, staring unseeingly into nowhere. She listened to her husband snore softly beside her.

A big bold orange band lay on the carpet—painted there by the strong dawn light pouring through the bright orange-curtained window.

Reluctantly, she focused her eyes. Her head was throbbing. She glanced at the alarm clock on the dressing table. God, it wasn't even five o'clock yet. How was she going to survive this day? she asked herself. Her right eye felt as though someone was poking a red-hot iron rod into it from the back of her head, where he'd first drilled a hole.

Irritatedly, she pushed her husband onto his side. Immediately, the snoring stopped. She listened to the drilling inside her head, assuming that with the noise of Mdlangathi's snoring gone, the pain would subside. And, indeed, it did appear to be in abeyance if not completely vanished.

She took a deep and noisy inward draw of breath. Cruel fancy played her tricks. She could swear the air was faintly laced with the barest soupçon of the bittersweet smell of coffee. Mmmhh! What she wouldn't give for just one cup. Just one.

Her stomach growled. Swiftly, she placed one hand on her still girlishly flat tummy. She felt the quick ripples of air bubbles in her bowels. When last had she eaten? And what had she had then?

Mdlangathi, her husband, lying next to her, mumbled something in his sleep and turned over to lie, once more, facing the ceiling, his distinctly discernible paunch hilling the blankets.

Immediately, the snoring resumed, provoking swift and righteous retaliation from his wife, reflex by now, after all the years with him and his snoring.

Mamvulane dug an elbow into his side, grumbling, *"Uyarhona, Mdlangathi. Uyarhona!"* for habits die hard. In their more than twenty years of marriage, among the constants in their relationship was his snoring whenever he lay "like a rat suffering from acute heartburn," her talking to him as though he were awake and the answers he never failed to mumble—pearls from an ancient oracle. She always chided herself that she actually listened, paid attention to the barely audible ramblings of a snoring man who'd gone to bed drunk. But she always did. And tonight not only was he drunk when he went to bed, Mamvulane told herself, but she had never seen him so agitated. Would she never learn?

Last night, however, was the worst she'd ever seen him. He'd returned positively excited, ranting and raving about the gross lack of respect of today's young people.

"Baqalekisiwe, ndifung' uTat' ekobandayo. Baqalekisiw' aba bantwana, Mamvulane."

"What children are cursed?" his wife wanted to know.

And that is when he told her of the curse the actions of today's children would surely invite onto their heads.

"Why do you say such a terrible thing?" his wife wanted to know.

"Now, now, just as the sun set, I was on my way here from the single men's zones, where I'd gone to get a little something to wet my parched throat. What do you think I should come across? Mmhhmh?" He stopped and considered her with his bleary eyes.

His wife conceded ignorance. "I'm sure I don't know. Why don't you tell me," she said. She wanted to scrape together what food there was in the house. And try to prepare a meal.

"Do you know that a group of boys accosted a man? A grown man, who was circumcised? Boys laid their filthy hands on such a man . . . a man old enough to be their father?"

"Where was this?" asked Mamvulane, not sure how much of Mdlangathi's ramblings she should take seriously.

"You ask me something I have already told you. Where are your ears, woman? Or else, you think I'm drunk and pay no attention to what I tell you? No wonder your children are as bad as they are, where would they learn to listen and obey since you, our wives, who are their mothers, have stopped doing that? Mmhhh?''

"Are you telling me the story or should I go about my business?" retorted Mamvulane. She was taking a risk, for she did want to hear the story. But she also knew that her husband rather fancied the sound of his own voice.

"If you want to hear the story, then pay attention. I told you I was from the zones. On my way here, I came across a group of boys, you know, these little rascals who are always passing by here, pretending to be visiting your son, Mteteli, when you full know it's your daughter they want. And they were manhandling one of their fathers.''

"Who was that?"

"Now, you make me laugh. You imagine I stopped and asked them for their *dompasses*? Am I mad? Or do you think I am a fool? Or is it your hurry to be a widow that is putting those stupid words into your mouth? Mmhh?''

With great deliberateness, Mdlangathi attended to the business of picking his teeth. First, he took out a match. Then he took out his jackknife and started whittling slowly on the tiny match, chiseling it till the back had a sharp point.

"When a woman told me what those dogs were doing, I knew enough to mind my own business, my friend. Today's children show no respect for their fathers.

"This man, the woman said to me, had had too much to drink. Now, mind you,'' quickly, he went to the defense of his fallen comrade, "the man drank from his own pocket, he didn't ask those silly boys to buy him his liquor. So what is his sin? Tell me, what is this man's sin when he has drunk liquor he bought with his own money? Why should these mad children make that their business, mmhhmh?''

"What did they do?"

"These little devils,'' bellowed Mdlangathi, eyes flashing. "Don't they force the sad man to drink down a solution of *Javel? Javel*, Mamvulane! Do you hear me? What do you think *Javel* does to a man's throat? To his stomach? I ask you, what do you think it does to those things? Just visit and make jokes with them, heh?''

He glowered at her as though she were one of the "little devils" and he was itching to teach her a lesson.

Bang! went his fist on the table.

"A grown man, no less! The boys make him drink that poison. They tell him, 'We are helping you, Tata, not killing you!' Then, when they see that his belly is well extended from all that liquid, they give him a feather from a cock's tail and force him to insert it into his throat, '. . . deep down the path the poison traveled,' they say to him.

"The man does as he is told. Only he is so enfeebled by the heaviness of his stomach and what he'd had before he drank the *Javel* solution that his attempts do not immediately bring the required results. Whereupon the urchins take matters into their hands.

" 'This poison crushes Africa's seed!' they say, one of them taking the feather from his trembling hand and pushing it down the man's gullet himself.

"Do you hear what I'm telling you, Mamvulane? Even a witchdoctor does not put his own hand into the throat of the man he is helping to bring up poison from his craw.

"But that is what these wretched children did. Put their dirty hands down the throats of their fathers and forced them to regurgitate the liquor they had drunk."

None too sober himself, Mdlangathi embarked upon a bitter tirade directed at all of today's children, miserable creatures who had no respect for their elders.

Recalling last night's events or the account her husband had given her, Mamvulane now looked down at him, asleep still by her side. Poor Mdlangathi. So vulnerable in the soft early-morning light. Poor Mdlangathi. He must have got the fright of his life, she thought, shaking her head in dumb disbelief at the things that were happening these days in their lives.

Her immediate problem, however, was what were they all going to eat once they got out of bed? She had all but scraped the bottom of the barrel last night. Her mind made an inventory of all the food they had in the house: a potato, by no means gigantic; two small onions; a quarter packet of beans but no samp; there was no salt; a cup or a cup and a half of mealie meal . . . And then there was no paraffin with which to cook whatever she might have, far from adequate as that itself was.

Three weeks now, the consumer boycott had been going on. Three weeks, they had been told not to go to the shops. She was at her wit's end. Mdlangathi and the children expected to eat—boycott or no boycott. Whether she had gone to the shops or not didn't much concern them. All they understood, especially the younger children, was that their tummies

were growling and they wanted something to eat. And their unreasonable-
ness, conceded Mamvulane, was understandable. Now, her husband's case
was cause for vexation to her. Wasn't Mdlangathi another thing altogether?
A grown man. With all that was happening. But still, he wanted and expected no changes in his life. Didn't he still go to work every day? That's
what he'd asked her when she told him they were running out of food.
What did she do with the money he gave her? As though, in these mad and
crazy days, money were the only issue, the sole consideration. And not the
very shopping itself—the getting of the food. With the comrades guarding
every entry point in Guguletu. And neighbor informing on neighbor. People
sprouting eyes at the back of their heads so that they could go and curry
favor with the comrades, giving them information about others, especially
those with whom they did not see eye to eye about things. Yes, it was so.
For the very people who denounced others to the comrades were not above
turning a blind eye to the same things . . . when the actors were people
they favored. But did her very reasonable, understanding, and loving husband, who always gave her his wages, understand that? No. He thought she
should just hop on a bus and go to Claremont and there go to Pick 'n Pay!
Mdlangathi was something else, concluded Mamvulane, shaking her head
slowly like one deep in thought. How did he arrive at thinking, at a time
like this, that food shopping was still a simple matter of whether one had
money in one's pocket?

The very thought of getting up was too much for her to entertain this
morning. Hunger has that effect. Her anger mounted with the growing
realization that she faced a hard day with no answers to the questions it
raised, that she had to feed her family and had nothing at all that she could
put together to make a meal.

It's all very well for the comrades to stop people from going to the shops,
she fumed. They were fighting the businessmen, they said. But as far as she
could see, it was only people like herself, poor people in the township, who
were starving. The businessmen were eating. So were their families. They
were getting fatter and fatter by the day. They had meat and bread and fruit
and vegetables and milk for their babies. They put heavily laden plates on
their tables . . . not just once a day, as most people like herself did in good
times, no, but each time they had a meal—several times a day. Oh, no, the
businessmen the comrades were fighting were in no danger of dying from
starvation. It was not their bowels that had nothing but the howling air in
them. And not their children whose ribs one could count.

Midafternoon that same day, Mamvulane said, "*I have to do something today!*" As there was no one else in the house, she was talking to herself. Thereafter, without a word even to her very good neighbor and friend, Nolitha, she made her way out of her yard. Looking neither left nor right, away she hurried.

She had her day clothes on, complete with apron and back-flattened slippers. The pale of her rather large heels showing, she flip-flopped down the road. Anyone seeing her thus attired would have assumed she wasn't going any farther than perhaps fifty or so meters from her very own doorstep.

It was a little after three—time to start the evening meal. For those who could do that. Not me, thought Mamvulane bitterly. Not poor me, she said under her breath, walking away as nonchalantly as you please.

NY 74 is a crescent street with three exit points: north, west, and south. Mamvulane's family lived directly opposite the western exit, separated from it by two large buildings, the Community Center in front of her house and plumb in the center of the circle, and the Old Apostolic Church behind it. In reality, therefore, from her house she could not see anyone coming or leaving from that exit which lay on NY 65. The other two exits were clearly visible from her house. And usually those were the ones she favored because, until she disappeared altogether, she could always turn back and yell for one of the children to bring her anything she might have forgotten.

But this day she slowly made her way toward NY 65, soon losing sight of her house. "*Andizi kubukel' abantwana bam besifa yindlala.*" And thus emboldened by her own thoughts, she went on her way. No, she was not going to watch her children starve to death.

Her plan was simple. And daring. Straight through NY 65 she walked. Into the zones, she went, her gait slow and steady, not once hesitating. Past the zones and into the Coloured township of Mannenberg. She'd gained enough anonymity, she deemed. Along Hanover Road she made her way until she found a bus stop. With a sigh, she stopped and leaned against the electric pole marking the stop.

Into her breast her hand fished for the little bundle, the handkerchief wherein lay her stash. Money. Bus fare and much more.

Carefully, she extricated enough for the fare and put the rest back where it had been, securely tied it into a knot at one corner of the handkerchief. And then back went the purse, safe and secure.

Her wait wasn't long. A bus came. She clambered on—one of only a few still making their way to the shopping suburb at that time of day, and

definitely the only woman from Guguletu (or any of the other African townships, for that matter) on that bus. The buses coming back from Claremont
were full with workers and shoppers returning home.

Mamvulane found a seat easily. Her heart was quite calm. Her chin quite
firm. Her head held high. She was amazed at how unbelievably easily she
had accomplished her mission thus far. But she knew that the real difficulty
lay ahead . . . in Claremont? Or would it be harder for her back in Guguletu? *Ndakubona ngoko.* That stubborn thought planted itself in her mind. *I'll
cross that bridge when I get to it.*

At Pick 'n Pay the aisles were full. She began to wonder whether the
boycott had been lifted and she and her neighbors were maintaining a boycott
long past because they had not heard the good news. But a closer look told
her the people milling about there were not from the African townships.
They were from everywhere else. And what they were doing there, they
were doing quite openly—freely and without one little qualm.

Soon, her own timidity left her. She forgot that what she was doing was
forbidden. Once more, it had become, to her too, a normal and very ordinary activity. Only the unusual exhilaration she felt, silent laughter of
parched gardens drinking in rain after a drought, gave any indication of her
deprivation. That, and the serious weighing of choices, which items to select,
which to discard, and which to ignore completely. Deep down, on another
level of knowing, she knew that she had to travel very light.

Her purchases made and paid for, Mamvulane went to the train station.
There was a toilet there that she could use. She had put back a lot of the
articles that, at first impulse, she'd grabbed and thrown into her trolley. Not
unaware of the dangers that lay in her homeward-bound journey, she saw
the virtue of ridding herself of most of what she wished for. It would be
stupid to make her venture that obvious that she ended up losing all she had
risked her neck for. The problem of packaging was of prime importance.

With her two Pick 'n Pay plastic bags, Mamvulane entered the toilet at
the railway station. Fortunately, there was no one there. In her mind, all
the way from her house, on the bus, and in the store itself, she had turned
and turned the problem of what to do with her purchases and now that the
time had come it was as though she had actually rehearsed the whole thing.
Several times over.

In less than ten minutes, Mamvulane left the toilet. She now carried only
one plastic bag. And it was not from Pick 'n Pay. To any eyes happening
on her, she was just a rather shabby African woman who might have gone

to buy some clothing, not much, from Sales House. For that is what the bag she was carrying said now: SALES HOUSE. And everyone knew Sales House was a clothing and drapery store. Indeed, since the bag had long lost its crispness it could be taken that she was a domestic worker carrying home goodies her madam had given her.

Deliberately avoiding the Guguletu bus line, Mamvulane made a beeline for the Nyanga bus. The line was not that long. Soon she would be home. Soon. Soon.

When the bus came she was one of the last to board it. But still found a seat, for most workers were already back in their houses, the time being half past six.

Ordinarily, she would have been concerned that her husband might get home before her. That was something he didn't particularly care for. Mdlangathi liked to get home and find his wife waiting supper for him, so that, should he feel in the mood for it, he could go back out again to get a drink from one of the *shebeens* nearby. To make matters worse, Mamvulane reminded herself, in her haste and caution, she had not told even one of her children where she was going. Ahh, silently she told herself, I'm sure when he sees where I've been he will not only understand; he will be mighty pleased.

The Nyanga bus passes Guguletu on its way to Nyanga, for the two townships are neighbors, with Nyanga lying east of Guguletu. Somewhere in the indistinct border between the two, there is an area neither in the one nor in the other, a kind of administratively forgotten no-man's-land. And there one finds all sorts of people, including some not classified as Africans or as Coloured—those who somehow escaped government classification. Some of them work, others don't. No one really knows what does happen in that place, which has come to be called *kwaBraweni*. How it got to be Brown's Place is a mystery, or perhaps a myth awaiting excavation.

Mamvulane let the bus ride past Guguletu with her, making no sign at all that that was where she was headed. Only when the bus came to *kwa-Braweni* did she ring the bell, indicating to the driver that her stop approached.

From the bus stop where she got off, it was less than a kilometer or so to her house. But Mamvulane was well aware that that was where the greatest challenge lay. In covering that distance that seemed insignificant and easy.

There was a shortcut through a thicket. Avoiding the road, where she risked running into people, she chose the shortcut. Here and there she had to use her hands to separate entangled branches of trees so she could pass. Dry twigs scratched her bare legs and she kept her eyes peeled for dog and human shit. Her slippers were old and torn and anything on which she trod would certainly get intimate with her feet.

In the middle of the woods, when she was halfway home, she heard voices, loud enough but still a distance away. Quickly, she stepped away from the path and went deeper into the woods. When she was a good few meters away from the path, she chose a well-leafed shrub and squatted in its shadow. In the case of prying eyes, she would look like someone relieving herself or digging up some root to use for an ailment. Either way, she should be left alone—unless the passersby happened to be people with more on their minds than she bargained for.

The foursome, two young men escorting their girlfriends somewhere, from the look of things, passed along. They were so engrossed in their discussion that they hardly paid her any heed. If, indeed, they saw her at all.

After they had gone past, Mamvulane resumed her journey, which was without event until she had almost cleared the thicket. She could plainly see the houses to the back of her own, on NY 72, when suddenly her ears picked up a not too faraway buzzing.

She stopped to hear better from which side it came. But even as she stood, her ears straining hard to pinpoint the source of the disturbance, the sound grew to a cacophony, discordant and threatening.

Right about the time her ears told her to look a little toward her left, in the bushes hiding Fezeka High School from view, her eyes picked up tumultuous movement.

She stood as though rooted to the spot. From sheer terror.

Mesmerized, Mamvulane watched as the unruly throng crowded in on her. Leading the rabble were a few women and one elderly man. She realized then that a few of those whose heels were chasing their heads were not just ahead of the group—they were actually fleeing from it.

She needed no further notice. Turning from the spectacle approaching her, she ran toward the houses, now so desperately near.

Mamvulane ran. The other women and the old man with them ran also. They all ran. But the army of young people at their heels had speed born of youth on their side.

Just as she came to the T-junction, where NY 74 joins NY 72, she found her way blocked. Some of her pursuers had taken a shortcut by jumping over fences from NY 75 to NY 74 and were now ahead of her. In seconds, she was completely surrounded.

Without further ado, someone snatched her plastic bag from her. "Let us see what you have in that bag, Mama?" he said, ripping it open.

Out spilled her groceries. And as each packet tumbled onto the hard, concrete road, it split or tore open, spilling its guts onto the sand, and there joined other debris that had long made its home there.

Happy and willing feet did the rest. Stamping and kicking at her food so that everything got thoroughly mixed up with the sand and with other food items. The samp and the mealie meal and the sugar and the dried milk and the coffee and the broken candles and the paraffin—everything became one thing. All those things, mixed together, became nothing. Nothing she or anyone else could use.

"*Sigqibile ngawe ke ngoku, Mama*. We are finished with you," announced her tormentors.

Walking home, her knees weak from the encounter, Mamvulane met one of her neighbors, attracted by the noise. "Mvulane, what is happening? Why are all these people staring at you?"

"I can't talk now, Mandaba," answered the other, not pausing in her unsteady walk. Mandaba, suspecting the cause of her neighbor's reticence and disheveled appearance, remarked, "*Hayi*, you are naughty, Mamvulane." To which the latter said not a word but just continued walking to her home as though the other had not spoken at all.

When she got to her gate, Mamvulane shooed away the straggling group, mostly curious children and one or two adults, that was following her. What the comrades had done to her had disarranged her. But her heart grieved. And that was definitely not on their account. About the comrades, she supposed she should be grateful they had done her no bodily harm. She remembered the man Mdlangathi had told her about the previous evening— the man the comrades had forced to drink *Javel*. That man, after he had brought up little chunks of meat, and of course the liquor that had caused him all the trouble to start with, had eventually brought up blood. His own. So, when all is said and done, I suppose I'm lucky, Mamvulane told herself after she had calmed down some. At her home. But, her eyes smarting, she could feel her heart bleed. Because of the other thing.

Her husband was home when she got there. "What happened to you?" he asked, seeing her disheveled appearance. For although she had not been beaten, she had been manhandled.

Mamvulane recounted her experience while her husband listened to her in dumb silence. And then she told him, ". . . and among the comrades who did this to me, there was Mteteli, our son." There, it was out in the open. She had mentioned the despicable, unmentionable thing that had gnawed at her heart since the comrades had fallen upon her.

When she said that, mentioned Mteteli as one of her attackers, she burst out crying. Mdlangathi started up and for a moment his wife thought he was going to go out of the house in search of their son right there and then.

But no, after two or three hesitant, halfhearted steps, he sat down again and quietly inquired, "You saw him? With your own eyes, I mean?"

"Oh, why wouldn't I know my own child, even in a crowd."

"Mmmhhmh." That is what Mdlangathi said. Only that and nothing more. On being told that his son was part of the crowd that had spilled his wife's groceries on the sand, all that was heard from him was that sigh. That is all.

Mamvulane waited for more reaction from her husband, usually so easy to reach boiling point. But no, not today. Today he kept so calm that his wife became resentful of exactly that calmness that she had so frequently and desperately sought from him. Today, when she least expected it or welcomed it for that matter, here was her priceless husband displaying remarkable sangfroid.

"I'm glad, Father of Fezeka, to see that you appreciate the risk I took, nearly getting myself killed by these unruly children, so that you would have something to eat." She spoke in a quiet voice. Inside, however, she was seething. What did he think! That she had gone to Claremont only so that she could buy a loaf of bread and stuff it down her own gullet? That would have saved her all the trouble and bad name she, no doubt, had earned herself.

But Mdlangathi would not be drawn to a fight and, after seeing that, Mamvulane soon found her anger dissipate.

When she had rested a little and was sure there would be no follow-up action on the part of the comrades, Mamvulane went to her bedroom and closed the door. When she emerged, in her hand was a tray full of sausage. There were also two loaves of bread and a plastic packet of powdered milk.

"That is all I was able to save," she told her husband, showing him her spoils. "To think I spent more than fifty rands at Pick 'n Pay . . . and that is all that I was able to save!"

"But how?" he wanted to know.

And she knew he wasn't talking about the money she had spent.

For the first time since she had come into the house, harassed and agitated, Mamvulane allowed a slow smile to appear on her face. Her eyes widening in mock disbelief, she exclaimed, "*Tyhini, Tata kaFezeka!* Don't you think that a woman should have some secrets?" And refused to divulge how she had achieved the miracle.

As she prepared the meal, she wondered what he would say if she were to tell him that she had girdled the sausage around her waist, put the packet of milk in the natural furrow between her breasts and carried the loaves of bread flattened in the hollow of her back, one atop the other so that they formed a pipe. Ah, Mdlangathi, she thought, feeling the smile in her heart, these are not times for one to be squeamish.

But thinking about the whole *indaba* later as she stirred her pots, now and then peering into this one and then, a moment later, the other one, she was a bit miffed. Mdlangathi had been more upset about the drunkard the comrades had forced to regurgitate his beer than over what they had done to her. Imagine that! A man to have more sympathy for someone like that than for his own wife. She was sure she didn't know what to make of it. His lack of indignation on her behalf galled her, though.

On the other hand, she had to admit relief that he had not carried on the way he had about the stupid drunk. A fight might have broken out between father and son. Mteteli had become quite cheeky with this new thing of children who had secrets from their parents and went about righting all the wrongs they perceived in society. Yes, she told herself, perhaps it was just as well his father said nothing to the boy, or didn't show anger on her behalf. Anger that he had participated in her humiliating attack, which had resulted in the loss of her groceries.

Mamvulane dished up and father and children fell on the food as camels coming upon an oasis after crossing a vast desert.

As usual, Mteteli had missed dinner—out attending meetings. "Wife, times have truly changed," said the husband. "Do you realize that all over Guguletu and Nyanga and Langa, not just here in our home, people are having dinner, with their children only God knows where?"

"You are quite right," replied his wife. But seeing that he was getting angry, she added, "But you must remember that our children live in times very different to what ours were when we were their age."

"And that means we must eat and go to bed not knowing where this boy is?"

Although he didn't name names, she knew he meant Mteteli, for he was the only one of the children not in. The girl, Fezeka, for some reason that wasn't clear to the mother, was not that involved in the doings of the students, although she was the older by three years.

"Well, that is what is happening in all homes now. What can one do?"

"Mamvulane, do you hear yourself? Are those words that should be coming from a parent's mouth? 'What can I do?' Talking about the behavior of her own child?"

"He is your child too, you know. But all these children are the same. They don't listen to anyone except each other."

"*Hayi!* You are right, my wife. I don't know why I argue with you when what you say is the Gospel Truth. Here I am, having dinner when I do not know the whereabouts of one of my own children. Very soon, dishes will be washed. Then we will say our evening prayers and go to bed. And still we will have no idea where Mteteli is. And you tell me there is nothing to be done about that. Not that I disagree with you, mind you."

"Well, what could you do, even if you knew where he was right now. What could you possibly do?" Mamvulane stood up, gathered the dishes, and took them to the kitchen, where Fezeka and the two youngest children were having their meal.

When Mamvulane returned to the dining room, Mdlangathi, who was smoking his pipe, said, "Do you know what's wrong with the world today?" And quickly answered himself, "All of us parents are very big cowards. The biggest cowards you have ever seen."

She hummed her agreement with what he was saying. But in her heart she didn't believe that what he said was wholly true. Powerless, perhaps. That is what she thought parents were—overwhelmed by a sense of powerlessness in the face of the children's collective revolt, where the mildest child had become a stranger: intransigent, loud of voice, and deadly bold of action.

"*Mama, kuph' okwam ukutya?* Where is my food, Mama?" asked a grumpy voice in the dark. It was Mteteli, all right. The mother knew at once. Only *he* had not had supper. Only *he* would come in the middle of the night, demanding food when no one had sent him on an errand anywhere that he should have been absent during dinner.

"My son," replied Mamvulane without bothering to strike a match and light the candle standing on a small round table next to the bed. "I am surprised you should ask me for food when *you* know what happened to the groceries I went to get in Claremont."

"Are you telling me that no one has had food tonight, here at home?" His tone had become quite belligerent.

Before the mother said a word in reply, Mdlangathi roared at his son: "*Kwedini!* What gives you the right to go about causing mischief that I, your father, have not asked you to perform and then, as though that were not grief enough to your poor mother here, come back here in the middle of the night and wake us up with demands of food? Where were you when we were having dinner?"

"*Awu*, Tata, what is this that you are asking me? Do you not know that a war is going on? That we are fighting the hateful apartheid government?"

"Since when is this woman lying next to me the government? Is this not the woman you and your friends attacked this evening?"

"Mama was not attacked. She was disciplined for . . ."

But Mdlangathi sprang out of bed and, in the dark, groped his way toward the door, where he judged his son was standing. Grabbing him by the scruff of his neck, he bellowed, "She was *whaat?* Are you telling me you have a hand to discipline your mother? What has happened to your senses? Have they been eaten away by intoxicating drugs?"

By now, Mteteli's teeth were chattering from the shaking he was receiving at the hands of his father.

Quickly, Mamvulane lit the candle.

Startled by the light, the two grappling figures sprang apart. Both were breathing heavily.

"Are you fighting me?" quietly, the father asked his son.

"You are beating me."

"I asked you a direct question. Are you lifting a hand, fighting with me, your father?"

"All I want is my food. I'm not fighting anyone," said Mteteli sullenly.

"I suggest you get out of my house and go and seek your food elsewhere. I do not work hard so that I shall feed thugs."

"Now I am a thug because I want my food?"

Mdlangathi had had enough of sparring with Mteteli. Abruptly, he told him, "Go and look for your food from the sand, where you threw it away when you took it from your mother by force." Fuming, he got back into bed and covered himself with the blankets till not even his hair could be seen.

"Yes, Mteteli," Mamvulane added. "Remember all the sand, and samp you and your group threw down onto the sand, *that* was to be your supper. You spilled your supper on the sand out there—birds will feast on it on the morrow."

"*Andithethi loo nto mna, ngoku.*"

"Mteteli, your father goes to work tomorrow morning. Leave us alone and let us have some sleep. You are the one who doesn't have time for doing this or that, you come and go as you please, but don't let that become a nuisance to us now, please."

"Mama, I don't know what all this fuss is about. All I said I want, and still want, is my food. Where is my food?" Mteteli had now raised his voice so high people three doors away put on their candles. The whole block heard there were angry words being exchanged at Mdlangathi's house.

Mteteli, angry at the reception he was getting, and hungry, having gone the whole day without eating anything substantial, approached his parents' bed and stood towering over them, his bloodshot eyes trained on his mother.

"*Hee, kwedini,*" came the muffled sound of his father's voice from under the blankets. "What exactly do you want my wife to do for you, at this time of night?"

"I want my food."

"That we tell you it is where you spilled it on the sand doesn't satisfy you?" Mdlangathi stuck his head out of the blankets again.

"*Andithethi loo nto mna, ngoku.* I'm not talking about that, now."

Under his bed, Mdlangathi kept a long, strong, well-seasoned knobkerrie. A flash of bare arm shot out of the blankets. A heave, and he'd strained and reached the stick.

Before Mteteli fully grasped what his father was up to, his father had leapt out of bed and, in one swoop, landed the knobkerrie on Mteteli's skull.

"CRRAA-AA-AAKK!"

The sound of wood connecting with bone. The brightest light he had ever seen flashed before Mteteli's startled eyes. A strong jet of red. The light dimmed, all at once. A shriek from the mother. In a heap, the young man collapsed onto the vinyl-covered floor.

"*Umosele!*" That is what people said afterwards. One of those cruel accidents. How often does one stroke of a stick, however strong, end up in a fatality? He must have ruptured a major artery.

The boy bled to death before help could get to him, others said.

Yes, the mother tried to get one of the neighbors to take him to the hospital, you know ambulances had stopped coming to the townships because they had been stoned by the comrades. But the neighbor refused, saying, "Your son can ask someone who doesn't drink to take him to hospital." Apparently, he was one of the men the comrades had forced to bring up, forcing them to make themselves sick because they had "*drunk the white man's poison that kills Africa's seed.*"

Of course, later, some people condemned the man who had refused to take Mteteli to the hospital. But others said he taught the comrades a lesson long overdue. And others still pointed at the father and said, "Why should someone else bother about a dog whose father wouldn't even ask for permission to come to his funeral?"

Yes, many wondered about that. About the fact that Mdlangathi was not denied permission to come to bury his son but had not requested that permission from the prison officials. That was something even Mamvulane found hard to understand. Harder still for her to swallow was his answer when she'd asked him about his reasons for the omission.

"*Andifuni.*" That was all he would say. "I do not want to."

However, so did she fear being bruised even more by events that seemed to her to come straight out of the house of the devil himself that she could not find the courage to ask what he meant: whether what he did not want was to come to the funeral or to ask to be allowed to attend the funeral. She did not know which would hurt her more. And did not dare find out.

—1996

Nuruddin Farah

(BORN 1945) SOMALIA

Often described as a writer's writer, Nuruddin Farah is one of the most prolific—and most influential—novelists from the continent. The praise and devotion of his readers have stemmed in large part from his extraordinarily sensitive portraits of African women. *From a Crooked Rib* (1970), his first novel, was welcomed by feminists as the groundbreaking story of a Somali woman constrained by her traditional world. Western readers, confused by the author's name, assumed that he was a woman and wrote him letters addressed as "Ms. Farah."

Farah's first novel was followed by *A Naked Needle*, in 1976, and then the trilogy subtitled "Variations on the Theme of an African Dictatorship": *Sweet and Sour Milk* (1979), *Sardines* (1981), and *Close Sesame* (1983). A second trilogy—again with strong political overtones—began with the publication of *Maps* (1986) and *Gifts* (1993) and will conclude with *Secrets*. Farah has also published essays and occasional short stories.

Farah was born in the Italian Somaliland, in Baidoa, in 1945, and grew up in Kallafo, under Ethiopian rule in the Ogaden. The ethnically and linguistically mixed area of his childhood contributed to his early fascination with literature. He spoke Somali at home but at school learned Amharic, Italian, Arabic, and English: "We learned that one received other people's wisdom through the medium of their writing. . . ."

From a Crooked Rib was written while Farah was studying philosophy in India. His second and third novels—including *Sweet and Sour Milk*, which won the English-Speaking Union Literary Award—were written in Rome. The latter novel made him persona non grata in Somalia and resulted in an exile of twenty years; he describes his life as a "nomadic existence." Typically, he spent part of each year in Africa and the rest in Europe or the United States. In the summer of 1996, he finally visited his native land. Well before that time, Somalia had become an international trouble spot, as reflected on the nightly news in Europe and America.

Farah articulated his ambivalence about the American troop "rescue" of his country in an article in *The New York Times*, saying: "The crisis in Somalia is one of its people's making and is native to the country's ill-run clan patronage. . . ." In an interview with Maya Jaggi, he further explained: "If you take the Somalia nation as a family, the betrayal is no longer that of colonialism, it is no longer from outside, but from within. And the cure must also be found within." More than anything else, he bemoaned the failure of Pan-Africanism, the inability of other African nations to deal with the crisis in his country.

In another context, in an essay titled "Childhood of My Schizophrenia" published in *The Times Literary Supplement* in 1990, Farah stated: "Colonial childhood such as mine is discontinuous: the child grows up neither as a replica of his parents, nor of the colonial ruler. I have remarked on my people's absence from the roll-call of world history as we were taught it, to the extent that we envied our Ethiopian, Kenyan and Arab neighbours the passing mention given to them in the textbooks we studied at school. It was with this in mind that I began writing—in the hope of enabling the Somali child at least to characterize his otherness—and to point at himself as the unnamed, the divided *other*, a schizophrenic child living in the age of colonial contradiction."

MY FATHER, THE
ENGLISHMAN, AND I

To Mina, all my love

I would have been as high, standing, as the knees of a full-grown pygmy sitting, when I first met a European, to wit an Englishman, the Administrator of the Ogaden, with whom my father worked as an interpreter. I wasn't quite three when, responding to an urgent summons, my father took me with him, well aware that I didn't want to meet up with the colonial officer. My mother's undisguised aversion to the white man was no secret, but this in and of itself could not explain why I declined the Englishman's offers of boiled sweets and other presents.

Being my mother's favorite child, I suspect I harbored resentments not only toward the Englishman but toward my father, too—what with my dad's unpredictable furies, his hopeless rages which I would encounter later in life, and his sudden loss of temper when he was not having his way with you. My father was kindness itself to non-family, temperamental with his dependents. But he cut the figure of a most obliging vassal to the Englishman. You might have thought he was the white man's general factotum, doing his bidding and never speaking an unkind word about him.

It was a feat of great magnitude to convince myself not to stuff the boiled sweet the Englishman had sent along with my father, because in those days mine was a mouth-centered universe. Not admitting to being tempted, I now had my right thumb shoved into my mouth and my left tight around the uneaten sweet, while I remained in contact with my father, who held on to my wrist, pulling me as though I were a sandbag. I had a great urge to eat the sweet but didn't, in deference to my mother's unspoken wish. Later I would realize that a history of loyalties was being made then.

I remember my parents raising their voices over the matter earlier, my mother disapproving of my father's wretched acceptance of his lowly status in the hierarchy of colonial dispensation. When, years later, in a heated argument, my mother accused my father of "political pimping," my memory revisited this incident.

Anyway, I would have stayed with my mother if I could, my mother who had lately been incontinent of sorrow, something I was too young to understand. I left the house wrapped in sadness. Often I had little difficulty getting my words out when in the company of my mother, whereas with others I had the habit of choking on my speech. Today it felt as though I had swallowed my tongue. I loved my mother, whom I thought of as my sanctuary, her silences generous as openings embracing my stammers.

I regret I do not have my mother to corroborate my versions of these happenings. As fate would have it, I was not able to exchange my memories with her before she died.

Above all, I remember hands: hands pulling me, hands pushing me. I see the Englishman reaching, striving to take hold of me. My father's open palm pushes me from behind, urging me forward toward the white man's looming face. Or are we dealing with memory as a rogue, memory willfully vandalizing the integrity of a remembrance and reshaping the past so as to confirm the present? Perhaps not. Because I am not the only one who associates my father with hands—hands not giving but reaching out to hit. One of my older brothers whom my father often struck for being mischievous reiterates that one did not know if our father's hands were about to make a monkey of one or, in a bid to encourage one, pat one on the head.

If I went with my father to be with the Englishman, it was because I was given little choice. I had to make do with the makeshift of emotions which I had built around myself, emotions meant to protect me from psychological harm. For I had wised up to this before my third year and knew, as though by instinct, that my father might punish me for my lack of deference toward the Englishman. Too clever by half, I took a step forward if only to humor him and made sure not a truant tear would betray my genuine feelings. By Jove, it was difficult not to submit to the desire to weep or to cringe with embarrassment as the Englishman embraced me.

It was such a relief to see that my father appeared pleased!

* * *

There was a pattern to the relationship between my father and the English-man, my father speaking only when spoken to or after he had been given the go-ahead. It struck me as if my old man stood in relation of a student repeating what a teacher had said. What I could not have known was that in his capacity as a vassal to the British Empire, my father translated into Somali whatever the Englishman had uttered in Swahili.

No sooner had the Englishman sat me on his lap than I sensed a change in my surroundings. For we were joined by the stifled murmurs of a dozen or so men, preceded by the noise of *jaamuus*-sandaled feet being dragged heavily across the floor. And I was suddenly heir to the sad expressions on the newly arrived men's faces, the sorrow of the eunuched. I might have thought that my sense of powerlessness was no different from theirs had I known then, as I know now, that the clan elders were gathered in the Englishman's spacious office to sport with the tangles of history, putting their thumbs to a treaty Ethiopia and Britain had prepared with the connivance of the Americans. I'm not certain of the fu-ture date in the same calendar year 1948 when the fate of the Ogaden was de-cided and put in the hands of expansionist Ethiopia.

What was my role in this ignoble affair? I lay in the embrace of the Englishman; I felt the tremors of words dressed in the garb of authority coming into contact with my heartbeat before they were translated into Somali by my father; and I did nothing. If I had resisted being the English-man's booty, which he received without firing a bullet, would matters have been different? If I had fussed so as to prevent my father from translating the ignominious words of the Englishman into Somali, would the Ogaden have been dealt a fairer hand?

I remember the elders of the clan entering into a cantankerous argument with my father, who in all likelihood was discouraging them from standing up to the Englishman. Left out of the debate altogether, the Englishman rose up to ride the high horse of rage the powerful so often mount: and there was silence. It was then that I entered the fray, letting out a shriek of outrage wrung out of the primeval beginnings of all my years. Apologizing to me, the Englishman adjourned the meeting till another day.

At a subsequent meeting, the clan elders placed their thumbs over the alloted space in the treaty they signed. Had I been present, or had my mother been consulted, maybe this would not have occurred.

—1995

Mandla Langa

(BORN 1950) SOUTH AFRICA

Mandla Langa was born in Durban in 1950. In 1972, he earned a B.A. in English and Philosophy from the University of Fort Hare. Two years later, he became director of the South African Students Organization (SASO), a position he held until 1976. Like so many writers who grew up under apartheid, Langa literally had to run for his life. On his résumé he states that in 1976—because of his political activities—he was arrested and served "seven months of a three-year sentence for sedition—a charge based on the cursory reading of a poem" he had written. After the months in detention, he was released "on stringent bail conditions pending an appeal," whereupon he went underground and fled South Africa.

His years of exile included time spent in Botswana, Lesotho, Zambia, and finally the United Kingdom. During the early years of his exile, he worked as an editor, speechwriter, and journalist. Increasingly, however, his political activities aligned him with the anti-apartheid forces outside South Africa. In the early 1990s, he was Deputy Representative of the African National Congress (ANC) Mission to the United Kingdom and Ireland. During all these years, he continued with his own writing and his education. In 1989, he earned a Postgraduate Diploma in Periodical Journalism from the London College of Printing; in 1993, he earned an M.A. in Modern English Literature from the University of London (Birkbeck College).

Langa's short stories and novels have been widely praised and honored with numerous literary awards, especially his three novels, *Tenderness of Blood*

(1985), *Rainbow on a Paper Sky* (1989), and *The Cult of Innocence* (1994). *Rainbow on a Paper Sky* tells the moving story of two brothers, Mbongeni, a musician, and Thokozani, a preacher-idealist, in the Northern Natal in the 1970s, during the time of increasing guerrilla activity. Although much of the setting is Durban, Langa's strength is also in depicting the everyday activities of village life. The rhetoric of the novel is muted, generally limited to terse statements such as: "The aim of the powerful of the land was to let everything look like internecine tribal fighting of black against black."

As in the past, Mandla Langa has always moved with the times. In his current position in Johannesburg, he is responsible for "lobbying on local and government levels." As much as anything, "A Gathering of Bald Men" provides a glimpse into post-apartheid South Africa, where things are (still) not always as they may appear to be.

A GATHERING OF
BALD MEN

Caleb Zungu was forty-three years old, married to Nothando for thirteen years, with two girl children, Busi and Khwezi, aged eight and fourteen, respectively. He owned a house in Norwood, a car, and two dogs of dubious pedigree. He was an insurance salesman for Allied Life, where he had worked for five years. He was overdrawn at the bank and hoped for an act of God, perhaps the death of a long-lost uncle who would leave him a handsome inheritance. Nothando had graduated from Kelly Girl to full-time employment in the Human Resources Department of TransStar, a transport company. The girls were on school holidays, it being April, and the dogs, which he addressed in imperatives such as *"Voetsek!"* or "Come here, boys," depending on his mood, were content with life.

On this late-April Monday, Caleb woke up, took a shower, brushed his teeth, and dressed. He cut a dashing if formidable picture in his navy-blue pin-striped suit, a white shirt, a red tie, and black shoes. He drank his coffee quickly and went back to the bathroom. Nothando almost dropped her coffee mug when she heard a shriek coming from the bathroom. Thinking that her husband might be suffering a stroke (it had killed two male members of Caleb's family), she spilled her coffee in her rush to see what was the matter.

She found Caleb, his head bent, gingerly feeling a bald spot the size of an old one-rand coin which had, it seemed, developed overnight on the crown of his head. Standing behind him as he lamented his loss of hair before the unflattering mirror, Nothando felt a pang of tenderness mixed with disappointment. Why were men such babies? She managed to coax him out of his dark mood, telling him that baldness was an attestation of virility, and that he looked very handsome and distinguished. Nothando resisted the temptation to kiss him on his pate, but firmly steered him to his car—a secondhand shocking-pink Renault he had never got round to repainting— with encouraging words. Standing on the doorway and giving him the obligatory goodbye wave, which he didn't reciprocate, she knew that Caleb was deeply troubled; he hadn't even taken along his mobile phone.

While she was preparing herself for work, her helper arrived and took over the necessary task of putting the kids within the straight and narrow. This might have seemed like heavyhandedness to the girls, especially Khwezi, who was spending too much time yakkity-yakking on the phone. This was a little worrying, especially since her daughter had taken to scribbling *I ♥ JM* on her trainers and listening to Seal's crooning with a rapt expression on her face. Nothando wondered who the hell JM was—probably one of those acne-ridden, foulmouthed louts in oversized jackets, baggy pants, and loose-laced, high-top trainers who slouched on street corners, wolf-whistling at women. Although Nothando had ascended to suburban respectability, she still maintained contact with a few of the heavy brothers on the streets. If JM messed around with her daughter, she did not rule out calling in a friendly neighborhood enforcer. It wouldn't do to let Caleb know of her anxiety; the way he felt, what with his loss of hair, they would have a homicide on their hands.

Nothando's lift came. Having negotiated the nerve-racking Johannesburg morning traffic, she and Marcia, who drove a new Toyota Conquest, made it to the office on time. The Marketing Manager, Mr. Peter Marshall, was forever bitching about punctuality, "The RDP will go down the tubes," he was fond of repeating, like a preacher invoking Holy Writ, "if you people keep this up." *You people!* Nothando would think bitterly, these bastards never change, even if they pretend to be Jay Naidoo's lieutenants.

Nothando mulled over her husband's difficulty, knowing that some men had committed suicide at the loss of their hair. A man who does that wasn't fit to live anyway, she thought unkindly. Suicide, she believed, is the highest form of self-criticism. Caleb had told her of many people who had posthumously tried to gyp insurance companies by making their deaths look like murder or accidents. There was no bonus in killing oneself; in the credo of the Catholic Church, you were even barred from entering that great festival in the sky. Nothando suddenly realized that she really didn't know whether

Caleb was a suicidal type. The morning's outburst in the bathroom had shown another side to him. She'd be supremely pissed off if he took this way out.

She wouldn't know, however, that exactly at that moment Caleb was in a boardroom where the Harvard-trained MD, Arnold Spicer, was reading everyone the Riot Act. The returns were low, much lower than had been forecast by the salesmen. When Sanders, a bright spark who specialized in retirement annuities, pointed out that there was a slump in the economy, Spicer retorted that he didn't give a rat's ass about the slump. "The population is increasing daily," he went on, "and more and more people are growing older; they worry about death, so they need insurance. And you all sit here warming your backsides, telling me about the slump." Well, thought Caleb, who was envious of the fact that the MD had a full head of hair on his shoulders, it's good of him to say that; he doesn't have to pound pavements looking for clients. Caleb felt especially vulnerable since his brief was to attract the black market. There was no percentage in this, for the simple reason that the black business he solicited seemed interested only in supporting the *black* market. Had he had it in him, Caleb would have informed Spicer that most black people also didn't give a rat's ass about insurance; some of those who did were slack in paying their premiums. When he called on policyholders on weekends, he was certain that they briefed their sons to tell him that no, Daddy's not home, he's gone to Thohoyandou. Caleb would know that he was being given a runaround, with the bastard who couldn't be bothered probably sleeping off a hangover. Personally, Caleb had no time to cultivate a hangover, he was too busy. In one weekend alone, two dozen defaulters had gone to Thohoyandou, maybe there was an anti-insurance convention there. He had to devise another strategy to flush them out.

Caleb imagined himself a tolerant man. His job called for this. But one thing which was guaranteed to get his goat was people laughing at him. It wasn't so much that people didn't have money as being lazy to reach into their jackets for the checkbook and sign on the dotted line. He remembered one office worker he had approached with the intention of selling him insurance. After the usual spiel, to which the man listened attentively, Caleb had switched to the politically correct tack of how insurance helps the RDP. The man had laughed so much Caleb had feared he would rupture himself. "You know what they call your RDP in the township?" he asked. "Real Dummies Pay." What was one going to make of these people? Small wonder he was losing his hair. For the first time after long months of abstinence, he felt like a drink.

As he drove along Empire Road, he cast around in his mind for famous men who were bald. There was Winston Churchill: *It will be long, it will be hard, and there will be no withdrawal.* That was a classic piece, and Churchill was regarded as a sex symbol. Gandhi? Well, Gandhi was famous for other things, his glasses and the *dhoti*, he couldn't go that far; nor could he imagine South Africans following a leader who wore nappies. Bruce Willis? He was an actor, there was no guarantee that his scalp wasn't also acting bald. Was Hitler bald, or did he wear a hairpiece? What about Rajbansi, whose wig had canted to the side when the *boers* manhandled him? Boy, that was sad— and on camera, too. If President Mandela were bald, maybe that would even the equation, lots of men like Caleb would walk with their heads held high. That De Klerk was no longer the top dog merely made matters worse. It made his baldness seem like a weakness.

He parked his car on Pretoria Street, in front of the Hillbrow meat market. Tossing a fifty-cent coin at one of those informal parking attendants lining the streets of the built-up areas of Johannesburg, he proceeded to the tavern at the corner. It was 11:30 in the morning; Caleb justified getting a drink this early on the peculiar nature of the day. Inside the bar, loud Zairian music issued from a stereo system. The interior lighting was rigged for a nightclub, strobe lights and weak bulbs dangling from the ceiling. This gave the bar a certain mysteriousness, a mixture of intimacy and menace. Dark men in the gloom drank their dark brews, speaking in low tones. The bar was a favorite haunt for drug dealers, illegal immigrants, people who operated on the periphery of the law. Two women in loud dresses and high heels danced without spirit, their eyes luminous, giving the effect of neon lights with some of the tubing missing. Caleb wondered if this establishment was insured against fire.

He chose a table that was farthest from the bar. The minute he was settled, a waiter ambled over and presented him with a menu. Caleb told him that he just wanted a drink. The waiter sullenly removed the menu and asked him what he wanted. Caleb settled for a beer, knowing that there was no trusting any bottled concoction. He recalled an English visitor who had ordered rum; on being supplied with a drink, the man took one sip and immediately passed out.

Caleb listened to the throbbing bass and the wailing guitars accompanying an aggressive male voice. He was on his third beer, when the dancing women were beginning to have a certain raw sex appeal, that he considered suicide. He cried into his glass as he thought of Nothando and the girls. What would happen to them? He was overdrawn at the bank; even if his credit status were stable, he reasoned, the funeral parlor would no doubt make a big hole in his bank balance. Nothando would be left destitute, the kids—especially Khwezi, who was already a very combative teenager—would spit on his memory.

But the alternative was as bleak. He knew that losing his hair was a portent of a greater, more devastating loss. With his luck having run out at the same speed as defaulting clients, he could easily conjure up an image of himself, a few months from now, when he would be standing on a street corner carrying a placard with a message detailing his woes. He visualized himself totally bald, in tattered clothes, tapping on car windows, rattling a tin up some driver's nose. Maybe he should start now, learning the tricks of the begging trade. He thought of his children seeing him in that state, denying any knowledge of him in their shame, wishing him dead. Yes, he thought, death was better.

Already feeling relieved, as if a great decision had been made for him, Caleb placed a few rand notes on the table, stood up, collected his briefcase, and buttoned up his jacket. It was then that a man entered and headed straight for Caleb's table. He was a gaunt white man about Caleb's age, with a weather-beaten, sallow face, his head as smooth as a billiard ball. The khaki overcoat, a yellow sweatshirt, ragged grayish trousers, and Converse sneakers from which small brown toes peeped like mischievous children gave him the look of an out-of-practice pickpocket. Rolled up under his arm was a piece of cardboard, greasy as if he had picked it up from the pavement. He gave off an odor of stale liquor, sweat, and inner-city pollution. But there was something about the way he carried himself, his piercing slate-gray eyes, which distinguished him from the regular station crusty.

"Do I pass the inspection?" he challenged, drawing a chair and sitting down, looking up at Caleb. When the latter hesitated, debating whether to respond to the newcomer or just continue on his way as he'd intended, the man waved a proprietary arm over the chair Caleb had just vacated. "Sit down, my friend. Sit down because you're going nowhere."

Caleb had encountered people of questionable sanity before, and he knew how to make short shrift of them. But this stranger's confidence, the way he seemed to take over, calmed him down. He sat down. "What's up?"

"You were thinking of killing yourself, weren't you?" the man asked, placing his cardboard scroll on the table. "Been following you all the time. Said to myself: "That bloke's gonna do it.' " He laughed; it was not a pleasant sound. "You don't need to be a genius to know if a guy's gonna pop himself." Then he turned and shouted at the barman, who was eyeing them with amused contempt. "Pilsner *moja, bareki-sana*. That's Swahili for I want a beer, tot-quick!"

"Fuck off, Ranger," the barman shouted back. "I'm not giving you a glass of water until I see some money first."

"O ye of little faith," the man called Ranger lamented. "Your obduracy will be your downfall yet, ye children of Mammon. Who says I need to produce money? My friend here"—and he tapped a long, bony forefinger against Caleb's shoulder—"is on his way to committing suicide—"

"Now, wait a minute—" Caleb started.

"—and I feel it's mighty unenterprising, certainly against economic growth, to die with a bundle of dough, don't you think?" Ranger was enjoying himself. "I mean, inflation will have reduced those rands to scrip by the time you hit the Pearly Gates." There was a general titter in the barroom; even the dancers paused mid-step in their uninspired gyrations to appraise this fool who wanted to take his money to heaven. "What's your name, friend?"

Caleb knew it was time he told Ranger where to get off. Pulling himself to his full height, he was about to let loose a salvo of imprecations when his gaze fell on the cardboard placard, which had unfurled itself on the table. Written in uneven block letters with the i's topped by small circles, it read: TOM RANGER BLIND EX-SOLJER DONT NEED YOUR PITY BUT MONY WILL DO I DRINK AND SMOKE JUST LIKE YOU.

"Christ!" Caleb said; he was uncomfortable with any form of disability. He was suddenly at a loss for words. "I'm sorry."

"Yeah," Ranger said carelessly, "that's the way it is sometimes. Hope you don't mind the spelling, 'cause I dictated the damn thing to some cretin who can't spell to save his life." He turned his sightless eyes to Caleb. "You haven't told me your name. Judging by your reluctance, it must be one of those well-kept state secrets." He let this sink in, and then said: "But first things first—am I getting my drink or what?" As if on cue, the brooding waiter was suddenly hovering around with a tray—like a surely genie, Caleb thought.

"Give the man what he wants, and I'll have another beer," he said to the waiter. Turning to Ranger, he introduced himself. "My name is Caleb Zungu."

Ranger raised two fingers in the general direction of the waiter. "Careful with the water." He rested his arms on the table. "And what do you do, Caleb Zungu?" Before Caleb would reply, he asked: "You're some kinda salesman, aren't you?"

"*Ja*," Caleb said. "I sell insurance." He paused. "Does it show?"

"Man," Ranger said, "when I came in through that door, I got this vibe of sadness, you know what I mean, and I sensed this boyo out there in the corner, either drinking himself to a standstill or contemplating suicide. Or both. We blind *ous* can get so bloody annoying." He gave a self-deprecating smile and spread his arms, his face lightening up the gloom. "This fucking perception, man."

Ranger was a hustler, Caleb judged, but he was of the honest type. The streets of Johannesburg teemed with people chasing the rand, some with ingenious schemes up their sleeves. The streets were also full of children who dared the unrelenting traffic, begging, making their plight known to all and sundry in the myriad tongues of the country. As a rule, Caleb never gave alms; the government had a responsibility for the destitute. Even if they didn't vote—and so much was done in their name—they were still the children of this Republic. Millions of rand were being squandered in buying military toys of destruction, in a country that claimed to have no external enemies. Departments of social welfare enriched consultants, the same way that other government departments were throwing good money after bad in grandiose schemes and white elephants. As for big business, the directors were drawing salaries which boggled the imagination—their cars and their houses in Sandton could keep whole populations fed, clothed, and sheltered for months on end. Furthermore, Caleb was damned if he knew now who was a genuinely deserving case. Most of the people on the pavements claimed they needed money for food; he was sure that, as soon as the coins added up, they would rush to the nearest liquor store. Once, in a rare moment of generosity, he gave money to a supposed beggar whom he later caught buying a copy of *Penthouse*. No sir, he wasn't a *moegoe*—a dummy. His mission on earth didn't include supporting someone's jerk-off habits. It wasn't lost on him that he was beginning to think like Spicer. Caleb had earned the money he didn't now have.

As Caleb and Ranger conversed about life and death while sipping their drinks—and as the latter made frequent tours to the toilet—more customers trickled into the bar, turning into a crowd. Men looked up and smiled or waved in recognition as Ranger became considerably louder, until Caleb told him to pipe down. He was entranced and repulsed in equal measure by this blind white man. *The blind eye of the seers.* This thought came to Caleb, unprovoked, a comment on the situation in which he found himself. Or on the condition of business, where there was no vision. He had badgered the company to allow him to go to Pretoria and Cape Town, where he was sure he would sell insurance to the batch of new parliamentarians. He had also been stopped from setting up a meeting with the RDP officers in Pretoria. Caleb had worked out a presentation he regarded as foolproof, where Allied Life would be seen to be an ally of the government's developmental program. "Johannesburg," Spicer had said, "or, more precisely, the township, is *your* bailiwick. Forget all that developmental stuff." Other insurance companies had good working relations with government. Even formations such as Cosatu made it possible for insurance salespeople to have access to the workers. He, Caleb, was supposed to do business via the phone or on foot. He was in effect given a task he was not expected to accomplish.

But since Caleb was still determined to kill himself, Spicer and the insurance company became part of that other life, as remote as the stars, which would discontinue with his own exit. It suddenly felt good that he would not even miss it, there would be no room for such indulgence in the afterlife. Caleb was a believer in life after death; he was convinced that ghosts walked in their midst, perhaps transmogrified into motes of dust such as these inside the bar which swirled desultorily in a single shaft of light. His grandmother had impressed upon him the need to have respect not only for life but for inanimate things as well. Would sober up some of these drunks, Caleb thought, if some of the inanimate objects in the bar suddenly sprang into life.

"I don't get it," Ranger drawled. "You mean you want to kill yourself just because you're losing your hair?"

"Is there any other reason?" Caleb felt it would be futile to volunteer information about his status with the bank or frustrations at work. "Isn't that enough?"

"I have helped many people commit suicide," Ranger said. "But it's been real desperate cases. Like this one guy who got impotent and his wife started playing around. Even if he could have regained his manhood, his marriage was gone, kaput. Because he would forever be haunted by images of his wife swinging with another fellow, enjoying it—know what I mean?''

Caleb nodded. He was familiar with the humiliation facing a cuckold. There was a time when he suspected Nothando of seeing another man. It was then that he learned the destructive nature of jealousy. When she dressed and applied makeup, he concluded that she was tarting herself up for a tryst with her secret lover. Two of his best friends intervened and advised him that he was acting like an idiot. Nothando was a solid woman. This warning was timely because Caleb had started following her, hoping to catch her in flagrante delicto. Caleb knew he was by now quite sozzled when he started thinking in correspondence-school Latin. His tongue felt as if it had swollen up in his mouth. Yet he took another draught of his beer, convinced that it was better to die non compos mentis. He liked that phrase. Were it up to him, he would make his insurance pitch in Latin, see how Spicer liked that up his bloody white bailiwick.

''Do you want me to help you?'' Ranger asked.

''Yes,'' Caleb said. ''I just don't need no preambles. No last-minute sermons about the sanctity of life, or that my wife and kids will be unable to make ends meet. Don't give me that. I won't buy it.'' A bad conscience nagged him, though. He knew that he had to devise a plan that would make his death look like an accident. The eyes of the children stared at him from the bottom of his beer tumbler.

''How do you wish to go? A bullet in the back of the head? Poison? A rope? Well, that's not really pleasant.'' Ranger bent forward in the attitude of a conspirator, managing, however, to look like someone suppressing a belch. ''You know that my dad was a hangman. He's unemployed now there's this moratorium on the death penalty. But in his heyday he was in great demand. He strung up a lot of fellows, even in neighboring countries.'' He nodded, agreeing with something that spoke deep, deep behind the sightless eyes. ''And did you know that when they hang you in Pretoria, it's not strangulation, as most people believe, but a broken neck which actually kills you?''

Feeling a little sick, Caleb admitted that he hadn't been aware of that. He regarded his strange friend with renewed respect. ''Is that where you learned this . . . helping people?'' He realized the stupidity of his question. ''You couldn't have, though, being blind and all . . .''

''No,'' Ranger said, his hand flitting across the face, shielding his eyes with splayed fingers. "This is a recent thing, five years back. I was in the army where I was training some rookies in handling explosives, you know, and the damn thing just went *ka-boom!* and that was it, bye-bye eyes."

Ranger then turned his eyes to Caleb as if he were seeing him. "I was lucky I didn't lose my hearing, or my life." He chuckled. "My old man would have been mortified." Then in a singsong voice so low that Caleb had to lean forward, Ranger intoned something which sounded like a prayer:

> *No longer mourn for me when I am dead*
> *Then you shall hear the surly sullen bell*
> *Give warning to the world that I am fled*
> *From this vile world, with vilest worms to dwell.*

Then the music stopped and the clock somewhere inside the bar chimed the hour. As if this was a signal, Ranger got to his feet, rolled up his placard. "Drink up, friend," he said. "Bill Shakespeare tells us it's time."

"Was that Shakespeare you were quoting back there, then?" Caleb asked as they made their way out of the bar.

"*Ja.* I felt it would be a good epitaph for you." Caleb said nothing for a while, feeling the weight of Ranger's words. The man was a crank, no doubt, but he possessed a deep well of intelligence and experience from which he could draw at will. Caleb suspected that his own failure in life could be ascribed to his inexperience. If he had meant to continue living, he was certainly going to spice dinner-table conversations with some of these gems which tumbled so effortlessly out of Ranger's mouth.

It was a clear, bright April day when they went out, and the sun shimmered upon Caleb's eyes. It seemed as if the population of the city had trebled since he entered the tavern; young men dressed for winter lounged around doorways. The sex industry, since the ushering in of the new dispensation, was blooming, with hoardings tacked against walls advertising stylized sex paraphernalia. Market stalls weighted down by gigantic avocado pears, cabbage, tomato, and an assortment of juicy fruit, replicated themselves on street corners. Rising above the purr and roar of traffic was the strident whine of the butcher's electric saw. Women and girls sat on woven mats along the pavements, selling bolts of cloth, cosmetics, watches, and tape cassettes. The heady Zairian rumba rhythms Ranger and Caleb had endured in the bar now reverberated from speakers articulated to shop fronts, significantly heightening the temperature of this autumn afternoon. Here, on the pavement and on the road, people walked as if this were the first day of creation, some toddlers straying off to touch flowers, tweak the cheeks of dolls, or feel the texture of calico prints; here, an entire lounge suite upholstered in carmine leather seemed naked on the open ground. An old man, like the victim of a recent eviction, sat in one of the armchairs reading the Bible, oblivious to the frenetic goings-on around him. This short walk to the car gave Caleb a strange thrill, where the pastel colors of walls reflected on the polished bodies of passing cars, a swift haze. He looked at all this energy, life in motion, stamping it in his memory as if with indelible ink.

As they neared the car, Caleb asked: "What do you do, when you're not . . . ?" He fumbled for a word which would be less offensive than either "begging" or "hustling."

"Ripping off you sighted buggers?" Ranger finished for him. "Playing Scrabble. Had meant to patent blind players' variant of the game, but some eyeless smartass beat me to it." He smiled. "My plan was for a multilingual game, and that means the value of the tiles would be different. I was already speaking to a Zulu teacher who wised me up to the preponderance of q's and z's in African languages. I'm still thinking of developing a slang, you know, *tsotsitaal* Scrabble."

Caleb knew it would be useless to tell Ranger that *tsotsitaal* was something which developed each day. And that, like Arabic, it took on new forms from region to region. The irony of it all, that the township slang had actually increased in use in direct proportion to the heightening of repression, was not lost on him. But he had other matters with which to wrestle.

"This your car?" Ranger asked, exploring the contours of the vehicle. He yanked the door handle and, when it didn't open, stretched out his hand. "Gimme the *fokken* keys, Zungu."

"*What?*"

"I said gimme the *fokken* keys, I'll drive." There was a suggestion of great violence barely held in check in Ranger's tone. Caleb had an image of crazy, blind fury unleashing itself upon him. He surrendered the keys. Ranger got into the driver's seat and adjusted it. He leaned sideways to unlatch the door lock and let Caleb in. Instinctively, Caleb pulled the seat belt to strap himself in. "No seat belts," Ranger said. "You want to die, don't you?" He turned his eyes in the passenger's direction. Then he inserted the key into the ignition, released the hand brake, and felt for the gears. "*Ja*," Ranger said as he steered the car slowly out of the parking space onto the road, "we're now in business."

Then Ranger stepped on the accelerator, sending the car shooting up the thoroughfare, scattering a group of Mozambicans like skittles. "Used to drive in New York," Ranger said as he gunned the car past the amber lights on the left into Abel Road, edging off a minibus. The taxi hooted as it avoided Ranger, almost cannoning into a Clover Dairies delivery truck. "Simple city to drive in, New York. Perfect for blind people like me, with all that Braille from the potholes." He paused to stick his head out of the window and curse the taxi driver. "What's the matter with you, man? You blind or something?"

While all this was taking place, Nothando was idly leafing through magazines such as *Cosmopolitan, Style,* and *Drum,* pausing to scrutinize the advice columns. She read Tom Crabtree's contribution regarding male baldness. Quickly tossing the magazine onto the desk, she put on her jacket and picked up her handbag. Marcia was in the office kitchen, drinking her umpteenth cup of coffee while holding forth about sugar daddies. Nothando caught her friend's attention, tapped her wrist to indicate that it was lunchtime, and retreated into the lobby. Most of the typists, young women who worshipped at the shrine of the shopping mall, had long since broken off for lunch. Only a few stragglers who were victims of tyrannical superiors were still at it, tapping at their keyboards and brusquely responding to telephone inquiries. Hell hath no fury like a woman done out of her lunch hour. Nothando remembered a story she had heard from one friend who was a returned exile. The secretarial staff at the ANC headquarters in Lusaka was sent on a course where people learned, among other things, telephone manners. The then President Oliver Tambo called his office. "ANC headquarters," a smooth voice said. "Dudu speaking, good morning, can I help you?" Tambo had to ask twice whether this was the ANC office, possibly wondering if his organization hadn't been taken over by the Swedish Embassy, before he was convinced that he was phoning the right place. Listening to the hum of computers and the constipated belch from the photocopier, Nothando marveled at the amount of paper that got pushed every day in the office.

Accompanied by Marcia, she now showed her pass at the security gate and waited while Marcia opened her door. Nothando felt unaccountably tired; the strain of work combined with what had become a thankless task of raising two headstrong girls was beginning to tell. Moreover, she had a feeling that Caleb was soon going to develop into a headache. Funny, she thought, how you marry someone and they look like your dream man; then, *bang!* something transforms them overnight into a potbellied, spindly-legged old man whose bristles irritate you. Many of the women in the office were unashamed about the means they employed to offset suburban ennui. But she was past playing games. Nothando had once seriously considered an affair, but her inner self had cautioned against it; an affair was a headache. And then there was that eternal, fatal advocate of chastity, AIDS. In her line of work, she was duty-bound to counsel the staffers on the hazards of casual sex. Even though she had been thoroughly grounded in the workings of the dread disease, and how it could be contracted, she couldn't quite see herself telling a man to wear a condom. She had once tried one on herself and quickly discarded it. It had felt as if she were walking with a Checker's rustly carrier bag between her legs. So, no extramarital *fickie-fickie*, as one of TransStar's more brazen Arabic customers would say.

Marcia interrupted her train of thought by suggesting that they skip the usual fare of spare ribs and chips and instead get some bagels with cream cheese from Feigel's kosher deli on Raleigh Street. The broad street of Yeoville was so full of people, some meandering aimlessly, that Nothando secretly hankered for the return of influx control. As she munched her bagel with the car rolling slowly down Hendon, she remembered the time when the sight of a uniformed cop meant that layabouts made themselves scarce. Now, she thought, *tsotsis* don't give a hoot; when they see a cop they try to sell him a stolen car radio. The spirit of new entrepreneurship, this morning's car attendant is tonight's mugger. Apartheid was bad, sure, but maybe it isn't right that people threw out the baby with the bathwater. Some of the laws needed to remain, else how can a woman feel safe? People should get their priorities right, stop picking on poor Winnie and . . .

Then she saw the car, there was no mistaking it was Caleb's pink jalopy. It streaked out of Abel into Harrow and almost flew into the brick wall behind which stood the Courtleigh luxury accommodation flats, narrowly missing a vendor who had been whistling as he stood on an unbroken line in the middle of the street. Marcia said: "Isn't that . . ."

"*Ja, uCaleb!*" Nothando screamed, reverting to Zulu, her primal comforter in times of crisis. "*Mlandele!*" She heard the screech of brakes and loud curses as drivers swerved to avoid the pink streak of madness bearing down on them.

Marcia caught the light before it went red, turned the wheel hard, and directed the Toyota down Harrow Road, herself missing a Volvo driven by

Hasidic Jews. Three cars ahead, the Renault picked up speed, heading south. Nothando read the overhead blue-and-white sign, DOORNFONTEIN; where was Caleb going to, and at such speed? Marcia overtook two cars. Nothando looked out of the window, seeing the old Albambra Theatre, a panel van reversing quickly into Bates Road. "Don't worry," Marcia said, beads of perspiration on her nose. "I used to moonlight with Maxi Taxis . . ." Then the skeletal railings on their left, beyond them the railway to Germiston, Brakpan, Benoni. Nothando looked at all these structures which were part of her city, strange now, much like the once-familiar car headed to hell. The mine dump, the old mine, the girders and cables bespeaking obsolete glories. Far ahead, above her husband's car, stood the rubber factory, Dunlop. She wondered why Americans chose to call condoms "rubbers." Caleb, you dumb son of a no-good bitch, she thought viciously, why are you doing this?

He's trying to kill himself.

This thought came to her just as she heard the sirens wailing behind. With it was a memory of Chris, an old childhood friend who had tried to kill himself. Having been jilted by his girlfriend, Chris announced to all and sundry that he was serious about suicide. Nothando and a group of friends— and Chris's reason for wanting to leave this cruel world—followed him unobserved as he sought a tree in Mofolo Park. They had never seen a person actually dying, this was going to be a golden opportunity. They watched him installing breeze blocks at the foot of the tree, loop the rope over the branch and secure the noose around his neck. Only the tree was a sapling; it sagged with Chris, making Nothando think of one of those ineffectual snares township boys set for birds. Having failed, Chris trekked to the railway line near Orlando Station. He stretched himself across the tracks and waited for the train. The sun was hot, which meant that the steel tracks must have been blistering. Chris left the rail tracks to look for pieces of corrugated paper in the bushes. While he was reaping his strange harvest, a train rolled past. He went back to the rails and made a bed for himself. Nothando and her friends crouched in the tall grass, also waiting for the train. What came was not the train but a platoon of railway workers in their ocher overalls, each with the SAR&H logo on the breast pocket. They carried signs which Chris would have gratefully added to his bedding. The South African Railways and Harbors Union had called a strike earlier in the week; hence the scarcity of trains. The singing and *toyi-toying* railway workers made a sound not unlike the Kiwis' rugby *haka* when they saw Chris. Since being torn limb from limb was not part of his suicide repertoire, he got up and dashed into the bush, over the fence, and onto steady township ground.

Nothando heard a loud crash as the pink Renault slewed off the highway into Rissik Street. The sirens got louder; the vehicles to their left skidded and tortured brakes screeched as each driver strove to avoid being embroiled in a pileup. Nothando couldn't remember when or how she had got out of the Toyota, but she found herself running toward Caleb's ruined car, which had hit the railings and edged a quarter way into space. Mangled steel and chrome, spinning wheels, scorpion-like breakdown trucks, flashing lights, and the incessant scream of the siren—all these sights and sounds blended in Nothando's mind, releasing an impulse that had been struggling for expression in her chest. She screamed: "*Caaaaaaaaleb!*"

This cry, coming from lungs which had been trained in church choirs, vigils, and admonishment of rebellious children, rang above the roar of traffic, almost shattered the eardrums of nearby police officers and onlookers, and caused a flock of pigeons to start in midair and soar into the sheltering sky. It was heard in the offices of the car dealers along Eloff and Albert streets. Commuters coming out of Faraday Station stopped in mid-stride, pricked up their ears, and rushed to the source of the scream. In an interview with *The Sowetan* later that afternoon, the chef who had been sweating in the kitchen abandoned his fried chicken at Chicken Licken because, for him, what he had heard was a trumpet heralding Judgment Day.

A burly policeman, Warrant Officer van Vuuren, stopped his squad car and rushed into the melee. He shoved the curious onlookers until he got to the crashed car. Working with the breakdown attendants, he prised the doors open, dragged the two men out, and laid them on the road. Nothando, breathless, rushed to Caleb's side, swabbing the blood off his brow with her jacket. Moaning his name repeatedly, she gazed upon his face, noticing as if for the first time that he had an old, cuticle-shaped scar above the left eyebrow. The realization that she had missed this little detail brought about a gush of emotions she had never suspected she possessed. Nothando knew then that she loved Caleb, this fool, her fallen hero, who now lay like a log, breathing the foul smell of unwashed socks and tar.

When he opened his eyes and smiled, Nothando almost wept with relief. Then her eyes were blinded by rage. She pulled him up until he was wobbling on unsteady feet. Pushing him against the car, she started pummeling him with her fists, shrieking, "You bastardyoubastardyoubastard," until, spent, she collapsed against him. Van Vuuren, who obviously hadn't read

Commissioner George Fivaz's latest tract on community policing, was busy slapping a groggy Ranger.

"You *fokken blerry mampara*," van Vuuren hissed, "how many times have I told you to steer off trouble? You know that you're giving us *wit mense* a bad name?"

"Officer," Caleb said, extricating himself from Nothando's arms, "you can't do that to Ranger. He was trying to help me."

Van Vuuren turned round and studied Caleb. "You stupid idiot," he said. "You must count yourself lucky that he didn't kill you. This man," he continued, pulling Ranger by one ear, "has been a *blerry* headache for us since leaving Sterkfontein."

"No matter," Caleb persisted. "The man is blind, after all . . ."

"Blind?" Van Vuuren laughed. "Is that the latest trick, now?" He turned to Ranger. "Tell me you're blind, you son-of-a-bitch, and I'll personally *moer* your eyes out."

"*Ag,*" Ranger said conversationally, "be reasonable, *Kolonel.*" He shrugged. "A *mens* has got to live, *mos.*"

The crowed which had collected petered out. An ambulance came and the two men were installed inside. Nothando climbed in and sat beside her stunned husband. Caleb still couldn't believe that Ranger was not blind. He wanted to dive across and beat him up, but he was feeling too weak. Even thinking about what he and Ranger had got up to was a strain.

A month later, Caleb resigned from his job at Allied Life and set up an organization called Progressive Hairlessness Educational Workshop. Head-quartered at a small office overlooking the new Constitutional Court in Braamfontein, PHEW, as it was popularly known, started off badly, with the media dismissing it as a monumental hoax. But they hadn't bargained for Caleb's tenacity. Working day and night, he canvassed his erstwhile insurance clients (and people didn't dodge him now that he was no longer a threat) and importuned bald celebrities in the Gauteng region to endorse PHEW. Ranger emerged from his adventures to lend a hand. The two men inserted advertisements in the papers, seized every opportunity to speak for the hairless on the radio. Using his insurance connections, Caleb patented a logo, an egg with a confident smile above and below, with PHEW and "pride of the hairless" in lowercase red letters.

Letters from interested correspondents flooded the office. A controversy broke out (by then Caleb had shaved off all his hair) whether people with receding hairlines could take up membership in PHEW. Some prankster, no doubt an infiltrator, boasted on Radio 702 that he had a database of top leaders in industry and government who wore wigs. *Is baldness a private matter?* read a headline in the *Star* the following day, responding to the idea of outing closet baldies. By now subscriptions were pouring in. Nothando's services were enlisted to deal with the increasing volume of work. After appearing in Dali Tambo's *People of the South*, Caleb and Ranger were invited on a nationwide speaking tour. A car company in Uitenhage purchased a franchise to market its latest model, exhibiting the PHEW logo minus the lettering. Caleb, Ranger, and Nothando registered PHEW as a listed company in the Johannesburg Stock Exchange.

Caleb Zungu was forty-five years old, married to Nothando for fifteen years, with two girl children, Busi and Khwezi, aged ten and sixteen, respectively. He owned a house in Norwood, two cars, and two dogs of dubious pedigree. He was the chief executive officer of PHEW Enterprises. Nothando and Ranger were junior partners in the company. J.M., who exhibited keen business acumen, was a favored future son-in-law. His ready acceptance into the Zungu family was due to his premature loss of hair.

And the two dogs were called by their real names, Baldy and Beauty.

—1996

PERMISSIONS

1984 West Mall
Room 200
Geography (Geog)
15:30